Advance Praise for *PrimeTime Women:*

"Marti Barletta—the First Lady of marketing to women—is back, and she's done it again. Marti calls marketing to 'PrimeTime Women' a 'radical opportunity'—and proves it. I not only agree, but also I would call anyone who does not make this extraordinary book the centerpiece of their marketing/strategic plans very, very foolish."
—Tom Peters, Author of *Re-imagine! Business Excellence in a Disruptive Age*

"Full of expert advice about today's PrimeTime Woman: who she is, what she cares about, where she shops, and what she buys—PrimeTime Women *is a must-read for advertising and marketing professionals who are determined to reach the hearts, minds, and wallets of today's most coveted consumers: women 50–70 who are in their prime!"*
—Dana Anderson, President and CEO, DDB Chicago

"PrimeTime Women *will no doubt change the way corporate America views and markets to today's Boomer women. Based on new research and her experience in the field, Marti Barletta opens our eyes to the immense power of this emerging marketing force. She reminds us that women over the age of 50 hold the power of the purse in their PrimeTime hands."*
— Lisa Bacus, Director, Global Marketing Strategy, Ford Motor Company

"With wit and wisdom, Barletta has pulled off the seemingly impossible: made the prospect of becoming an 'older' woman sound like fun. Marketers, take note: a horde of PrimeTime Babes, with passion, power, and bulging pocketbooks, is heading your way."
—Linda Tischler, Senior Writer, *Fast Company*

"Anyone trying to build their business over the next 20 years should start by reading PrimeTime Women. *There isn't a more relevant, insightful, and just-plain-useful book on how to effectively connect with this economic tour de force. If you don't have a plan yet for PrimeTime Women, you will. If you have a plan, this will make it better."*
—Matt Thornhill, Founder & President, Boomer Project

"Marti Barletta has done it again. Within the pages of this book, Marti has given every business the roadmap to success with this dazzlingly wonderful group of consumers. Take the insights in this book to heart. Apply them thoughtfully and passionately and watch your efforts drive your success!"
—Susan Sweetser, MassMutual

"Marti Barletta once again breaks the mold and takes us to the edge of a new frontier in consumer behavior. No one who gives this book serious attention will fail to shoot forward at warp speed in their understanding of the largest market on the planet—Prime Time Women."
—David B. Wolfe, Principal, Wolfe Resources Group

"Marti Barletta's new book, PrimeTime Women, *offers a fascinating perspective on an overlooked—yet vital—segment of the market. Marti effectively demonstrates that all marketers need to look beyond the 18–49 demographic: PrimeTime Women are the newest force in the marketplace."*
—Teresa Smith, AARP Foundation Director of Philanthropic Outreach

"Just like Marti Barletta's powerful and engaging presentations, this book is chock-full of breakthrough insights and practical ideas to stimulate marketers. PrimeTime Women *makes you think and offers the strategies you need to move ahead with today's most powerful and influential target, Boomer women."*
—Roger J. Dow, President & CEO, Travel Industry Association of America

"A great read with fascinating detail and data. But best of all—now I actually look forward to aging, after learning that PrimeTime Women statistically are feistier, more fulfilled, less anxious, and overall happier than their younger selves. And they're an increasing financial force marketers must reckon with and cater to! A must-read for women and all marketers!"
—Cynthia Good, CEO & Founding Editor, *PINK* magazine

"Written in a conversational, story-telling style, Marti's book delivers a compelling business case and an engaging look at what drives this powerful yet underserved segment of buyers."
—Cathy Benko, National Managing Director, Deloitte & Touche USA LLP

"Like Marti's previous books, PrimeTime Women *brilliantly continues the story of how and why to market to women. This book focuses on the PrimeTime in the lives of women ages 50–70. Finally a book that tells you where the dollars really are and the best strategies to capture them."*
—Marsha Firestone, PhD, President and Founder, Women Presidents' Organization

PrimeTime
WOMEN

HOW TO WIN THE HEARTS, MINDS, AND
BUSINESS OF BOOMER BIG SPENDERS

MARTI BARLETTA

KAPLAN) PUBLISHING

This publication is designed to provide accurate and authoritative information in regard to the subject matter covered. It is sold with the understanding that the publisher is not engaged in rendering legal, accounting, or other professional service. If legal advice or other expert assistance is required, the services of a competent professional should be sought.

Editorial Director: Jennifer Farthing
Acquisitions Editor: Karen Murphy
Production Editor: Caitlin Ostrow
Production Artist: the dotted i
Cover Designer: Carly Schnur

Published by Kaplan Publishing,
a division of Kaplan, Inc.

Printed in the United States of America

07 08 09 10 9 8 7 6 5 4 3 2 1

Library of Congress Cataloging-in-Publication Data

Barletta, Marti.
    Prime time women : how to win the hearts, minds, and business of boomer big spenders / Marti Barletta.
        p. cm.
    ISBN-13: 978-1-4195-9330-7
    ISBN-10: 1-4195-9330-7
    1. Women consumers–United States. 2. Middle-aged women–United States. 3. Marketing–United States. 4. Baby boom generation–United States. I. Title.
    HF5415.33.U6B37 2006
    658.8'34082–dc22

                                                                    2006027371

Contents

Dedication

To my mother, Jane Radcliffe, an amazing woman who has climbed the tall pyramids of Macchu Picchu, canoed the headwaters of the Amazon, traveled through India, served as a mission volunteer in Kenya (in her 70s!); has worked as a runway model, professional dancer, massage therapist; has taught yoga, journalism, creative writing, and English as a second language; and has distinguished herself as a Fulbright scholar, published poet, museum docent, and student of Native American languages—thank you for being an inspiration and a role model, both personally and, along with your sisters in the so-called Silent Generation, to the first generation of PrimeTime Women.

Foreword

The three strategic keystones of modern marketing are Segmentation, Targeting, and Positioning (STP). Each keystone is oriented around gaining and applying an understanding of the customer. In a world that is no longer plagued by a shortage of goods but faces a shortage of customers, customer focus is critical.

In focusing on the customer, marketers have to go beyond the superficial markers of people in a segment. They need to search for insights into the customer's deeper motivations, however subconscious or unspoken.

Sometimes these insights are surprisingly obvious in hindsight. It was only about six years ago that marketers of big-ticket consumer items and business-to-business products and services realized that their primary buyers or deciders were women. Those who realized it first, and applied fresh marketing and communications strategies, gained a competitive edge.

Marti Barletta is a key thought leader when it comes to gaining insights about marketing to women. In her first book, *Marketing to Women*, she presented numerous relevant and actionable insights into women. She presented a compelling case for viewing women as the primary buyers in the consumer, corporate, and small business sectors. She amassed findings from a variety of disciplines on how women differ from men, and on women's distinctive priorities, preferences, and buying processes. She was the first in her field to provide concrete strategies and tactics for reaching and motivating women in ways consonant with their desires and activities.

In this book, *PrimeTime Women*, Barletta takes the next step by narrowing her focus to that segment of the women's market with the most buying power—women 50–70 years old. She calls them "Prime-Time Women" for two reasons: first, contrary to popular opinion, they are active and energetic, and consider themselves in the prime of their lives; second, they handle the buying decisions for households enjoying their peak income, assets, and spending power, making them marketers' prime prospects.

Yet most marketers neglect this group, preferring to focus on the 18–54 age cohort. They are late in recognizing that the average age of women buyers is approaching 49. They mistakenly apply their understandings of younger women to women over 50 as if they haven't changed. Those who read this book will look back and wonder how they could have ever decided to cut off their prospecting just at the age when their best prospects are in a position to start spending some real money.

Barletta goes beyond a presentation of the business opportunity to provide a detailed understanding of the PrimeTime customer and, specifically, of PrimeTime Women.

Midlife men and women are different from younger adults. They have more experience, they buy more intuitively, they rely more on gut feel, they behave more independently of social conventions, they crave authenticity, and they seek ways to create a legacy. Additionally, PrimeTime Women experience the midlife transition to what psychologists call their Second Adulthood very differently than their male counterparts, in ways that significantly affect both their social and economic behavior. An understanding of their underlying issues, motivations, and decision-making processes is the key to unlocking the powerful marketing potential of this customer segment.

When all is said and done, segmentation is a search for insight into customers and customer types, and it can provide a rich reward for marketers who are the first to identify new variables for classifying customers. Barletta dispels the myths, delivers the research, and details the specific strategies and actions that savvy marketers can use to outflank and outrun the conventional efforts of their outdated competitors. By finding a new key to understanding the customer, she has unlocked a wealth of new ideas and opportunity for marketers in many industries.

Philip Kotler
S. C. Johnson Distinguished Professor of International Marketing
Kellogg School of Management, Northwestern University

Acknowledgments

Many Thanks

To Robyn Hall, my writing partner, whose comprehensive background research, exceptional command of the concepts, and organizational genius made this book possible—really;

To the other members of the book support team—Linda Packer, who crafted first drafts of several chapters; Angel Gibson, who developed the proprietary research included in the book, including partnering with DDB on the GirlFriend Groups; and Amy Acri, whose relentless pursuit of permissions allowed us to share a wealth of examples;

To the rest of the TrendSight Group team—Jane Demakos, Marcia Sutter, Paula McLeod, Betsy Westhoff, and Michaela Shaw, whose professional excellence kept the business going and growing through the months that I couldn't give it as much of my attention as usual;

To Jeff Kleinman, the world's best agent, whose patience, tact, responsiveness and great suggestions continue to merit my undying gratitude;

To the talented staff at Kaplan Publishing—Karen Murphy, the acquisitions editor who has championed the book internally and to the book world; Mary Good Palmer, the development editor whose good judgments and insightful suggestions greatly improved the work; Caitlin Ostrow, the production editor who kept this complicated project smoothly on track; Margaret Haywood, the copy editor who minded all our p's and q's; Krystal Villanosa, who organized the galley review process; Eileen Johnson, the business development driver who keeps us all in business; and Courtney Goethals, the PR maven who gets the word out, which, after all, is what it's all about;

To my fellow members of the Women Gurus Network—Sally Helgesen, Connie Glaser, Gail Evans, Bev Kaye, Susan Bird, Jeri Sedlar, Susan RoAne, Margaret Heffernan, and Robyn Waters—a mutual admiration society whose mutual support of books and businesses has helped to elevate the word about women in the workplace and the marketplace . . .

Many, many thanks to all of you!
Marti Barletta

Introduction

Women—ya gotta love 'em. Especially if you're a marketer. Or a salesperson. Marketers and salespeople are all about selling stuff. And women buy most of everything. Match made in heaven!

Looking back, it's a little hard to believe that just four years ago when my first book, *Marketing to Women*, came out, marketing to women was pretty much a new idea to marketers in a lot of categories. Everybody knew women bought most of the "little stuff"—housewares, family apparel, and the packaged goods you get from grocery stores and mass merchandisers. What a lot of marketers didn't know, however, was that women were taking on primary purchasing responsibilities for the big-ticket items as well: health care and home improvement, insurance and investing, and computers and consumer electronics.

Marketing to Women

The premise of my first book, *Marketing to Women*, can be summarized in three points:

1. Women buy most of almost everything, not only in the consumer market but also in the corporate and small business arenas.

2. Women are different from men in their attitudes, priorities, communication patterns, and decision styles. These differences, and the differences in how women respond to every element

of the marketing mix, are synthesized in the GenderTrends™ Marketing Model.

3. Marketers who apply the insights and principles of the Gender-Trends Marketing Model will boost the return on every dollar in their marketing and sales budgets because their programs and communications are more relevant, credible, and appealing to their primary buyers—women.

Let's look at each of these three points a little more closely.

Women Buy Most of Almost Everything

Just a few years ago, I always had to start all my speaking programs and corporate presentations with a fairly extensive overview of women's earning and buying power. These days I don't. The research is clear; the numbers are huge. When it's about following the money, marketers are pretty fast learners.

Women Are Different—from Men

With the premise that "women are different," I wanted to go beyond simply understanding women to a deeper-rooted perspective of understanding in what ways women are different from men. My intuition told me that the marketing messages designed to reach the traditional buyer—men—weren't effective with the new primary purchaser—women. When I would read studies and conclusions based on talking only to women, I couldn't help feeling "Yes, I believe women are like that. But so what? Who says men aren't exactly the same way?" It's not enough to talk to 5,000 women, or to deeply understand women's attitudes and practices in a given category. Talking only to women doesn't deliver the kind of sharp focus and subtlety you need to hone a marketing insight that matters.

I'm a skeptic, and I wanted evidence. I was looking for differences based on more than someone's casual observations or opinions. So I set out on a search that encompassed not only marketing studies, but also published research in fields as diverse as anthropology, biochemistry, brain structure, human development, organizational behavior, psychology, and sociolinguistics. The findings were fascinating.

The most interesting aspect of my research came from synthesizing the findings across disciplines. It's a little like looking at an Impressionist painting: up close, all you see are small strokes of color—some blue here, some green there. Step back and a picture emerges of a cathedral on a river bank.

To illustrate: when you put together (1) the United Nations study on how women prefer and are better at multitasking; (2) the neuroscientists' learning that women's brains often have multiple processing centers for a given function, whereas men usually concentrate all of the process in a single center; and (3) the buying studies from two different categories showing that women usually require more time and more visits to reach a decision on a big-ticket item, a picture emerges of how and why women's "multiminded" decision style is so different from men's.

Yes, women are different, sometimes in ways you'd suspect and sometimes in ways you'd find surprising. The important thing is, many of the learnings have major implications for marketing and selling. In *Marketing to Women,* I synthesized these learnings into my Gender-Trends Model, grouping the findings into four essential categories: Social Values, Life/Time Factors, Decision Styles, and Communication Keys. Some examples: When considering a big purchase, women seek advice and information, while men see asking for advice as compromising their independence. Women search for "The "Perfect Answer™," while men opt to stop when they find a "good solution." Women see shopping as a process of exploration; men see buying as a process of elimination.

Women like to get together to talk, while men like to get together to do things. Women tend to feel the full context of a communication is as important as the key point; men want to know the top line, and only a limited amount of detail. Women respond more to "warmer" messages that highlight the connections among people; whereas men respond more to "winner" messages based on getting ahead of other people.

Understanding Gender Differences Boosts Marketing and Sales Impact with Your Primary Buyers—Women

These and similar insights can and should upset the applecart on a lot of what you took for granted as fundamental marketing. Turns out that many of the principles we've all been using, while well-aligned with male gender culture, have little to do with the ways that women respond, shop, and choose brands. My premise is that going beyond "understanding women" to "understanding how women are different from men" allows you to sharpen your focus on how to adapt and customize your marketing tools. And because nobody else does it that way, it gives you a truly innovative way of looking for your next big idea—the kind of idea that can blow the doors off your next ad campaign or marketing program. The kind your competitors haven't even thought to look at. Yet.

Marketing to Women: The Next Generation

Marketing to Women focused on "women" in general. Admittedly, I'm using the term *focused* a little loosely. At 51 percent of the population—that is, the majority—women as a whole are hardly the sort of "segment" that marketers can target effectively (though you'd be surprised at the number that say they'd like to do exactly that).

People at my presentations often ask if the GenderTrends principles vary by age, ethnic background, nationality, or socioeconomic status. Of course they do. Obviously, not all women are the same.

Marketing to Women, and the six or seven similar books that followed it, represents the first generation of understanding how to market to women differently than to men. The next step is to refine the insights for different target segments within "women."

Women Are Different—From Each Other

Companies with brands that have traditionally focused on women—food, diapers, apparel, health and beauty care—have some pretty comprehensive knowledge bases on the women who buy their products. They have them segmented every which way—geographically, demographically, psychographically, generationally. In other words, there actually is a fair amount of work in existence on how women are different from each other—up to a point. And that point is 54.

Fifty-four years of age has been the highest cut-off point for any marketing initiative I've ever been involved in or even read about. Sometimes it's as young as 49. Which is pretty weird when you consider age 50 is right about when people who have worked all their lives start to have some money to spend!

The Invisible Woman

We in the Western world have a bad case of youth myopia. Because marketing as a discipline came of age about the same time the Baby Boomers did, a lot of our marketing thinking is rooted in how to market to young people. Boomers, the product of a substantial surge in birth rates following World War II, were also the first beneficiaries of a new consumerist society. At the time, marketers were choosing between the "old folks" and the kids. Boomers' parents had suffered the ravages of the Great Depression and the deprivations of a world war, so what money they had, they saved. Naturally, the admen who invented mass marketing turned their focus on the large, young population with the big fat wallet, which made sense—at the time.

But lo and behold, the Boomers grew up. And as marketers, we've let ourselves fall behind. Stuck in the stereotypes of a bygone day, we're letting our outdated language and imagery get in the way of our biggest opportunity.

Why Consumers Don't Want to Be "Mature"

People are at a loss to describe "consumers over age 50" in ways that don't conjure up negative associations. Terms like *middle-aged, mature market,* and *senior market* come freighted with unappealing overtones. *Middle-aged* calls up images of dowdy, lumpy frumpiness. *Mature* suggests someone who is serious, sober, sedate, and stately—in other words, no fun. And while being a senior in high school or college is a status that underclassmen aspire to, perversely, *senior citizen* in the context of older consumers connotes a nominal acknowledgment to the tottering old dears, a condescending head nod, a senior discount—gee, thanks.

People say Boomers are resisting growing older. That's not it at all—in fact, it completely misses the point. Boomers, particularly women, are fine with growing older. What they're resisting is being labeled with language loaded with the patronizing images and attitudes above—*frumpy, sedate, tottering*. It's not how they feel, it's really truly not who they are, and they're not inclined to put up with anyone implying otherwise. What they're resisting is being talked down to.

Unfortunately, so far, those words are all we've had to work with. We need some new lingo, words that tell it like it really is; words that capture a personality that is positive, dynamic, and savvy—in short, words that make a woman feel good about saying, "Yup, that's me!"

Introducing PrimeTime Women™

So let me introduce you to PrimeTimers, in particular to Prime-Time Women—women from 50 to 70 years old. I coined this term because I like the way it connotes vitality and primacy, which aptly describe this group on not one, but two levels:

- They are in the **prime** of their lives. It comes as a surprise to most pre-Primers that people in their 50s and 60s report these two decades are the happiest of their lives and, as you will see later, women experience this phase even more positively than men do.[1]

- They are the **prime** target opportunity for marketers in almost every category, because they handle 80 to 85 percent of the spending decisions for households in the peak years of their income, wealth, and spending power.[2]

Moreover, although most of this book focuses on consumer spending, I should also note PrimeTime Women's preeminent purchasing role on the business-to-business side of the economy. Women overall hold 50 percent of managerial and professional positions these days,[3] and, among them, PrimeTime Women are in the most senior positions with the most spending authority.

And among women business owners—who, just so you know, have been starting 70 percent of all small businesses for the last couple of decades—a significant number are PrimeTime Women who have exited those big corporate jobs to bring their considerable business experience to their own table. Moral of the story: for those marketers among you who sell B-to-B, chances are a large and growing number of your corporate and small business buyers are PrimeTime Women too.

So, exactly who are these PrimeTime Women? Bear with me for a couple of clarifications about who they are *not*.

Not "50+"

First, they are not "50+." When I say PrimeTime, I'm not talking about everyone over 50; I'm talking specifically about that segment of men and women who are between 50 and 70 years old. I'm already in trouble with my 73-year-old mother, who thinks I should make the span an even quarter century—50–75. The truth is, Prime-Time is more a state of mind than a strict chronological age. More on that in a moment.

For now, my point is to highlight that, while a lot of studies and statistics are reported as simply "50+," most Mature Market experts agree that within "50+" there are roughly three age strata, sometimes referred to as the *young-old* (50–70), the *middle-old* (70–85) and the *old-old* (85+). The way I look at it, PrimeTime is a stage of *midlife;* there's nothing "old" about it.

Not "Boomers"

Second, PrimeTime is not synonymous with "Boomer." Recently, the press has given lots of attention to Boomers, a generational cohort defined as people born between 1946 and 1964. *Newsweek, TIME,* and *BusinessWeek* have all run cover articles on the "news" that the leading edge of the Baby Boom turned 60 in 2006. Apparently this is a big surprise. Seems to have crept up on people.

Boomers are a generational cohort who, like all generational cohorts, started out young, are passing through midlife, and will someday move on through old age to . . . how shall I say it . . . the big Woodstock in the sky?

PrimeTime, on the other hand, is a life stage. At the moment, Boomers are moving through it—hence the subtitle of this book, *How to Win the Hearts, Minds, and Business of Boomer Big Spenders.* So far, about half of them have gotten their PrimeTime papers. In a little less than 10 years, the first Gen Xer will put a toe over the Prime-Time threshold. Then 11 years after that, Gen Y will hit "the big 5-0" and enter into their PrimeTime phase.

Each generation will bring a slightly different outlook to Prime-Time, because each cohort brings with it some unique attitudes and outlooks that are a product of world conditions and milestone events during their so-called formative years. But for the most part, the qualities and characteristics of PrimeTime will stay fairly constant, because almost everyone evolves through two common progressions over a lifetime: the "second adulthood" stage of psychological human development and, more or less simultaneously, the "post-family/peak career" life stage.

The key take-away here is that, while "Boomer Marketing" books and newsletters will give you good insights into this decade's Prime-Timers, the marketing principles of this book are timeless. You won't have to learn a whole new set of rules to reach Gen X in PrimeTime, then yet another approach for Gen Y. As long as your target is high-spending households ages 50–70, these principles apply.

I keep saying "PrimeTimers." I wonder if you're wondering, "What happened to the 'women' part?"

Well, here's the thing—actually, two things:

Cherchez la Femme

The thought leaders of mature marketing (or its cousin, Ageless Marketing, as my highly esteemed friend David Wolfe has conceived of it) have created and validated an impressive body of work on how to market to older people. Indeed, David's books, along with those by Gail Sheehy, Ken and Maggie Dychtwald, Carol Morgan, Brent Green, and Jean-Paul Tréguer, have been among my most invaluable resources as I've researched this book.

But the thing is, for the most part, these books all discuss older people in general. Nobody has honed in on women.

From a marketing point of view, that distinction is far from academic. As I said upfront, and documented in *Marketing to Women:* (1) women buy most of everything, and (2) women are different from men. Moreover, women experience midlife very differently from men. Marketers want to reach and influence the people who make the purchase decisions. And that means they want to reach PrimeTime Women with programs and messages that PrimeTime Women find compelling.

A Radical Opportunity

As I said above, following Boomers, there will be generations of PrimeTime Women to come. However, in a certain sense, Boomer women are actually the pioneers of PrimeTime Womanhood.

Boomer Women represent a true inflection point in history. Barring unforeseen catastrophes, from this point on, women will never be the same. Striding smartly through the doors of opportunity opened by their mothers, Boomer women came of age during the radical 1960s and '70s, during the height of the Women's Movement. They have had choices and made decisions that their mothers only dreamed of. It cannot be overstated how dramatically life has changed for, and has been changed by, Baby Boomer women. They are the first generation of women to have:

- **College educations:** graduating from college at rates that substantially exceed their brethren.

- **Serious earning power:** currently bringing home half or more of the household income in over half of U.S. households (yes, you read that correctly).

- **Reproductive rights:** family planning with the ability to control if and when to have children, which in turn determines if and when to take a career hiatus.

- **Property rights:** as of 1973, a woman could not get a bank loan without a signature from her husband or father. Until 1981, state laws designated a husband "head and master" with unilateral control of property owned jointly with his wife. Think about that: in 1981, I was an adult, 27 years old, with a Wharton MBA and a great brand management job. My husband and I had just purchased our first house together, and *he* was recognized as the *only* "owner" of everything we had. Whoa.[4]

Book Tour

As with *Marketing to Women,* the premise of this book can be outlined in three statements:

1. PrimeTime Women spend at the high-dollar end of the consumer, corporate, and small business markets.

2. Most marketers are sadly unaware of the power of the Prime-Time market, who the PrimeTime Woman really is, and how to effectively capture her business.

3. Marketers who get smart about applying the principles of this book will be getting more bang from every dollar in their marketing and sales budget as they focus their efforts on the highest spending segment within the women's market—PrimeTime Women.

Part I: Understanding PrimeTime Women

In Chapter 1, I hope to get you motivated to seize this market opportunity by quantifying the scope of PrimeTime Women's demographic and financial power. Chapters 2 through 5 take you on a tour of the behavioral, attitudinal, physical, mental, and life-stage changes that occur in women in PrimeTime and the marketing implications that arise from these changes. Chapter 6 gives you a look ahead at what PrimeTimers are planning for their retirement years and a glimpse into the future and its dramatic effect on the housing, real estate, and home furnishing markets.

Brand New Research. In particular, I want to highlight Chapter 2, contributed by agency powerhouse DDB Worldwide, which summarizes findings from new, never-before-published research. We partnered with them to develop three sets of qualitative Girlfriend Groups, with women in their 40s, 50s, and 60s, respectively, so we could observe whether and how women's attitudes toward growing older evolve as they go through each stage. Further, they have tapped their proprietary Life Style Study^{SM}, which is longitudinal quantitative research that spans the past 30 years, to shed further light on PrimeTime Women's attitudes and behaviors. David Polston and Martin Horn, both senior vice presidents, DDB Chicago, synthesized their findings into five illuminating insights that shed additional light on Prime-Time Women's state of mind and how it differs from that of younger women. In addition, throughout Chapters 3 to 6 we provide real world comments from our own PrimeTime Women 50/50/50 panel—50 fabulous women, ages 50–70 and proud, answer 50 thought-provoking questions.

Rose-Colored Glasses. This book intentionally and unabashedly looks at the bright side of the midlife market. It's a point of view that's desperately needed. The general press is full of head-shaking and hand-wringing over Boomers' vanity (not true), self-centeredness (typical of youth, but not of PrimeTime), soon-to-be crushing burden on the U.S. economy, Social Security, and the healthcare system (not going to happen), upcoming health challenges (much less incidence than they'd have you believe at this age), and various other topics meant to raise readership by provoking alarm.

Unfortunately, that has obscured the marketing opportunity. The simple fact of the matter is that the *women currently in PrimeTime are the healthiest, wealthiest, and most active, educated, and influential generation of women in history.* I emphasize that phrase and alert you now that you will see it throughout this book, because it is the core, the essence of the opportunity I am trying to convey. If marketers were more aware of the bright side, they'd understand what incredible money there is to be made. Sue Shellenbarger, the esteemed *Wall Street Journal* writer, sees the silver lining (lining of PrimeTime Women's purses, that is!): "You can make a ton of money . . . Let's face it. These women with their fat pocketbooks approach the age of

50 and lose their inhibitions. Imagine that! That's a lot of spending. If you strike out in new directions . . . you spend. If you are pursuing a dream, your primary focus is not going to be frugality. You're going to be out there buying stuff."[5]

Part II: The Field Guide to Marketing to PrimeTime Women

Chapter 7 will start with a quick overview of the GenderTrends Marketing Model from *Marketing to Women,* which highlights how women are different from men and then customizes the model to refine the GenderTrends principles specifically for PrimeTime Women. Chapter 8 is where I deliver the goods—the nuts and bolts of how to tailor your marketing tools, including advertising, promotion, and sponsorships—to boost your sales and marketing results among PrimeTime Women. If you don't have time to read the whole book, this is the one chapter you don't want to skip! Chapter 9 illustrates best practices applications of these principles with two in-depth and integrated case studies that, between them, cover most of the tools in the marketing toolbox. And Chapter 10 closes the book with Notes to the CEO, a feature that readers of my first book told me was particularly helpful in introducing the business case and key learnings to others in their organizations.

Who Am I to Say So?

People at my presentations are often curious about how I found my passion for marketing to women and came to start my company, The TrendSight Group. I'd have to say, I'm kind of surprised myself at how I got here.

After earning my MBA from the Wharton School of Business, I launched my career in corporate marketing at Clorox. After about four years in brand management, I moved from the client side to the agency side, first joining McCann Erickson in San Francisco, then advancing to positions at TLK, Foote Cone and Belding, and Frankel. At Frankel, I created a marketing to women strategic capability as a new business platform for the agency and named it Frankly Female. The initiative was very successful in achieving its visibility, credibility, and prospecting goals, but when the agency was sold to new owners, they made the decision to focus on other areas. With their blessing, I decided to pursue the business opportunity on my own.

I went solo in 1999 and was gratified to find there was already enough interest in marketing to women to keep me busy as an independent consultant without too much difficulty. Over the next couple of years, I continued to add to the body of knowledge on the topic, and soon clients were suggesting I capture it all by writing a book.

Marketing to Women was released in early 2003. Shortly thereafter, the professional speaking side of my business took off, and I spent most of my time tailoring my insights and implications to the interests of my various audiences. While the core findings stay more or less the same, each presentation is customized by about 25–30 percent because each audience has different needs and applications.

The variety of industries I have spoken for is one of the most fascinating and rewarding parts of my work. In the course of one six-week busy season, I spoke to an association of bank marketing directors, a convention of pest control operators, an annual meeting of top financial producers for an investment company, trade shows of hardware store franchisees, of photo shop owners, and of fine jewelry store operators, a conference on future trends, and a chamber of commerce of women business owners.

My clients have continued to broaden the range of topics I speak on, with requests that go beyond marketing to women, advertising to women, and selling to women consumers to recruiting, retaining, and managing women in the workplace, selling to women executives who buy multimillion dollar professional service contracts, and helping companies get more value from their support of women vendors in their supply chain.

Since I was often preparing presentations at the rate of more than one a week, I had my hands full keeping up with my speaking and wasn't able to pursue the frequent consulting inquiries that often followed a speaking gig. To be honest, I was enjoying my freedom from managerial duties and was reluctant to take on the responsibility of bringing in additional people to the business.

I have been enrolled in an entrepreneur development program called The Strategic Coach for about three years now and, although the program has been spectacularly successful in helping me grow my business in more ways than I can count, one particular insight motivated me to expand my services into consulting: Always make your future bigger than your past.

With that in mind, I knew I needed to find a way to leverage my expertise to create more value, and the only way I could do that would be to bring in some bench strength. I was fortunate to find a remarkable team, all with senior marketing and management experience in a number of different industries and environments.

With clients like Serta, Volvo, Ford Motor Company, Toys R Us, Logitech, Deloitte, Regis Corporation, and GE Appliances, The TrendSight Group has grown by leaps and bounds over the past few years. We love our work, we love our clients, and we love working together as a team.

The second edition of *Marketing to Women* was released in 2005. It gives me a thrill to note that it was reprinted eight times in three years and is now available in 15 foreign languages.

In addition, I was honored to be invited by Tom Peters to coauthor a book with him. *Trends* was also released in 2005 and provides a quick capsule of why and how to market to the two largest, fastest growing consumer demographic trends of the next two decades: women and the mature market. While that book top-lined the key insights on marketing to PrimeTime Women, it only scratched the surface of what proved to be a compelling story that needed telling. There was so much more to learn, so much more to share—and hence, here we are.

In case you're wondering, I'm a PrimeTime Woman myself. I recently turned 50 and couldn't help noticing it didn't hit me nearly as hard as it had hit my husband. (He claims it's purely coincidence he bought his first convertible that year; but I can't help noticing that sometimes he calls it his "midlife Chrysler.") Like most PrimeTime Women, I have more time these days because my kids are both teenagers with driving permits and have *very* busy school and social schedules. I also have more money now because the business I started six years ago is growing exponentially. No doubt about it—life is grand.

But enough about me. Let's get on with winning the hearts, minds, and business of Boomer big spenders—PrimeTime Women.

PART I ONE

UNDERSTANDING PRIMETIME WOMEN

CHAPTER ONE

The Power of the PrimeTime Purse

I don't know how you developed your images of so-called "middle-aged women;" in fact, I don't even know how I developed mine. All I know is that when I started my search for the golden bull's-eye of target marketing—a substantial segment within the women's market with money and the moxie to spend it—I never would have predicted I would follow the dollar trail to PrimeTime Women.

My ill-informed assumptions would have been that "old folks" didn't have much money, and middle-aged women didn't have much moxie. Shame on me. From Chapter 2 onward, the rest of this book will focus on sharing a more informed picture of who middle-aged women—women between 50 and 70 years old—really are. And for the record, they've got plenty of moxie, so from now on, we'll stick to calling them PrimeTime Women because:

- They are in the **prime** of their lives.

- They are the **prime** target opportunity for marketers in almost every category.

This chapter dispels the myth that PrimeTime Women don't have much money. My own impressions would have been based on dim memories of 1970s news stories raising the alert about the many retirees who lived below the poverty line. There was a great deal of worry—both among them and about them—and scary stories about their having so little money for food that some were buying cans of cat food instead of tuna to eat as the minimum subsistence source of nutrition.

Now no disrespect intended to those in need, and I know there are many who deserve our concern and our help, but the reality is that newspapers need to sell papers, and provocative stories of human distress sell a lot more papers than celebrations of prosperity. And while there's always more than one side to a story, no matter what the topic, you will always see more stories and find more facts about the bad than the good. In hindsight, I realize now that my impression that "all old people live in poverty" was based on coverage definitely skewed toward the "poor story." And the same is true of news reports today.

In all reality, things actually were different in the 1970s. Households generally had only one earner—the husband—and thus at the end of the day, only one Social Security check. Life insurance wasn't all that well-established; not too many people had it. And the concept of investing as we know it today—even simple instruments like mutual funds and money market accounts—really weren't in general use. My grandparents lived on a pension and a Social Security check, with maybe a savings account for rainy days and emergencies.

Things have changed—quite a bit, actually. And there is definitely another side to the "poor story," which I call the "power story."

The crux: PrimeTime Women stand at the intersection of the two most powerful and prosperous consumer segments in the world today:

1. the younger, midlife decades of the so-called "Mature Market," people 50–70 years old, whose numbers are growing exponentially and who enjoy above average income, wealth, and spending power; and

2. women, whose earning power has accelerated like a rocket over the past 30 years, and more important, who act as chief purchasing officers in almost every household, as well as in many small businesses and corporate buying functions.

Business guru Tom Peters says that these two trends—Women and the Mature Market (he calls mature folks "Boomers and Geezers," actually!)—are the demographic drivers of the next 20 years. I don't know if you've noticed, but Tom has a tendency to be right about things like that. In fact, that's why we pooled our efforts last year and co-wrote our book *Trends,* a top-line look at the why, who, and what-should-I-do of these two mighty markets. That book was the freshman introductory course; this book is for the marketing majors.

A Few Words about Definitions

Getting data on this group of women has not been easy. Actually, let me back up a step: there *is* no data on PrimeTime Women, *per se;* that is, on women 50–70 years old. As a matter of fact, there is very little data even on the broader group, women 50+.

What we do have are data on various definitions of the Mature Market and data on women. In this chapter I present a snapshot of each of those groups in their own right and cut and paste a composite picture of PrimeTime Women.

Data on the Mature Market. People who look at the 50+ population don't break out age segments consistently. Everyone presents the data in a different way, all valid but not consistent with each other. Throughout this chapter, throughout the book, you'll find the facts I quote flitting maddeningly from "50+" to "55+," sometimes swooping down to "45+" or up to "65+." Every governmental and statistical bureau defines their data differently, not to mention the variability in published corporate and association studies. Almost nobody uses an upper end cut-off point. (Except, of course, for advertisers, who cut off their interest in "older consumers" at 54!) Frustrating? No kidding.

Data on Women. Rarely does anyone break out data on women 50+ from women in general. Lest we forget, until four years ago, there was little recognition of women as an important buying target. When I wrote my first book, it was often difficult even to find data on women broken out from data on men. Little by little, we're seeing advances in that arena.

The resolution on this portrait isn't as clean and clear as I'd like it to be. But here's the big picture: PrimeTime Women are the mightiest money machine on the planet. If they had their own country, their spending power would rank their economy as the sixth largest in the world, outstripping the GDPs of Spain, Saudi Arabia, and Switzerland.

Population: The Mature Market Moves into Midlife

Boomers Move into PrimeTime

No single figure captures the true magnitude of the PrimeTime population. Here are a few choice facts concerning the 50+ demographic and the Boomers who are steadily joining its ranks.

Going "Boom." In all, there are about 78 million Baby Boomers. In 1996, they began to turn 50; as of 2006, more than half have handled that milestone. In 2011, a mere five years from now, the first Baby Boomer will turn 65, reaching the traditional age of retirement.[1]

Hitting the Half-Century Mark. Every seven seconds, another Boomer in the United States turns 50. In 2000, 38.5 percent of the U.S. adult (18+) population was over 50; by 2010 that percentage will rise to 43 percent, and by 2026, it will rise again to 49 percent.[2] By 2009, the *majority* of U.S. households will be headed by someone over the age of 50.[3]

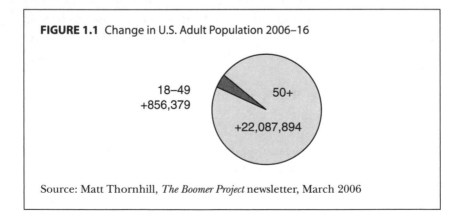

FIGURE 1.1 Change in U.S. Adult Population 2006–16

18–49
+856,379

50+

+22,087,894

Source: Matt Thornhill, *The Boomer Project* newsletter, March 2006

The new majority. According to Matt Thornhill, editor of the very useful newsletter *The Boomer Project,* between 2006 and 2016, the U.S. adult population will grow by 22.9 million people. Of this growth, an astonishing 22.1 million will be in the over-50 group. Yes, you read that right. Fully 96 percent of the growth in the U.S. adult population will come from the 50+ market as the Baby Boomers leave behind the "junior leagues" and move up into PrimeTime. The 18–49 segment is expected to increase by only 856,379 people (4 percent). (See Figure 1.1.)

Women: PrimeTime "Femographics™"

Keeping It All in Perspective. As noted above, there are lots of ways to look at the data on this market, so you have to be really rigorous about quoting the stats exactly the way they are reported. Sometimes it seems like numbers are conflicting with each other, when actually they are consistent but just reported on a different base. For example, women over 50 are 16 percent of the U.S. population, 22 percent of the U.S. adult population, and 41 percent of the U.S. adult female population.[4] To help us all keep things in perspective, Figure 1.2 is a comprehensive summary chart showing how it all shakes out.

FIGURE 1.2 PrimeTime Population Comparisons

	Percent of			
Category	Total Population	Adult Population	Female Population	Female Adult Population
50+	29	41	—	—
Women	51	51	100	—
Women 50+	16	22	31	41
Women 50–70	11	15	21	27

Source: U.S. Census Bureau, 2005 Estimates

There are two key take-aways that should knock your marketing socks off:

Every Fifth Adult in the United States Today Is a Female Over 50.[5] There are more American women over 50 than the entire population of Australia, or Argentina, or even Canada. And thanks to the population bulge called the Baby Boom, lots more are on their way. So before you spend all those billions to expand into those difficult foreign markets, you might have a look to see if you've maximized your opportunity with the heretofore invisible women in your own backyard.

As More Boomers Move into Midlife, Women Will Constitute an Increasing Percentage of the U.S. Population.[6] From birth to burial, the population ratio of females to males increases with age. At birth, there are about 5 percent more boys than girls—about 105 girls born for every 100 boys. From birth through adolescence, more boys than girls succumb to infant mortality challenges, the diseases of youth, and acts of violence. (Some scientists speculate that's **why** there are more boys at birth: nature's way of ensuring that roughly equal numbers of males and females make it to the mating years.)

At around 20 years of age, the ratio stabilizes and changes at a much slower rate. Coincidentally, it's right at the half-century mark that the ratio changes from less than 50 percent (women are the minority of the cohort) to greater than 50 percent (women are the majority). The reason is simple: On average, women live longer; their life expectancy at birth is seven years higher than that of men.[7]

Right now, according to the U.S. Census Bureau, of the 87 million adults over 50 years old, 40 million are men, and 47 million are women. In a population of people aged 55–74, the female/male ratio is 54/46. That means for every 100 women of that age, there are about 85 men of the same age. Or looking at it the other way around, for every 100 men there are about 117 women. (See Figure 1.3.)

Single Women. Many PrimeTime Women find themselves single in midlife, either by choice or by chance. According to the U.S. Census Bureau, 35 percent of all women aged 50–70 in the United States are single—whether divorced, widowed, or never married.[8]

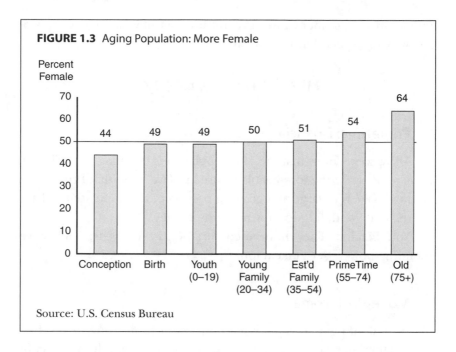

FIGURE 1.3 Aging Population: More Female

Percent
Female

Source: U.S. Census Bureau

And before you go feeling sorry for them, you should know that, for the most part, they are not leading the stereotypical sad, lonely life you might imagine. PrimeTime Women are smashing the myth of the "old maid." For example, they are not desperately seeking the man of their dreams; instead they enjoy their autonomy and are not eager to reassume spousal obligations. Nor are they clueless about finances; as a group, women actually make fewer investment mistakes than men. They are not huddled in their houses with half a dozen cats, as a recent AARP survey laughingly suggested; instead, they are reinventing themselves, returning to prior interests and activities as well as discovering new ones. They recognize that it is increasingly likely for all women to end up on their own, and they are creating clubs, communities, and support groups to maintain and expand their social ties.[9]

Single PrimeTime Women in the United States will become an economic force in their own right. Savvy marketers need to keep in mind that they are the *sole* decision makers in a substantial percentage of 50+ households. Two industries in particular had better be ready for single PrimeTime Women—housing and real estate. Already, single women own almost twice as many homes as single men (22 percent vs. 12 percent).[10] With midlife bringing a higher ratio of women to men, and a greater number of women who are single, we can expect that number to soar.

It's the Money, Honey

PrimeTime: Financial Force

Okay, so we know that the 50+ population is booming and will continue to do so for the foreseeable future. And we know that PrimeTime Women make up a large and growing portion of the population. That's all well and good, but do they have any money?

You betcha! They have income; they have assets; they have spending power. Let's take a look.

Money In: Income

In evaluating a consumer segment opportunity, one of the first criteria marketers use as a leading indicator is household income. In fact, income is normally a *mis*leading indicator in assessing the Mature Market because, whether defined as 50+ or 55+, average income for the segment generally looks significantly lower than the average for the general population.

But that doesn't matter. Because when you define the market that way, most of the consumers in that group are retired. Of *course* they have lower income; they've quit working. What often gets overlooked is that the retired population doesn't live solely on its income; it lives on pension payouts, Social Security, and the savings it has accumulated over a lifetime of working—its assets. Marketers (and newspaper reporters, for that matter) shouldn't assume that lower income by itself equates to lower spending power.

Interestingly, when you look at people in *mid*life, you're less likely to fall into this error, mainly because there is an upper end to the age range. This excludes the many millions of people older than the age cut-off, most of whom are more likely to be retirees, whose inclusion would bring down the income average for the segment. As you can see from the following data, midlife households (age 45–64 according to this data) actually have higher household income than the national average.[11]

2002 Income

Total Households	**$42,209**
Age <25	$27,828
Age 25–35	$45,330
Age 35–44	$53,521
Age 45–54	**$59,021**
Age 55–64	**$47,203**
Age 65–74	$28,173

Sources: Fourth editions of *Older Americans*, p. 114; *The Baby Boom*, p. 89; *Generation X*, p. 89–90; *Millennials*, p. 166–67 (Ithaca, NY: New Strategist Publications, 2004).

PrimeTimers, people age 50–70, straddle three of the segments broken out above. They start in the middle of the 45–54 segment and end in the middle of the 65–74 segment; a population-weighted average of the three segments would put their income at about $45,400. Their above-average income is due to three key factors:

1. PrimeTimers are at the peak of their careers and are enjoying the highest earning power of their lives. Among men who work full time, those with the highest incomes are aged 55 and older.[12] In fact, many older households are affluent; 21 percent of householders age 55 to 59 have annual incomes of $100,000 or more, significantly higher than the 6 percent among the population as a whole.[13] Incomes have steadily grown for people 55 to 64 years old, particularly among women 55–64. Women aged 55 to 64 saw their incomes rise 8.5 percent from 2000–2002, while men saw only a 1.6 percent increase.[14]

2. PrimeTimers are dual income households. Household incomes are higher for older households not only because more are still in the workforce, but also because there are usually two earners per household. Whereas in previous generations there was usually only one earner per household, among Boomers, 70 percent of households have two paychecks.[15] (Remember the yuppie DINKS, "Dual Income No Kids," back in the '80s? A Boomer original.) These two-paycheck families bring home a lot more money. Married couples account for 82 percent of households with income of $100,000 or more.

3. The long-term trend toward early retirement has eased off. Today, about 50 percent of women and 65 percent of men ages 60–64 are in the workforce.[16] As you will see later, Boomers have no intention of retiring at age 60 or 65, as has been traditional in the past. Actually, the whole notion of "retirement" is getting fuzzy: ABC News reported recently that most Baby Boomers expect to retire around the age of 63, and yet 66 percent of the survey participants intend to work for pay after retiring. Peter Francese, founder of *American Demographics* magazine, predicts that nonretiring Boomers will add another 9 million workers aged 60–69 to the workforce, which will in turn contribute at least $400 billion a year to consumer spending.[17] In other words, expect 50+, and especially PrimeTime Women's, income to continue to grow due to their continued presence and power in the labor force.

Money Building Up: Assets and Net Worth

Yes, 50+ consumers are still bringing home the income, but importantly, they also enjoy the greatest assets and net worth (assets minus debts) of any age group.

In 2001, households headed by people in the 55–64 age group had the highest median net worth of $182,500—more than double the net worth of total American households, and 16 times as much as the $11,600 in median net worth reported for the under-35 age group.[18]

Consumers aged 50 and older have much higher net worth due to:

• The appreciation they've captured in the value of their homes, which they have generally owned longer than younger households have owned theirs.

• Their greater grip on the financial assets in this country. While they make up "only" 41 percent of the adult population,[19] people over 50 own between 70 percent and 79 percent of all financial assets, depending on whether you get your number from Ken Dychtwald or the AARP, both equally good sources.[20] In addition, they control 80 percent of all the money

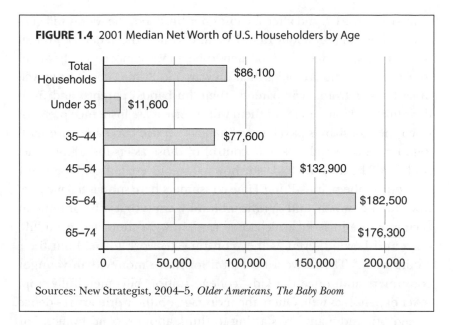

FIGURE 1.4 2001 Median Net Worth of U.S. Householders by Age

Total Households	$86,100
Under 35	$11,600
35–44	$77,600
45–54	$132,900
55–64	$182,500
65–74	$176,300

Sources: New Strategist, 2004–5, *Older Americans, The Baby Boom*

in savings accounts,[21] 62 percent of all large Wall Street invest-ment accounts,[22] and 66 percent of all dollars invested in the stock market.[23] The 50+ crowd leads all other groups when it comes to liquid assets as well (cash and short-term securities). They are 36 percent more likely than average to have liquid assets of more than $100,000 and 20 percent more likely to have liquid assets of $250,000 or more.[24]

Moreover, their net worth continues to grow. In 2001, the popu-lation aged 50-plus held $29.1 trillion in net worth, or 69 percent of the U.S. total—up dramatically from 56 percent in 1983.[25]

Money Handed Down: Double-Dipping Inheritance

Over the next decade or two, Boomers will be on the receiving end of the largest intergenerational transfer of wealth in history[26] as they inherit money from their high-saving parents. Experts debate the exact number to be inherited, but it ranges from 14 to 25 trillion dol-lars.[27] (What's a few trillion here or there? It's all in the family, right?)

And in the decade or two that follow, Boomer women will in turn inherit from their husbands. The average age of widowhood in the

United States is 67; and after she loses her husband, the widow will generally outlive him by about 15 to 18 years.[28] Life expectancy for women is about 7 years longer than for men to begin with; moreover, they tend to marry men who are older than they are. So PrimeTime Women will inherit assets from their parents, their husbands' parents, and from their husbands, and many of them will receive a life insurance payment when their husbands pass on. As financial service companies are starting to note, they will have sole control of those assets for a long time. And they'll be the ones to decide how to save, invest, gift, and spend it.

You get the point—PrimeTime consumers have substantial income, towering net worth, and significant family assets that will continue to accumulate and from which they can draw in their active midlife years and beyond, even as they continue to work throughout their "retirement." They have a heck of a lot more money than younger consumers and, once the kids' college tuition bills mercifully stop, fewer expenses as well. Often, the mortgage on their primary residence is paid off, and many are starting to think about second homes. For most—not all—the kids leave the nest at some point. Their smaller households spend less on daily expenses such as food and utilities, leaving more money to spend on their own interests and activities.

The Youth Market: Highly Overrated

Despite the youth obsession that started with the Baby Boomers and should have ended with the young dot-com millionaires of the '90s, wealth patterns today match the dominant patterns throughout history: *Older people control most of the money.*

But older people have an image problem. As a culture, we're conditioned toward youth and accustomed to admiring young people. When we think of youth and the young, we think "energetic and colorful;" when we think of middle age or "mature," we think "tired and washed out." And when we think of "old" or "senior," we think either "exhausted and gray" or, more likely, we just don't think.

The financial numbers are absolutely inarguable—the Mature Market has the money. Yet advertisers remain astonishingly indifferent to them, and television networks continue to party like it's 1975, scrambling to develop shows that deliver audiences that are 18–34 or, worst case, 25–49.

One particularly puzzling category of youth obsession is the highly coveted target of men 18–34, and it's *always* referred to as "the highly coveted target." Marketers have been distracted by men 18–34 because they are getting harder to reach. So what? Who wants to reach them? Beyond fast food and beer, they don't buy much of anything. I didn't say they don't buy *anything*—sure, they do a little of the household grocery fill-in shopping, and they buy more apparel and personal care items than in the past. But relative to women? Forget about it! If your budget is so large you can spread it around indiscriminately, go ahead and "covet" men 18–34. But, if your funds are limited and you need to focus money where it will be most efficient and effective, go for PrimeTime Women.

It's ironic, really. Everybody claims they're looking for ways to build sales. In these competitive times, even a partial share point can mean millions of dollars. But marketers' obsession with youth is blinding them to the big bucks right in front of them from PrimeTime Women. Billions and billions of dollars, and nobody's going after them!

That irony is compounded by another irony. Marketers focused obsessively on Boomers back in the 1960s, 1970s, and 1980s, when that generation was first making its way up the economic ladder. But now that they have reached the top, the peak convergence of their lifetime income, wealth, and discretionary spending power, marketers have dropped them like a hot potato. What gives?

The theory is that if you "get 'em while they're young, they're yours for life." What nonsense. *Maybe* it was true in the 1950s, when there were only three brands of crackers and two choices of washing machines. I doubt it—one of the characteristics of youth as they are trying to define their identity is the drive to experiment. So while getting them to try your brand is better than not getting them to try it, don't rationalize it by telling yourself that you've locked in their loyalty for life.

Even supposing the "cradle-to-grave" theory were true, it would mean you're spending today's dollars in the hope of generating tomorrow's sales. A worthy principle, to be sure, but one rarely encouraged by today's quarterly minded shareholders. When you spend your budget on the youth market, you're putting money into your successor's success—again, a noble notion, but a questionable career strategy. You might as well put your brand's budget into 25-year savings bonds as that's how long it will take the youth market to have the buying power PrimeTime Women have right now.

Money Out: Spending

Income and assets are all well and good, but what matters to marketers is spending. According to a U.S. Consumer Expenditure Survey, today's consumers over 50 have accumulated more wealth and have more spending power than any other cohort in history.[29] At 29 percent of the total U.S. population, the 50-plus crowd accounts for more than 40 percent of total U.S. consumer spending[30] and controls 50 percent of all discretionary spending.[31] They buy $2 *trillion* worth of goods and services each year.[32] That's a lot of cash.

You would expect 50+ consumers to be buying more than younger consumers in categories like health care, travel, and insurance. But that's just the beginning. In fact, from 1997 to 2002, inflation-adjusted spending among householders aged 55 to 64 rose at *double* the rate of increase for the average American householder.[33]

To illustrate, here are some spending facts that may surprise you. When you compare the average annual spending for householders 55–64 to their younger counterparts 25–34, you find that the older group spends

- **20** percent more on new cars and trucks;
- **29** percent more on meals eaten at full-service restaurants;
- **38** percent more on airfare;
- **58** percent more on sports equipment;
- **100** percent more on coffee;
- **103** percent more on motorized recreational vehicles;
- **113** percent more on wine consumed at home;
- **127** percent more on maintenance, repairs, and home insurance;
- **258** percent more on owned vacation homes; and
- **250–500** percent more on housekeeping and yard services.[34]

The 50+ segment comprises 40 million credit card users, who own almost half of the credit cards in the United States. In fact, those in the

45–65 bracket own and use credit cards at a higher rate than any other age group.[35]

In addition to buying new things for the first time, older consumers buy stuff to replace older stuff, often trading up in the process. Let's look at the car industry, for example. According to an article in *The Wall Street Journal,* of the 13 cars that a typical U.S. household buys over its "lifetime," seven—*the majority*—are bought after the head of the household reaches 50.[36]

PrimeTimers' substantial spending power gives them the luxury of being generous gift-givers; that is, they spend not only on themselves, but on others. According to *New Strategist,* 55- to 64-year-old households are the second biggest gift givers (slightly behind 45–54 year olds), and they are the only demographic segment actually increasing its gift-related spending.[37]

Here, the big story is the grandparents' market. By 2010, there will be an estimated 80 million grandparents in the United States. Already, spending by older Americans on their grandkids amounts to about $30 billion annually, and as more Boomers become grandparents, more grandkids will find themselves on the receiving end of that indulgent impulse.

And it's not just Thomas the Tank Engine, Barbie, and Disney World who will reap the rewards of the grandparent bonanza. Research has shown that PrimeTime Women's influence continues to grow exponentially with age, as their hefty wallets and sense of responsibility also increase. PrimeTime Women will be helping out their children and grandchildren financially and contribute important funds to everything from private school tuition to the latest and greatest minivan, from sending them to summer camp to footing the bill for a volunteer trip to Costa Rica.

PrimeTime Women: "Just the Facts, Ma'am"

Boomer Women: The Inflection Point

Speaking of grandmothers means you're speaking of PrimeTime Women. And they're very different from what probably popped into your head when you heard the word *grandmother.* While yesterday's grandma may have sat in a rocker reading a book and sipping tea during her leisure hours, today's grandma is more likely to be sitting at her computer checking on her investments and sipping Evian, having just come in from her tennis match.

Today's woman 50–70 years old is very different from women of previous generations. In fact, it may be said that this is the first generation who can legitimately be called "PrimeTime," for two reasons:

1. As recently as 40 years ago, 50–70 wasn't really the "prime of life." Boomer women are the first generation of women to have the benefit of recent significant advances in health, fitness, and nutritional awareness, as well as access to miracles of modern medicine like knee replacements and heart transplants.

2. Additionally, 40 years ago, 50–70 wasn't really a "prime marketing target," either. The things we buy now with our discretionary income simply didn't exist then. There were virtually no consumer electronics—no cell phones, no personal computers, no PDAs, no GPS devices, no Internet. There were no spas, no cosmetic surgery, no gourmet grocery stores, no home furnishing stores (except for Sears), no Home Shopping Channel, no personal trainers, no venti decaf nonfat vanilla lattes. There were few real investments besides one's own home, little participation in life insurance, and a good deal of reluctance to get involved in the stock market. (Remember, the great stock market crash was still fresh in a lot of minds.)

Forty years ago, the relatively recent innovation of Social Security enabled most people to retire at 65. Note that when Social Security was established in 1935, the average life expectancy was 61.[38] So for most people, there were at best only a few years between retirement and death. Travel, hobbies, and socializing were modest.

In the introductory chapter, I touched on the point that Boomer Women represent an inflection point in history—a dramatic, radical change from those who went before them. To give you a little better sense for that, let me fill in a few facts for you:

- **College Education.** Before Boomer women, most college students were men. While about 26 percent of women aged 55–59 today have degrees, that number rises to 30 percent among women 50–54, which is more than double the 14 percent of women 65+ with degrees.[39] For the last two decades, women have been earning the *majority* of college degrees, 58 percent, while men account for 42 percent.[40]

- **Serious Earning Power.** Boomer women are the first generation of women in history to enter the workplace en masse and to command better paying and more secure jobs. Women in the workplace surged from just 30 percent in 1950 to 59 percent in 2004.[41] These Boomer women have broken barriers in almost every field dominated by men. They now account for 50 percent of managers and professionals,[42] and there are more female doctors, lawyers, engineers, computer scientists, CEOs, astronauts, politicians, and high-powered consultants today than ever before.[43]

- **Business Ownership.** For the past 15 years, women have been starting 70 percent of all new businesses. Forty-eight percent of all privately owned businesses are majority- or equally owned by women. Relative to the economy at large, woman-owned businesses are growing twice as fast in number, three times as fast in employees, and four times as fast in sales revenues.[44] Nearly three-quarters (73 percent) of women business owners in nontraditional industries, such as construction and transportation, are age 45 or older.[45]

- **Reproductive Rights.** Birth control radically changed the roles, expectations, life-stage assumptions, and routine patterns of women. It's hard to have a career if you have to keep dropping out of the workforce every two years to have a baby.

- **Property Rights.** It's amazing to see the changes in just the past 20 to 30 years—within my adult lifetime. Can you believe that as recently as:

  - 1970, the Ohio Supreme Court held that a wife was "at most a superior servant to her husband . . . only chattel with no personality, no property, and no legally recognized feelings or rights."

– 1974, the Georgia legislature approved a statute that defined the husband as "head of the family" with the "wife . . . subject to him; her legal existence . . . merged in the husband, except as so far as the law recognizes her separately, either for her own protection, her own benefit, or for the preservation of the public order."[46]

– the mid-1980s, newspapers were still ignoring the Equal Employment Opportunity Commission's 1968 ruling that it was illegal to run newspaper Help Wanted ads segregated into "Help wanted—women" and "Help wanted—men." Regrettably, the EEOC had little enforcement power, so for decades, there continued to be pages and pages of jobs for which women could not even apply.[47]

Women: The Power of the PrimeTime Purse

Money Talks

Thanks to the dramatic developments above, PrimeTime Women have had a much greater role in contributing to family income than prior generations of women, most of whom did not work outside the home. Between 1990 and 2003, women's inflation-adjusted median income grew 26 percent, while men's grew a modest 8 percent.[48]

This decided skew is driven by a couple of key changes: First, on average, college graduates' lifetime income is approximately twice the income of people with only a high school degree, and as you just saw above, substantially more college graduates are women. Second, in recent years, there's been an evaporation of many of the high-paying blue-collar jobs men have relied on for their big paychecks.

Interestingly, the *greatest* income growth was experienced by women 55–64, whose income grew more than 58 percent during that same time frame.[49]

All that has substantially changed the dynamics of family decision-making, because there's always an unspoken understanding that he who brings in the bread gets more say in how it's sliced. Boomer women in particular are seven times more likely than the prior generation to share planning and financial decisions with their spouses.[50]

These days, the unspoken understanding in most households is that the woman of the house is its "Chief Purchasing Officer." As I established in my first book, *Marketing to Women,* women in general control an estimated 80 percent of all household spending. In addition to the traditionally female-purchased categories, like groceries, cleaning supplies, and kids' clothes, women are assuming responsibility for big-ticket buying decisions as well, even in historically male-driven categories:

- 53% of investment decisions[51]

- 55% of consumer electronics[52]

- 60% of home improvement buyers; 80% of home improvement purchase decisions[53]

- 60+% of new cars[54]

- 66% of computers[55]

And since, as we'll soon see, their influence on buying decisions doesn't wane in later years but actually grows, it means that Prime-Time Women control even more than 80 percent of the spending in the PrimeTime households, which are at the peak of their income, assets, and spending power.

By the way, a quick note to the fashion industry, which, as you will see throughout the book, happens to be a particular hobbyhorse for me: Overall, women's apparel spending is on a downward trend, with average household spending dropping 8 percent between 1997 and 2002.[56] So you might want to take note that households of 55- to 64-year-olds spend *more* on women's apparel than any other age group, in fact, fully 64 percent more than women 25 to 34. PrimeTime Women are offering you a lifeline, and other than the spectacularly successful Chico's, the best you can do so far is Gap's tentative and slightly terrified venture to reach women 35+ with Forth and Towne, a new retail chain that claims to target women who don't want to look like 24-year-olds. Don't let your stockholders find out that you've let your infatuation with size four models blind you to the market with the money—even if you do have to cut the clothes a size or two larger.

Keep in mind that PrimeTime Women have no plans to retire anytime soon. They'll be bringing in more income and wielding even weightier wallets. According to the U.S. Bureau of Labor Statistics, in the mere ten years between 2002 and 2012, the number of working women aged 55 to 64 is projected to increase by an astounding 57 percent, more than any other age group of women.[57]

PrimeTime Women: The Perfect Storm

Women today who have passed the age 50 mark—or who will be passing it in the years to come—are the healthiest, wealthiest, most active, independent, and influential generation of women in history. Here's why:

Healthiest. The average life expectancy for women in the United States is now 79.7 years.[58] As quoted in Gail Sheehy's *New Passages,* if a woman reaches her 50th birthday without cancer or heart disease, she can expect to reach the age of 92.[59] This generation of women— with their walking and swimming, their yoga and Pilates—will stay healthy and active for many years to come.

Wealthiest. Women in the United States earn half or more of household income in the majority of U.S. households.[60] They are gathering considerable assets in their midlife years, both through their own earning power and through inheritance. Now add in the fact that, having raised their kids, they can finally begin to spend time, energy, and, yes, money on themselves again. Talk about pent-up demand!

Most Active and Independent. Not only are PrimeTime Women more physically active today than ever before, they are also remaining economically vital to an unprecedented degree. For all Americans over 50, the labor force participation rate in 2003 was 46.3 percent, up nearly 7 percentage points from a mere decade ago.[61]

And according to the Bureau of Labor Statistics, the number of women aged 55 and older in the workforce will increase by a whopping 52 percent between 2000 and 2010—from 6.4 million to 10.1 million.[62] Whether they work out of choice or out of necessity, PrimeTime Women possess both self-reliance and purchasing power that far exceeds those of their mothers and grandmothers.

Most Influential. For the next two decades, PrimeTime Women will occupy the center of gravity in the United States and in the developed world by virtue not only of their preponderance in the population, but also because of their consolidated weighty wallets. And as gravity tends to do, PrimeTime Women will draw the values, priorities, and purchasing practices of the rest of the world towards them.

PrimeTime Women are large in numbers. They have lots of money to spend. They have long years of experience as confident consumers. They are growing more assertive. And they are entering a stage of life in which they are free from old responsibilities and eager to embrace new adventures.

Message to marketers, especially those of you who sell big-ticket items: *learn to communicate with PrimeTime Women.* Get gender-savvy and age-savvy—and do it fast. If your business is financial services, for example, or real estate (second homes, retirement communities), you will find that PrimeTime Women make up an ever-growing portion of your market, as they take on a greater role in managing not only their own money, but the entire family's finances. Follow the dollar signs, and they will point you to PrimeTime Women.

CHAPTER TWO

Shattering Conventions

This chapter is contributed by David Polston and Martin Horn, both senior vice presidents, DDB.

Introducing My Esteemed Contributors

As I said before, it's very difficult to find any real research about Prime-Time Women. I've read every book and every study I can get my hands on. I like to think this book does a pretty good job pulling together what exists and translating it into insights.

But I wanted to know more. I had some hunches and no way to confirm them—specific questions that needed specific answers that could be obtained only through primary research. Lucky for me, I have friends in high places. One of them is David Polston, Group Account Director at agency powerhouse DDB Chicago. When I approached him about partnering on an initiative to gain more insight on the world's biggest spenders, PrimeTime Women, he was not only open, he was enthusiastic.

I asked him if DDB would be willing to sponsor three sets of qualitative Girlfriend Groups, with women in their 40s, 50s, and 60s respectively. I had a hunch that a lot of the angst that conventional wisdom accepts as "every woman hates growing older" originated in the 40s crowd, evaporated in the 50s, and was actively repudiated in the 60s. I had another hunch that, while PrimeTime Women, currently in their 50s and 60s, brought with them many attitudes and behaviors acquired during their Boomer formative years, the 1960s and '70s, they also had changed a good deal and now see things quite differently from how they did when they were younger. In other words, they're not only different from younger women today, they're also different from their younger selves.

When he heard that, David raised his eyebrows and invited DDB Director of U.S. Strategic Insights Marty Horn to join us. Turns out, previously unbeknownst to me, DDB has a remarkable research knowledge base in their proprietary Life Style Study^{SM} that has captured a treasure trove of consumer and category data for over 30 years.

The long and short of it is, in this chapter DDB has melded the learning from the Girlfriend Groups (expertly conducted and interpreted by Caryn Harbour of Candid Conversations) with quantitative findings from their Life Style Study^{SM} to uncover realities about PrimeTime Women that defy stereotypes. My special thanks to David and Marty, who have been not only insightful but truly delightful to work with.

So far, you've gotten to know PrimeTime Women as a demographic group and as an economic force. You've learned about their growing numbers and increasing spending power and that Prime-Time Women are **the** market of the future.

However, if you hope to tap the awesome potential of Prime-Time Women, you need to know them not solely as a *demographic,* a *market segment,* or a *target consumer;* you need to know them as **individuals** with hopes, dreams, aspirations; with concerns and fears; and with an outlook on life that is often quite different today from what it was when they were younger. You have to have an appreciation for what's going on in their heads and in their hearts.

It's tempting to think of marketing as a process for selling goods and services to millions of people. But marketing is, fundamentally, *communication between two people*—the marketer and the customer. The better the marketer knows the customer, not just as a consumer of goods and services, but as a **person** who brings life experience to the purchase process, the more likely the marketer will make a sale.

Effective communication with the PrimeTime Woman can only be achieved by viewing many facets of her personality, her innermost thoughts, what she enjoys doing, and what keeps her up at night.

So let's get an up close and personal look at the PrimeTime Woman.

Getting to Know the PrimeTime Woman

Over the years, we've done a lot of research with women of all ages, so the PrimeTime Woman isn't exactly a stranger. However, we wanted to get to know her even better. To that end, we conducted several rounds of Girlfriend Groups with PrimeTime Women as well as "40-something" women. As the name suggests, Girlfriend Groups consist of four to five pairs of long-time friends. Girlfriend Groups are enlightening (and fun!) because women in these groups really enjoy sharing stories with others and are not as shy about opening up in front of friends as they might be with strangers. Hearing these women talk about what they think and feel as they move into their 50s, 60s, and 70s; what they laugh and cry about now versus when they were younger; and how they have rearranged priorities as they age was incredibly revealing.

Insightful as these Girlfriend Groups were, we weren't content to stop there. We also needed **data** from a large and representative group of Prime-Time Women. If we hope to better communicate with PrimeTime Women, we needed to truly understand how widely held their attitudes, interests, and opinions are on key issues; how prevalent certain behaviors really are; how great the lifestyle differences are between PrimeTime Women and younger women; and what it is that really gets the blood pumping through their veins.

To get a better measure (literally) of PrimeTime Women, we turned to the DDB Life Style Study[SM]. DDB has conducted the Life Style Study[SM] annually since 1975, surveying 3,000 men and women nationwide each year. Respondents answer over 1,000 questions about diverse topics such as health, family finances, shopping, work, self-image, child care, religion, leisure activities, product use, and media habits.

This wealth of information makes it possible to paint a vivid, detailed, multidimensional portrait of nearly any consumer segment. So, in profiling Prime-Time Women, we went into the Life Style database, looked specifically at women 50 to 70 years old, and then compared and contrasted their responses to the 1,000-plus Life Style questions with those of younger women, the Gen X and Gen Y generations, 25 to 49 years of age.

Conventional Wisdom Isn't So Wise!

A big advantage of a large and nationally representative study such as Life Style is that it allows us to more easily separate fact from fancy, reality from myth, issues that are known to be true that really **are** true from issues that are "known to be true" but aren't! Life Style can tell us when conventional wisdom is right, and when it's not.

For example, conventional wisdom about women 50 to 70 years old holds that PrimeTime Women tend to be quite reflective and introverted and pine for the good old days. This "wisdom" typically concludes that, having already lived a large chunk of their lives, few PrimeTime Women believe that they still have new horizons to explore or a lot left to accomplish in life. Faced with an ever-shortening future, conventional wisdom argues that these women are fairly worried, passive, and perhaps even a bit depressed (since depression has been reported to be an unfortunate part of aging). PrimeTime Women simply aren't in control of their lives the way they were when they were in their 20s, 30s, and 40s.

But in these and many other instances, conventional wisdom is wrong. Dead wrong.

Women 50 to 70 years old are called PrimeTime Women for a reason! Surprising insights from the DDB Life Style Study and the Girlfriend Groups reveal that these women strongly feel that they are in the **prime** of their lives, not the downward slope that so many people imagine. PrimeTime Women firmly believe that they are savvy from experience and are better able to handle what life throws at them, and that they are young enough in spirit—if not always in years!—to embrace life and tackle challenges in ways that younger women don't or can't.

So, much of what passes as gospel about women entering "prime time" just doesn't hold up under close inspection. Are PrimeTime Women different from younger women? Of course, but not in ways we might expect.

What Makes PrimeTime Women Tick

The PrimeTime Woman is so multifaceted in so many unexpected and intriguing ways that we could go on forever. But neither paper nor patience is infinite. So we offer you five interrelated and interdependent insights, a mere sampling, into the PrimeTime Woman that are particularly cogent for any marketer who hopes to have a meaningful conversation with her.

Before we begin, though, here's a little quiz for you. Go ahead and fill it out. We'll give you the answer later on.

> What percentage of PrimeTime Women, women 50 to 70 years old, in the DDB Life Style Study agree with the statement *My greatest achievements are still ahead of me.*
>
> A. 21%
>
> B. 31%
>
> C. 44%
>
> D. 59%

OK. Let's get started.

1. Experiencing the Joy of Being. What is particularly striking about the PrimeTime Woman is the contentment, joy, and enthusiasm with which she lives her life. Although she describes herself as *serious,* being serious does not equate to being negative. You could even say that she lives by that old Johnny Mercer classic, "Accentuate the positive, eliminate the negative."

She's happier and more content and possesses a brighter, more optimistic disposition than Generation X and Generation Y women who are many years her junior. And she's less apt to be on edge or off-kilter. She's come to accept her age (and some of the physical and emotional challenges that come with it) with a dignity, grace, and an **enthusiasm** that belies that Rolling Stones (of all people!) refrain "What a drag it is getting old."

As we heard in our Girlfriend Groups, PrimeTime Women have learned to find happiness wherever and whenever they can, whether that's helping a daughter by taking in her children, buying a new pair of shoes, or, yes, starting to date **online!**

How PrimeTimeWomen Feel

	PrimeTime Women (50–70)	Younger Women (25–49)
	%	%
Cheerful	**77**	68
Optimistic	**74**	68
Content	**53**	47
Unhappy	**31**	39
Discouraged	**28**	36
Bored	**22**	30

Source: 2006 DDB Life Style Study

Note: Data in this table and all others in this chapter, unless otherwise noted, are from the 2006 DDB Life Style Study. All differences between PrimeTime Women and Younger Women reflected in this table and other tables in this chapter, unless otherwise noted, are significant at a confidence level of .90.

Sure, some PrimeTime Women still struggle accepting their crow's feet, wrinkles, and sagging muscles. Yet, most have gotten past the point of needing to look young. **In fact, PrimeTime Women are just as likely as their younger counterparts, 58 percent versus 57 percent, respectively, to boast that "When I look in the mirror, I like what I see."**

I love being 50; I love this time in my life. I feel stronger, I do more now than I used to. I am more active, mentally stronger. I don't think, oh God, I'm getting old. I look in the mirror and see wrinkles and I'm okay with it.

Lynn, 50

Just about every woman we spoke to said that she gets aches and pains and that getting up in the morning takes more time than it used to. But they adjust by getting up a little earlier or planning their days to start a little later. They get up, get dressed, and put on their makeup, a routine that makes them feel better and more alive than does sitting around in a house dress or muumuu!

I can feel arthritis and the aches and pains, but I still don't think of the age.

Rachel, 60

You take a hot shower. You put your high heel house shoes on. You're groomed and you can answer the day because you are ready.

Leanne, 69

Even if they don't look it on the outside, most PrimeTime Women feel like 30 on the inside. Their psychological age is much younger than their chronological age, and in many respects, their psychological age is more youthful and vibrant than that of women 20 and 30 years their junior.

Drinking from a Psychological "Fountain of Youth"

	PrimeTime Women (50–70) %	Younger Women (25–49) %
I feel a lot younger than my age	82	68
I do everything I should to take care of my health	70	55
I have more energy than most people my age	66	48

Source: 2006 DDB Life Style Study

Experiencing the joy of being means that each day is special:

I really didn't give it a thought [what being 64 would be like]. *I love it. I mean, it's a blessing to live to 64. Age is just a number.*

Ruby, 64

The first thing I do in the morning is say "Thank you, God" for another day.

Rachel, 60

And to punctuate their joy of being . . .

- 44 percent of PrimeTime Women in our Life Style Study believe that they will live to 100, compared to only 38 percent of younger women who think they'll be centegenarians.

These days, it's more about PMA (positive mental attitude), and less about PMS!

What accounts for this joy of being, this passion for living, this youthful spirit that the PrimeTime Woman possesses? As we'll see later, a lot of the joy she gets from living stems from keeping busy, staying curious, remaining active, and living life "in drive."

But another reason she's happy and content is a newfound sense of freedom to be herself.

2. Relishing Liberation. PrimeTime Women are redefining "women's liberation," at least as it pertains to this phase of their lives. They are enjoying what we call a "liberation from expectation."

Before we go any further, we have to emphasize that PrimeTime Women have a lot to wrestle with. Financial pressures for some are very real, and several women mentioned having to work beyond the typical retirement age of 65. Though many women dream of total freedom from having to care for others during these years, they are finding themselves still taking care of their children. Some are responsible for tending to ailing parents (and husbands) as well as to their grandchildren. One of the hardest transitions for women to deal with at this time in their lives is going from caregiver of children to caregiver of their parents.

Yet, even in the face of these huge challenges, most PrimeTime Women still say that they feel freer than they did when they were younger. The women we spoke to felt that when they were younger, they were "required" to consider others before themselves—children, husband, parents. Now they are experiencing a newfound freedom and control over their lives. They do not feel as constrained as they once did by familial and societal pressures to act in a prescribed way.

When I was younger, I was always thinking about what the next person was thinking and now, I don't care what they think.
Mary, 68

Mary's point is driven home by the fact that

- only 39 percent of PrimeTime Women in our Life Style Study, versus 55 percent of women 25–49, say "I'm so busy trying to make everyone else happy that I don't have control of my own life."

It's not as if the typical PrimeTime Woman doesn't care about her kids, her husband, her friends, or her job. Hardly. It's just that the demands—or at least the pressure she puts on herself to meet those demands—have eased up to some degree. The surging confidence she feels in her life skills (which we'll elaborate on later) and the rising independence and self-reliance she possesses enable her to more easily deal with others on **her** terms. She is quick to please herself and less driven to serve the whims of others. External pressure is giving way to internal pleasure.

> *[When you are younger] there is such a focus on your self-esteem and proving yourself before you are 50. When you get to a certain age, you realize you're never going to please everybody. You finally have time to think, 'How can I make myself feel good?' And that may be helping someone else. You're not going to be in a position where everyone likes you, so live with it and get over it. So you think, 'What can I do to please myself?'*
>
> Monika, 60

Monika goes on to say, with much head-nodding from the other women in the Girlfriend Group:

> *I'm at a point now where I'm in control of doing what I want to do. It seems like there is a freeing moment [emphasis ours] at 50.*

As the PrimeTime Woman becomes more liberated, a desire for greater **independence** is becoming more central to her self-concept.

- A whopping 81 percent of PrimeTime Women, compared to 72 percent of younger women, describe their ideal selves as *independent.*

And it's this freedom to be herself and her blossoming independence that the PrimeTime Woman credits for allowing her to live in a more "Angst-Free Zone."

The "Freedom to Be" Relieves a Lot of Stress

	PrimeTime Women (50–70) %	Younger Women (25–49) %
I feel I am under a great deal of pressure most of the time	42	65
I wish I knew how to relax	47	55
I get more headaches than most people	16	37
I worry that something bad will happen to me or a family member	55	66

Source: 2006 DDB Life Style Study

What's particularly refreshing about PrimeTime Woman's "freedom to be myself" is that it hasn't devolved into mindless self-indulgence. Rather, her liberation from expectation allows altruism, not egotism, to play a bigger role in her life. She's not just active; she's a bit of an activist.

3. Rocking Her World. PrimeTime Women who came of age in the 1960s and 1970s grew up in a time of tumult: the Vietnam War; racial unrest; the 1968 Democratic National Convention; Watergate; the burgeoning Women's Liberation Movement, to name just a few. Many of them demonstrated, carried protest signs, fought for social change, and dramatically redefined their expectations of what women were "supposed" to do in society.

While we would by no means characterize them these days as fire-breathing radicals (we probably wouldn't have exactly characterized them that way back in the '60s or '70s either!), PrimeTime Women

Will the Real Women's Lib Generation Please Stand Up?

We should pause for a moment and look at who was at the forefront of social activism in general and the Women's Movement in particular. Women currently in their PrimeTime years constitute two cohorts: the older end of the Boom Generation (50–60) and the younger end of the so-called Silent Generation (61–70). In the latter case, we say so-called because the Silent Generation was anything but. The Silent Generation spawned the Women's Movement, Boomer claims and egos notwithstanding! Boomers certainly took up the cause, but it was Silent Generation luminaries such as Betty Friedan and Gloria Steinem who led the way. And let's not forget Helen Reddy of "I Am Woman" fame, the anthem of the Women's Liberation Movement. Reddy was born in 1941, making her another member (albeit an Australian one) of the Silent Generation.

Hear them roar!

still want to make their voices heard—be they liberal or conservative. Many of the more activist attitudes and behaviors that were formed when PrimeTime Women were in their youth have stayed with them as they've gotten older.

The social and political activism that was the imprimatur of the 1960s and 1970s in general, and the Women's Movement specifically, is still alive among PrimeTime Women, and beating with a much stronger heart than is the one beating in today's Gen X and Gen Y women.

Energized and Engaged

	PrimeTime Women (50–70) %	Younger Women (25–49) %
I am interested in politics	64	54
My vote counts	81	73
I need to get the news every day	74	55
Wrote a letter to the editor	32	23

Source: 2006 DDB Life Style Study

PrimeTime Women may be doing more things for themselves these days and are less concerned about fulfilling the expectations of others, as we said above, but that does *not* preclude them from investing time and energy in their community or in altruistic pursuits.

For example, PrimeTime Women are more likely than younger women to

- do volunteer work, 61 percent vs. 57 percent.

- belong to a club or organization, 51 percent vs. 42 percent.

Over one in three (36 percent) have been involved in community projects during the year, a bit more than younger women (34 percent).

Earth Day was first celebrated in 1970, when PrimeTime Women were quite young and developing an environmental consciousness. Like many of their political and social attitudes, their concern for the environment is still with them more than 35 years later.

PrimeTime Women are a decidedly green bunch who are significantly more attuned to "saving the planet" than are younger women. They more readily buy from businesses that are environmentally conscious, more apt to recycle as much as they possibly can, and are more willing to conserve energy even if it means a lower standard of living.

One more thing every marketer should know: PrimeTime Women are particularly sensitive to corporate behavior. As indicated in the following table ("Going Green"), PrimeTime Women will go out of their way to buy from companies that are environmentally conscious. It's fair to say that this favoritism also extends to corporations that are socially responsible in other areas.

Unfortunately, PrimeTime Women, like the vast majority of all Americans, have an unsettled feeling, to put it mildly, about corporate America.

- Over eight in ten (83 percent) PrimeTime Women (and 86 percent of younger women) feel that "most big companies are just out for themselves."

The moral: behave yourself! Being a good corporate citizen is critical to winning over PrimeTime Women, as well as women and men of all generations.

Going Green

	PrimeTime Women (50–70)	Younger Women (25–49)
	%	%
I make a special effort to conserve energy	91	80
I make a strong effort to recycle everything I can	70	63
I make a special effort to buy from businesses that are environmentally conscious	68	58
I would be willing to accept a lower standard of living to conserve energy	54	49
Donated money to environmental or conservation organizations	42	35

Source: 2006 DDB Life Style Study

4. Brimming with Confidence. PrimeTime Women tell us that getting older better equips them to make decisions more confidently than when they were younger. They know how to handle unexpected turbulence and how to get around obstacles in ways that younger women have yet to figure out. With age comes experience. And with experience comes wisdom. This wisdom has given them confidence and control over their lives, indeed a swagger that, in some respects, makes younger women look a touch wimpy!

When adversities such as dealing with financial pressures, caring for an ailing spouse or parent, having to support kids or grandkids, and recovering from a layoff rear their ugly faces, PrimeTime Women steadfastly believe that the maturation process and their life experience have given them the coping skills and the confidence to handle almost anything that's thrown their way.

A "Can Do" Swagger

	PrimeTime Women (50–70) %	Younger Women (25–49) %
I have a great deal of self-confidence	69	63
I can easily handle whatever tough things come my way*	81†	77
Sometimes I feel as if I don't have control over the direction my life is taking	53	61

Source: 2006 DDB Life Style Study
*From 2005 Life Style Study
†Significant at .70 confidence level

. . . there's a magic to getting older in that in time of crisis you know it will pass and it won't be forever. When things go wrong, it's not the end of the world, as I used to feel in my 20s.
Sandi, 61

Now that I am older, I feel good about myself. I have confidence emotionally and am at a better place than when I was younger. I like being this age. I am much more self-confident. It comes from just living, learning about other people and their motivations. A sense of how the world works.
Anne, 62

Further, the "sense of how the world works," as our Girlfriend Group respondent Anne so eloquently put it, enables the PrimeTime Woman to be less apoplectic when something disrupts her normal routine.

- Whereas 48 percent of younger women agree that "Changes in routine disturb me," only 38 percent of PrimeTime Women are upset by interruptions to their routine.

There is significant power in the realization that they can master the curveballs and "high hard ones" that life throws at them, and that they can do it with a high degree of equanimity and aplomb. It also gives them the drive to keep their lives moving forward.

5. Living Life in "Drive." We'll conclude this discussion about PrimeTime Women with some findings about going forward. But first, let's go back to our quiz.

> What percentage of PrimeTime Women, women 50 to 70 years old, in the DDB Life Style Study agree with the statement *"My greatest achievements are still ahead of me."*
>
> A. 21%
>
> B. 31%
>
> C. 44%
>
> D. 59%

When we give this quiz to clients or to trade groups, the vast majority of people select either A, 21%, or B, 31%. A few give PrimeTime Women more credit and select C, 44%.

Only a tiny minority know enough about PrimeTime Women (or are just really good guessers!) to pick the correct answer—**D, 59%.**

When we ask people who chose incorrectly (many of whom are half the age of PrimeTimers) the reasons for their selections, invariably they offer explanations such as

- "I think of getting older as a time to reflect."

- "When you get to 'that age,' you tend to look back on your life."

- "Well, when you hit 50, you start to wonder about the road not taken."

- "Because, let's face it, by that age your best years are behind you."

Sadly, few people ever consider that a woman in her mid-50s or late 60s, or a woman who has just turned 70, would actually have a lot left to accomplish.

Yet, as we've just seen, nearly three out of five PrimeTime Women we've surveyed affirm that their greatest achievements are *not* behind them. They lie ahead!

Further, PrimeTime Women have a very clear idea of what it is they want to achieve and how they are going to get there.

- Over two-thirds (68 percent) of PrimeTime Women say "I am the kind of person who knows what I want to accomplish in life and how to achieve it," while 62 percent of Gen X and Gen Y women feel this way.

Of course, each PrimeTime Woman has a very personal definition of what it means to achieve; however, a pattern we saw in our focus group discussions was that achievement for a PrimeTime Woman is *not* necessarily some tangible goal or definitive end point that she checks off a "To Do" list. She believes that achievement can also be an ongoing process of discovery, exploration, learning, and growth. A PrimeTime Woman is likely to consider any goals she has, whether it's taking an art class after a long hiatus, starting a workout program at the gym, or learning a new skill that will feed her desire to be more creative as works in progress, things that will either continue forever or that will lead her to another step in the process.

Once the children are out of the house, or at least old enough to fend for themselves, or once she retires or cuts back on her work hours, the PrimeTime Woman is open to new opportunities and is willing to try things she couldn't when she was younger. Back then, family and job obligations and a lack of time to pursue her own interests stymied her. Now that she is "free to be" she is less constrained.

> *I just got into this new hobby, making glass beads. I have a lot of free time and I enjoy it. I always liked glass and there was this girl at this meeting and she was showing her glass. I asked if she would teach me.*
> Joanne, 52

I went back to school to get my master's. You know, at 52 I wondered if I could do it. It was very stimulating; I learned about myself and got straight A's. It just built up my confidence. You don't have to check out just because you got older.

Becky, 56

I just started an art class, illustration. I went to a class about 30 years ago, but I started again.

Anne, 62

The penchant that PrimeTime Women have for living life in drive also extends to the workplace. PrimeTime Women who do have jobs or own their own businesses are *much more passionate* about what they do than are younger women.

We ask several questions about work in our Life Style Study. One pertains to how people view their work: as a career or just a job. Another asks how much people enjoy their job.

The Life Style Study revealed that PrimeTime Women, many of whom came of age when greater professional growth and career mobility were available to women than had been available before, are more career-focused than the generation of women who came afterwards.

PrimeTime Women and Work: It's Not Just a Job

	PrimeTime Women (50–70) %	Younger Women (25–49) %
Do you consider your work . . .		
A career	**58**	51
Just a job	**42**	49
How much do you enjoy your work?		
A lot	**66**	56
A little	**32**	38
Not at all	**2**	6

Asked of women who work
Source: 2006 DDB Life Style Study

Further, PrimeTime Women enjoy their jobs more than younger women do. Perhaps the new generation of women in the labor force take for granted what many PrimeTime Women feel they had to fight for, and thus are less likely to view their work more favorably.

So, the PrimeTime Woman is hardly living life in reverse. She keeps moving forward, living life in drive. Even overdrive! Her greatest achievements really are ahead of her. And this drive, which for many younger people can result in tension, frustration, and unhappiness, actually seems to be a tonic for the PrimeTime Woman!

* * *

By now, just part way through this book, it should be clear that marketers who hope to tap the vast potential of PrimeTime Women have to toss aside most of the conventional wisdom about them. Contrary to well-embedded stereotypes and assumptions, the PrimeTime Woman is

- **experiencing the joy of being.** Rather than being in denial, she revels in her age even in the face of the challenges that come with it. She lives her life with abundant contentment, joy, and happiness.

- **relishing the liberation** and independence from expectation that this time of her life provides. She feels free to be herself and to pursue whatever it is that makes her happy. External pressure is yielding to internal pleasure.

- **rocking her world.** Forget any notions about the demure and retiring lady who'd rather rock in her chair than rock the boat. The PrimeTime Woman wants her voice to be heard and her opinions to count. She's involved in her community. She exercises her right to vote not only in the political arena but in the marketplace as well, preferring to buy from companies who exhibit forthright corporate behavior.

- **brimming with confidence.** The PrimeTime Woman will tell you that getting older can be a blessing. With age comes experience and with experience comes wisdom, the wisdom to handle adversity in ways she wouldn't have been able to when she was younger. Now that she's older, she feels she can confidently navigate turbulent waters in her life and maintain balance and equanimity in time of crisis.

- **living life in drive.** The PrimeTime Woman is hardly moping around pining for the good old days. She's spirited and energetic. She has things to do, places to see, and possibilities to explore. The PrimeTime Woman feels that her greatest achievements are still ahead of her. Life is for living. Continually moving forward is a reward in itself.

Understanding these qualities of the PrimeTime Woman, along with the other lessons in this book, and having a deeper understanding of how she thinks, how she behaves, how she lives will help any marketer to better communicate with her and, in turn, win her trust, her confidence, her friendship—and her business.

CHAPTER THREE

What's on Her Mind

Freedom, Friendships, and Fulfillment

With healthier diets, different lifestyles, and advances in health care, we're all living longer. While at first glance this would seem to be adding an extra decade to the end of life, in actuality, it's more like adding an extra decade to the middle, somewhere around age 50. These days, 55 is very alive. While the stereotype of ages 50–70 may be "the sunset years," the reality is that it's more like high noon!

PrimeTime Women encounter the added decade of life very differently from the way midlife men do. While both men and women approach their 50th birthdays with a good deal of apprehension, as it turns out, the midlife transition is a good deal easier on women, who, in a way, have fewer challenges to deal with and more resources available than men do.

Most men reach 50 alarmed about sliding downhill for the rest of their lives. They want to stay where they are, to keep what they've got. Status quo is good; change, especially getting older, is bad. Some try to recapture the feelings of their youth—they act on their rebellious impulses. Some don't know what to do with themselves after they have retired and no longer have a power role in society. They stay at home and putter around the house, declining to exercise or socialize. Many midlife men refuse to take their health seriously, say-ing things like "I'm going to keep going until I crash and burn."[1] (Oh, those daredevils.)

To women, 50 comes as a gift. For most, it's a major life shift, from the "mom" mode to the "me" mode. (Incidentally, in case you think I'm overgeneralizing about the mom mode, you might be inter-ested to know that by the age of 40, 84 percent of women have had children.) At the same time as the kids are leaving home, leaving mothers with more time, those moms get a little extra boost of post-menopausal zest. They use the added decade of life to go back to col-lege or start new businesses. It's finally "my time," and they make the most of it, pursuing old passions, exploring new ones, spending more time with their friends, and seeking out ways to give back. They feel lucky to have the luxury of focusing on themselves, finding their inner individuality, and fulfilling long-suppressed dreams. For women, 50 opens new doors, presenting vistas of endless possibility.

As detailed in *Marketing to Women,* the most powerful way to cre-ate relevance and appeal for women is to elicit "that's me" moments, when she sees herself in the situation and your product or service as the solution. The bar is set a little higher for PrimeTime Women than for women in general because midlife marks the emergence of the human drive for authenticity. Men and women who have spent the first 40 years of life constructing a social identity now feel the urge to develop and express their "real selves." For marketers, that means they are less interested in, and less tolerant of, the contrived personalities that are often used in commercial communications.

Marketers seeking to engage the PrimeTime Woman in their brands need to have an accurate and empathetic understanding of her mindset. So far, those marketers are few and far between. If she's not invisible, which is the usual state of affairs, she's portrayed as an object of humor, condescension, or pity. "Edgy" young marketers sometimes think it's funny to use older people as a foil—she's a cranky old lady or a doddering idiot. Those who are trying to be respectful err on the side of serenity, portraying PrimeTimers as slowing down, craving relaxation and quiet. As for pity, well, "I've fallen and I can't get up" is a national joke.

Don't forget why you're here: PrimeTime Women are the golden bull's-eye of target marketing. They make over 80 percent of the buying decisions for the households that have about 80 percent of the money. "Can you hear me now?" If you want her business, you'd better understand who you're really talking to.

Midlife Madness

The Menopause Monster

When I was growing up, the common understanding was that only women had a midlife crisis. It was called (s-h-h-h) *the change of life*, which was code for *menopause*. Sounded awful. Apparently, women went crazy—mood swings, crying spells, all kinds of erratic behavior.

Of course, there was a scientific explanation for all of this: ancient Greek philosopher and physician Galen originated the theory that because the blood vessels of postmenopausal women couldn't discharge accumulated blood, the congested blood went to their brain and caused insanity—a common belief until the 1920s, believe it or not.[2] And if you think that was bad, it's still better than the alternate explanation that linked menopause to witchcraft, an accumulation of evil humors that, if not purged, "might encourage doubly shameful conduct by the weaker, less rational sex."[3] And you know how they purged witchcraft—drowning, hanging, burning at the stake.

By the 1950s, '60s, and '70s, modern thinking had concluded "the obvious:" women went crazy with grief and worthlessness when they realized they could no longer bear children—their primary, if not sole, reason for existence. This lined up well with the theory published in 1968 by famed developmental psychologist Erik Erikson that a woman is psychologically complete only when she attains the roles of wife and mother.[4]

Menopause left her bereft with no reason for being. Uh-huh. As you'll see in a moment, that's not exactly the way PrimeTime Women see it today.

There's More to the Midlife Crisis

For the most part, researchers in developmental psychology haven't allocated much attention to adult development in midlife or later.

Jean Piaget, the psychologist who so greatly advanced our understanding of child development, assumed that cognitive development stopped during young adulthood. Erik Erikson, who mapped out eight stages of psychosocial development, allotted only two pages of his classic work *Identity and the Life Cycle* to later life.[5]

If little was known about midlife in general, even less was known about women. Carl Jung postulated that personality was continually shaped throughout our lives.[6] Yet, his findings on how it was shaped are based on his own *male* experience. As late as 1990, expert Kenneth Gergen noted that if academic research and developmental theories were our only measure of reality, it might appear that only *men* survive past the age of 40.[7]

The current idea of the "midlife crisis" came to popular attention via books such as *Passages* (1976) by Gail Sheehy and *The Seasons of a Man's Life* (1978) by Daniel J. Levinson. According to this thinking, we all go through two transition "crises:" the classic adolescent identity crisis and a midlife identity crisis, both characterized by about equal parts panic and searching. The adolescent identity crisis is triggered by the separation from parents ("Yikes! I'm on my own!") and the need to settle into an identity ("Who am I going to be, now that I'm grown up?"). The midlife crisis is triggered by a realization of mortality ("Yikes! I could die any day!") and a craving for meaning ("Is this all there is? Shouldn't there be some more important point?")

The timing of the midlife crisis varies with each individual, of course, but generally this feeling hits sometime in the mid- to late-40s and is experienced by both men and women. This is a time of discontent, of frustration with reality, of disappointment with oneself. Both men and women see and feel the evil effects of gravity on their physiques and physical abilities. Men lose their hair and gain a paunch; women lose their youthful figures and gain some crow's feet. All but the most diligent lose muscle tone, stamina, and agility.

Both men and women approach their 50th birthday with dread, recognizing it as a milestone when they are going to have to come to terms with who they really are, whether they like themselves or not. Before they can allow themselves to develop into their real "personal best," they have to let go of who they were "supposed to be."

So far, they're arm in arm. But then, contrary to popular opinion, men and women part ways.

Men in Midlife: A Rocky Road

In their 50s, men and women experience the midlife transition very differently. Men take it hard; they have more challenges to deal with and fewer mechanisms to help them cope. They make it through, obviously, and, like women, report their 50s and 60s to be the happiest decades of their lives. Women, on the other hand—well, more about them in a moment.

Greater Challenges

The Higher They Reach, the Harder They Fall. Because men are oriented toward a more hierarchical worldview than women are, they have higher expectations for themselves to begin with. Guys who make a great salary working on the assembly line for an auto company were "supposed to" have quit and opened their own trucking business years ago. Guys who own their own McDonald's franchise were supposed to have six stores by this time in their lives. Guys who are VPs in an ad agency were "supposed to be" SVPs by now, managing the accounts with the highest billings and fielding the most headhunter calls.

The really frustrating thing is, for the 20-year span of their corporate careers, many men have dedicated themselves almost single-mindedly to moving along this path. More than most women, men are willing to make the trade-offs and to compromise in other areas of their lives in order to actualize this vision of themselves.

Women have high expectations for themselves too, of course. But they don't tend to be as "comparative" as men are, nor do they tend to be as single-minded. A woman who is making a good salary as VP of marketing at a global food manufacturer is less likely than a man to be kicking herself because she doesn't have the CMO job. Her regrets are more likely to be in the personal arena: that she didn't keep up with her dance lessons, that she hasn't gotten involved enough in the kids' school activities or in community affairs, that she never got around to organizing that family reunion at Disney World for her parents' 25th anniversary.

Because men set the bar so high (by definition, it has to be "higher than the other guy"), they are more likely to fall short. In midlife, most have to face their reality and relinquish their dreams of exceptional achievements, universal admiration, and living an uncommon life. To make themselves feel better, many midlife men are moved to acquire external signs of success, youth, and freedom, like younger women, faster cars, or flying lessons. It's hard to say whether it's to convince others or themselves.

Unexpected Changes. Many midlife men are shocked to experience diminishing physical prowess in the bedroom. Men peak sexually at 18, whereas women peak around 35.[8] What makes it so much harder for men is the importance men put on this "prowess." To women, sex is an act of pleasure; to men, it's a point of pride. (It has always perplexed me that men talk about their "performance" in bed. Who is the audience, exactly? Have you *ever* heard a woman talk about her "performance?" No? Neither have I.)

In addition, men are unprepared for and apprehensive about the change in roles many of them experience with their wives, orchestrated by the gradual but ultimately substantial hormonal shifts that both experience in midlife. Men's testosterone levels begin to ease off, and they find themselves becoming more laid back and less driven. (Lower testosterone probably has something to do with the "prowess" too.) Women's estrogen levels drop, unmasking their testosterone (yes, women produce it too) and they find themselves becoming more assertive and less accommodating.[9]

For most couples, there is a gradual and subtle shift in the household dynamics. For one thing, decisions she used to discuss with him—when they will take their next vacation, what contractor they will use to remodel the basement—now she makes on her own. She finds it more efficient, and he doesn't really mind or care to be involved.

For another, his wife is morphing into a new person. Out of nowhere she is developing new interests and activities, and being quite insistent on pursuing them. This can take her husband by surprise and require quite an attitude adjustment. Jed Diamond, author of *Male Menopause, The Irritable Male Syndrome* and many other books on the topic, explains:

> *I had always thought of myself as the hero figure in my own action movie and everyone else as supporting characters. But it was becoming*

very clear that my wife was becoming the leading lady and I was moving into a new role, a role I never thought I'd play. Look, I only play leading men. I don't do secondary spots.

But, the truth was, I was slipping into . . . into what? I wasn't sure what it was, but I was damn sure I didn't want to have anything to do with it.

But little by little I found myself moving in a new direction. It's taken me many years to begin to get accustomed to this role. My wife is the new action hero and my job is to ride shotgun. She is the leading lady and my job is to bring her roses. Well, I got a clear vision of what was needed. In truth, a man's gotta do what a man's gotta do. For her 50th birthday I sent her to the Bondurant racing school. It was the best $2,000 I've ever spent.[10]

So all in all, midlife men have some substantial challenges and unexpected changes to deal with. They feel a real sense of disappointment and a loss of control, and naturally, they hate it. What's worse, they're missing an important mechanism for helping them get through a tough time: intimate friendships.

Who Ya Gonna Talk To?

The dictionary shows two definitions of the word *intimate:* Definition one is "friendly, warm, close, dear;" you can feel like that about someone simply by sharing some good times together. Definition two is "personal, confidential, private, secret," and that one pretty much requires talking.

They Can't Tell the Guys. The nature of friendships among men doesn't lend itself well to providing support and comfort when men are frustrated, troubled, or in distress, because their idea of *intimate* is definition one. Men bond with their male friends by *doing* things, not by talking. In fact, most of the time they're kind of opposed to too much talking.

What that means is that when men have a problem, they're not inclined to turn to their male friends to talk about it. They're well aware the guys don't really want to hear about it. Moreover, because male gender culture is hierarchical, men are conditioned to conceal any signs of weakness or vulnerability, especially from other men. Even though they're your friends and you trust them, you don't want to come across as not being able to handle your own life.

So they turn to women.

Women bond with each other by talking. Oh, there may be an activity involved—dining, shopping, working out—but it's all a background to the conversation. To women, "definition one" above hardly counts—that's what you have with the sales clerk, or the waitstaff at a restaurant. Without the personal exchange, the confidences, the intimacies, there is no real personal relationship. In fact, women often share personal information, worries, and confessions even with relatively casual acquaintances. On the flip side, they *like* hearing another person's stories and problems because it builds an empathetic connection—it's one of the things women are wired for. Women friends are great when you're feeling low; they're like your own personal psychotherapist.

The problem is, once they're married, men generally don't sustain one-on-one relationships with women friends.

No Women Friends. During the dating and mating stages of adolescence and the 20s, single men and women often hang out in groups, and it is common for both men and women to have friends of both sexes. But once people start to couple off, whether married or cohabitating, there is an unspoken rule: generally speaking, people in a committed heterosexual relationship socialize either in couples, or with friends of the same sex. They don't usually maintain close friends of the opposite sex, as they did when they were unattached. Men hang out with other guys; women hang out with their girlfriends.

That suits everybody fine most of the time, when life is smooth sailing. But when things are rough, like when you're going through a midlife crisis, a woman has a whole network of personal therapists to draw on. A man might have a wife. And even with her, it's hard to talk about this stuff, because men by choice just haven't had as much practice with sorting out and articulating emotions. Not to mention, chances are her head is in a whole different place right now.

PrimeTime Women: A Different Path

Until recently, everyone just assumed women experienced the midlife transition pretty much the same way men did: frustration and apprehension, compounded by the sad abandonment of "the empty nest syndrome." In the past year or two, however, a new point of view has started to emerge, based—finally!—on research with actual PrimeTime Women. Gail Sheehy's newest book, *Sex and the Seasoned Woman,* describes midlife for women as dynamic and full of vitality. Dr. Carol Orsborn, author of numerous books on success, leadership, and resilience and senior partner of the Imago Creative agency, has recently completed a psychological research study that confirms our findings and articulates three stages of midlife women's transition: Original Programming, The Reactive Response, and Integrity.[11]

One of the most quoted studies on midlife transition in women was conducted by Mills College in the late 1990s. Ravenna Helson, the lead researcher, reported that while "people generally describe personality change in middle age as a midlife crisis, with all its negative connotations . . . in the Mills women, the change was *positive* [my emphasis]—*a reorienting, not a crisis.*"[12] This confirmed what Helson had found in another study, which revealed that women moving into midlife become more self-sufficient, more decisive, more self-assured and secure, and less critical. These positive changes were accompanied by increased coping skills and increased comfort and stability.[13]

Why is the midlife experience so different for women?

Why Women Have It Easier

I believe the difference in men's and women's midlife experience is not rooted in a difference in underlying human development, but rather stems from three simple circumstances: more control, more support, and believe it or not, menopause.

More Control. Despite the fact that fathers these days are helping out more with shopping, chauffeuring, cooking, and housekeeping than their fathers did, in the average household, women still spend almost twice as many hours a week on these tasks as their husbands do—27 hours and 16 hours respectively.[14] In addition to chief cook and bottle washer, most women are the family's health guardian, school liaison, housekeeper, vehicle upkeeper, home services coordinator, inventory manager, bill payer, chief purchasing officer, travel/vacation planner, and social scheduler. Most men keep their lives a little more streamlined: in addition to their job outside the home, their responsibilities around the house typically include lawn care, home and car maintenance, everything electronic, sports coaching, and . . . oh, right: barbecuing. (Did I miss anything?)

When the kids get older and more independent, and especially when they launch their own households, the demands on mothers' time drop significantly, but because of the nature of their chores, and because they put in fewer hours in the first place, fathers' commitments and schedules are relatively less affected. So while both midlifers are thinking longingly about what they coulda-woulda-shoulda done with their lives, only the women get an "empty nest bonus" of extra time to look into new options, interests, and activities.

Perhaps this is why research shows that men's "dream fulfillment" peaks in their mid-30s, while women's "dream fulfillment" increases with age, reaching the pinnacle during PrimeTime.[15]

More Support. That network of personal therapists I mentioned above? A lifesaver—literally. As one of the participants in our Girlfriend Groups said . . .

> *My friends and I meet and walk for an hour five days a week. We all try*
> *to touch base and be our own therapy group. It's so healthy for me.*
> *We don't always feel it's beneficial to our bodies, but it's good for*
> *our mouths. It's like bringing your worries [for others to help you].*
> *We have helped each other out.*
>
> Lynn, 50

And from our 50/50/50 panel . . .

> *My friends (are one of the most important elements in life) . . . without*
> *them, I would be a basket case and much much lonelier.*
>
> Anne, 54

Research shows that friendship lowers blood pressure, boosts immunity, and promotes healing. It may help explain one of the mysteries of medical science: why women, on average, have lower rates of heart disease and longer life expectancies than men.[16] Because of the gender culture dynamics discussed above, men in midlife are at a distinct disadvantage when it comes to their social and support networks. A consistent body of empirical literature confirms that older women have more people in their social support networks, and that they rely far less on spouses for support than older men do. In fact, men tend to rely exclusively on their wives for social support.[17]

Post-Menopausal Zest. While a woman no longer has reproductive fertility, researchers have found that in menopause a woman enters a time of enhanced psychological and creative fertility. Margaret Mead coined the term *postmenopausal zest* to refer to the surge of energy and excitement accompanying this release from what could be termed the biological burden of womanhood. She found this elevated spirit manifested in midlife women across cultures. It may be fueled in part by the change in ratio of testosterone to estrogen.[18] Perhaps it's what writer Isak Dinesen was talking about when she said, *"Women, when they are old enough to have done with the business of being women, and can let loose their strength, may be the most powerful creatures in the world."*[19]

So all in all, while the PrimeTime Woman certainly goes through the human development stage known as the *midlife identity transition* along with her male cohorts, she is fortunate to have more time and flexibility to cope with it, a strong social support network to help her emotionally, and a biological bonus of post-menopausal zest. As we will see in a moment, her experience of this transition is less like a crisis and more like a chrysalis—the pod that unfolds to reveal that the caterpillar has become a butterfly. "Midlife Chrysalis"—I like that.

PrimeTime Women: Weathering the Whirlwind

Of course, women don't go from dread to delight overnight. As women in their 40s approach their 50th birthday, many of them are definitely not seeing the world as a happy place.

We suspected as much, when we structured three sets of Girl-friend Groups of women in their 40s, 50s, and 60s, respectively. Our intent in this qualitative research was to try to understand the various mindsets, and the differences between those mindsets, *before*, *during*, and *after* "the big 5–0." We didn't want participants at one stage of the transition to influence or intimidate participants at a different stage.

As you'll see in a moment, women in their 50s and 60s embrace PrimeTime with passion and pride. But those women in their 40s—whew. When talking about aging and its effects on appearance, life-style, finances, and so on, they're either in complete denial and want to remain that way, or they're filled with fear and anxiety; they expect the worst and are devastated by the mere thought of turning 50.

> *I just kind of believe in the Scarlett O'Hara approach—*
> *I'll worry about that tomorrow.*
>
> Carolyn, 46

> *The 40s are pretty good. I like the 40s. I don't know about 50. Time will*
> *go so fast . . . you might get sick . . . The older you get, the more you*
> *think like that . . . It's going to be scary.*
>
> Mary, 49

> *[When you're 50], you don't feel like a sexy lady anymore,*
> *you're grumpy.*
>
> Luz, 46

In talking with the women in their 50s, it was clear they had crossed the threshold and found a brave new world on the other side. In fact, the National Center on Women and Aging at Brandeis University discovered that more than half of women over 50 felt that "getting older is 'much' better than they had expected."[20] They are accepting themselves, even celebrating themselves, and are excited about the possibilities and blessings that age has brought them.

> *For me, turning 50 was like coming into your own. You stop worrying*
> *about a lot of things and do what you want.*
>
> Debbie, 54

The thing that struck us most about the women in their 60s was that, more than the other groups, they were the *most* likely to be looking forward, not back.

> *I am blessed with a lot of friends. God has been good to me and*
> *I am looking forward to 60 more years.*
>
> Shirley, 66

> *I'm 68 years old and I'm a practicing nurse and I have a family of four*
> *. . . I'm a widow, and I'm retired and I'm happy about it. I thought*
> *you'd be old [at 68]. When I got to be 62, I thought, 62 is not old.*
> *68 you're just beginning to live.*
>
> Leanne, 68

I think of women's midlife transition a little like Dorothy's journey in *The Wizard of Oz*. The 40s are like the dark foreboding world at the beginning of the movie. There you are in Kansas, minding your own business, and suddenly you're caught up and tossed around in this powerful tornado. It's violent and frightening and you have no idea what the future will bring.

Your 50s are like landing on the Wicked Witch. You step out the door and all of that dark commotion and turmoil has been transformed into a bright and colorful world. It's a little strange, with the munchkins and all, but it's a lovely place, the natives seem surprisingly cheerful and oh! Look at those cute ruby slippers—got to have 'em!

And then you have your 60s when you set off on a new adventure, following a yellow brick road of infinite possibility, gathering friends along the way. Sure, there are the occasional flying monkeys and worries about brain, heart, and courage, but with friends, determined optimism, and a little dog too, life is pretty darn good—a lot better than you would have expected in the aftermath of that wicked twister.

Happier Than When They Were Younger?
The Gifts of Midlife

New research conducted by AARP among women 45+ found that the majority (65 percent) are "happier now than they have ever been." One of the respondents was quoted as saying, "To me, life right now just seems so wonderful."[21] Gail Sheehy found that today's midlife women "are at the peak of their lives . . . they are happier and more productive than they have ever been before."[22] She reports that "over and over again, with conviction, women who have actually crossed into their 50s tell me, 'I would not go back to being young again.'"[23]

How can this be? What's so great about being older?

Well, to start with, there are the three freedoms: freedom from family chores, freedom from social conventions, and freedom to get real. Beyond these, PrimeTime Women receive two more gifts from midlife. Relative to their younger selves, they have a sense of greater personal resilience and a more conscious appreciation for life.

Freedom from Family Chores.

- **More time:** Up until this point, women have made their priorities their kids, their husbands, their own parents and siblings, the PTA, the Girl Scout troop, the swim team, their kids' college applications, and so on. Their orientation toward others and their commitment to making a nice home for their families don't leave much time for their own interests and activities. However, once they are able to scale back their responsibilities as mother, room mom, soccer mom, and so on, PrimeTime Women find themselves with whole heaping handfuls of time they can use to explore their options, rekindle old interests, and experiment with something new. And they mean to use it.

- **"My time":** Men have always been more "me" focused, but now it's women's turn. While men's responsibilities don't change much in midlife, once the immediate family needs ease off, PrimeTime Women's focus changes dramatically. This point in life marks a *beginning* for PrimeTime Women, not an ending. PrimeTime means "My Time." It's no wonder women love it!

You wake up and do whatever you feel like doing. I do a lot of walking outside for myself, walking the dogs for an hour. Meet friends for lunch, go shopping, read, cook. Whatever I feel like doing.
Barbara, 55

*I spend more today . . . I had to provide for other people,
and now I don't have to.*

Leanna, 68

I have more time and money to indulge my priorities.

Mary, 62

• **Return to self:** In many respects, the PrimeTime Woman is able
at last to return to who she was before she married and had
kids—a dancer, a traveler, an actress in community theater.
She can read until two o'clock in the morning and sleep late
on weekends if she wants, because nobody has to be at the soccer field by 8 AM. If all she wants for lunch is asparagus, there's
no one to insist on hot dogs and mac 'n cheese. Nothing for
kids to do on a wine tour through Tuscany? So what? Let's go!

The ad folks at Celebrity Cruises clearly understand the Prime-
Time Women "freedom from family chores" attitude. A recent ad
features a woman relaxing in beautiful blue water and captures the
midlife transition from "taking care of everyone" to "having someone take care of me" with the headline: "Somewhere between Monte
Carlo and Mykonos, 'mom' becomes 'madame.'"

Freedom from Social Conventions. As they come to accept
themselves for who they really are, men and women in midlife become more comfortable behaving the way they really want to. I'm
not talking about some kind of crazy anarchy here; more like taking
a few liberties with the social conventions. One friend told me, "Being
older is great. I intend to develop all sorts of interesting eccentrici-
ties . . . now that I can get away with it!"

This comes partly from their 50 or more years of experience that
tell them that, no matter what you do, you can't please everybody
anyway, so you might as well please yourself. Gail Sheehy associates
this with reaching what she calls the "Age of Mastery," which takes
place between the years of 50 and 65:

*The great transition in the passage to Second Adulthood for women is
to move from pleasing to mastery. In our First Adulthood, we survive by*

figuring out how to please and perform for the powerful people who protect and reward us: parents, teachers, and bosses. But by our mid-forties, we are all looking for greater mastery over our environment—emotional, physical, and vocational.[24]

Moreover, relative to their younger selves, PrimeTimers are more conscious that life is finite and time is precious, which gives them less patience with the nonsense of daily life, and more likelihood of saying so.

The Freedom to Get Real. One characteristic of midlife is the drive for greater authenticity. You don't "decide" to be more authentic, any more than you "decide" to be hungry. It evolves in the individual, like the drive to learn or to express oneself.

Up until midlife, the individual is developing the "social" self, which is defined by the need to fit in, belong, and be accepted by others. Authenticity is a matter of finding one's "real" self and involves integrating the internal, or "secret," self with the external, or "social," self.

Interestingly, finding what Carl Jung calls the "real self" is about *letting go* of the ego.[25] PrimeTimers are not as compelled to make social statements by their brand choices, and PrimeTime Women are no longer controlled by the need to have perfect looks and perfect behavior.

Looking for the long-submerged "secret self" is also about listening to one's own counsel rather than listening to others. PrimeTimers are more individuated, more autonomous, and less influenced by peers and celebrity endorsements.[26]

You learn with age, you listen to yourself.
Lynda, 57

I don't doubt myself. Go with my intuition. Know that inner person.
It takes a long time to know who you are. Because we have
experienced ourselves for 50 odd years.
Lynn, 50

With apologies for playing a bit fast and loose with serious concepts of psychology, the youthful focus on one's "social self" basically means that young people feel it's more important to be seen as the "right" sort of person, however that is defined—successful, rebellious, winning, and so on. Older people have been there, done that, seen through it a billion times.

In midlife, you want more. You want people to know you for who you really are, and to like the real you, not the "pretend" you that you built in your younger days. You want to be your "real self," all the time. You want to be dealing with other "real selves," and don't have a lot of patience with contrived personalities (as in perky TV people extolling their fascination and enthusiasm for a product).

Without this merging of the "social self" and the "secret self" into the "real self," the disconnect between the internal and external selves makes people feel like a fraud and creates anxiety about being revealed for who they really are. When people are successful in the merger, they achieve a state of integrity, of wholeness. They feel strong, complete, uncorrupted, and more confident.

PrimeTimers, men and women, know themselves, accept themselves, want to be themselves and express themselves and—importantly for marketers—want to be seen accurately for who they really are.

Getting Stronger Every Day

The next gift is a sense of greater personal resilience. As we saw in DDB's research in Chapter 2, PrimeTime Women have survived adversity and hardship, learned from it, and emerged with the knowledge that "What doesn't kill you will make you stronger." Interestingly, this boost in confidence delivers some noteworthy health advantages as a side effect. The MacArthur Foundation Study on Aging, the most extensive, comprehensive study on aging in America, shows that increased mastery or control over one's destiny leads to

- sustained mental ability;

- increased productive activity with age;[27]

- better health and strengthened immune system; and

- greater self-efficacy—a person's belief in his or her own ability to handle various situations, one of the four key factors of successful aging.[28]

To quote author Dorothy L. Sayers, "Time and trouble will tame an advanced young woman. But an advanced old woman is uncontrollable by any earthly force."[29]

A Greater Love of Life

Last but far from least is the gift of a more conscious appreciation of life. Sometime in your 40s, it dawns on you that you're going to die someday—and it's distressing! Usually, the big revelation is triggered by some brush with mortality, such as a friend stricken with cancer; a colleague, 48 and very fit, dies on the racquetball court; a neighbor loses her daughter in a freeway accident that was not her fault. The "not her fault" part is an important component, actually, because it's what brings home to you that you cannot control or predict how much time you have left. You can do everything right and still exit the planet in a matter of moments.

No doubt about it—it does focus the mind. But it's not all bad. In your 40s, you're mostly upset by the randomness of it all; by the time you've reached your 50s, you've processed your way through that and can see it as a gift. More than in their youth, PrimeTimers are aware that their days are numbered; and as with luxury goods, rarity and scarcity increase perceived value. "Life is short," the T-shirt says, "Eat dessert first."

When you're younger, you set goals. I don't know that it's something I do anymore. From one day to the next you know there's a whole bunch of stuff that can happen that can alter your life. You don't take anything for granted, not even being able to work.

Barbara, 55

Don't postpone experience. We just lost my husband's mother and we have three young friends with cancer—examples of how short life is. We both now feel like we have to do more, travel more, make more plans to see out-of-town friends, etc.

Susan, 59

If you want to do anything, don't worry about tomorrow.
You don't know what will happen.

Willia, 67

I am not unique in having discovered that life is shorter than we
think and all of a sudden you are 60 and you have wasted time
on priorities that don't matter at all.

Anne, 64

PrimeTime Women seek to savor every moment. They've got the time, the money, and the drive to make it count. So what do they do with all that PrimeTime zest?

PrimeTime Zest

PrimeTime Women are using their newfound freedom, high energy, and well-established confidence to pursue old passions and explore new possibilities, to continue their lifelong learning, to spend time with their girlfriends, and to expand their life impact by giving back.

Pursuing Forgotten Passions

As we discovered in Chapter 2, PrimeTime Women "live life in drive." One of the first things PrimeTime Women do with their new "My Time" is to return to some of the activities and passions they set aside when they got overcommitted with work and family responsibilities. They remember how much they used to like to write or sing or teach or belly dance or climb mountains. Among participants in our 50/50/50 panel, one woman told us she was starting piano lessons over again and made a point of practicing an hour a day. Another decided she wanted to prepare for retirement by taking business seminars! Another has taken classes in computers, photography, handicapping (when a new horse track opened in her area), and adventure (parachuting, rock climbing, rappelling). Wow. And our Girlfriend Group participants were returning to passions like art, glass beads, and history.

Exploring New Possibilities

Many PrimeTime Women are seeking out new directions. They recognize the world of possibilities before them and are unconcerned about starting fresh, being novices at something they've never tried before. They feel open to any opportunity and are willing to take risks the way they did when they were younger. The irony is that when they were younger, they were unafraid because they thought they were immortal and couldn't conceive of failure. Now they are unafraid to take risks because they know they won't live forever and they know failure is OK.

In 1970 the enormously popular book *What Color Is Your Parachute?* was published. It offered thought-provoking new perspectives and, most interestingly, tons of exercises designed to get you to think creatively and without constraints about what workplace occupation could fire up your sense of passion and enable you to live the life you wanted.

So where is Part II, *What Color Is Your Clock?*, or something like that? (Terrible title, I know. Just work with me on the concept here.) The idea would be to apply the same or similar exercises to help PrimeTimers visualize the second half of their lives, and it would be tailored, like this book, to their different priorities and attitudes.

I suggest that marketers craft campaigns based on stories of people who are exploring new possibilities and achieving their dreams.

But what have we here? The Microsoft campaign "Your Potential. Our Passion." Their advertising follows many of my GenderTrends principles (see Chapter 7). It's people-powered, focusing on the prospect, not the product. They show real people, with concrete visions of their future, and include PrimeTime Women in their ads—acknowledging that dreams and passions are not just for the young. One of my favorites is the one that shows an African American PrimeTime Woman gazing out the window of the diner where she works; there's a slight smile on her face, and the graphic designer has drawn in a mortarboard on her head and a diploma in her hand. The headline reads: "We see a Master's in comparative literature. Microsoft." Perfectly PrimeTime.

Love of Lifelong Learning

According to David Wolfe, esteemed author of *Ageless Marketing* and one of the thought leaders in the Mature Marketing arena, learning for personal growth and for the sheer pleasure of learning is stronger in the second half of life. The most common motivations for learning in midlife and beyond are

- to keep up with what's going on in the world (63 percent strongly agree);

- to experience spiritual or personal growth (62 percent);

- to simply enjoy learning something new (60 percent);

- to enjoy my hobbies or recreational activities better (53 percent); and

- to manage everyday life better (50 percent).[30]

Many PrimeTime Women have returned to school full time to pursue degrees that they put on hold in their child-rearing years; or part time to take advantage of the intellectual stimulation that a class-room setting provides. Full-time college enrollment by older women is up 31 percent in the past decade.[31]

There are many other ways to keep lifelong learning going. Here are a few providers that are helping PrimeTime minds thrive:

- Harvard University Institute for Learning in Retirement was established almost 30 years ago. This program offers no grades or degree at the end, but provides an idea-centric curriculum that changes all the time. Limited to 500 members to keep it a manageable and close community, HILR is a peer-learning mem-bership organization that is self-governing. Members develop their own curricula (50 courses each semester), teach each other and learn from each other, all for the joy of it. In 1977, the HILR was one of a handful of lifelong learning institutes; today there are more than 500 such institutes, and that number is growing.

- Elderhostel is the not-for-profit leader in educational travel for older adults. Unlike tour companies, Elderhostel offers in-depth and behind-the-scenes learning experiences for almost every interest and ability—history, culture, nature, music, out-door activities such as walking and biking, individual skills, crafts, study cruises, and so on.

- SeniorNet is a nonprofit organization of computer-using adults age 50 and older that uses an operating model of "seniors teaching seniors." Students learn new skills such as communicating online, sharing pictures with grandchildren, or saving money on airline tickets. Support is provided by many large organizations including IBM, various telephone companies, Microsoft, Charles Schwab, and local governments.

The Home Depot has tapped into PrimeTimers' life-long aptitude for learning and, in conjunction with the AARP, has set up a series of workshops to help older consumers with home improvement projects that are geared toward their particular needs. (See Figure 3.1.) According to AARP, more than 89 percent of those 50+ want to remain in their current homes as they age. To make this a reality, the majority realize they will need to make changes to their home in order to

FIGURE 3.1 Home Depot: Life-Long Learning

Source: The Home Depot

ensure that it is comfortable, functional, and safe.[32] The new work-shops are part of an ongoing alliance between The Home Depot and AARP which began in February 2004 with a national hiring initiative intended to attract, motivate, and retain eligible older workers. In addition to The Home Depot-AARP Workshops, an in-store informa-tion resource center with information on home modification projects relevant to consumers over 50 launched in approximately 80 Home Depot stores in Florida beginning in fall 2005.

Furthermore, as The Home Depot has confirmed with its Do-It-Herself workshops, women like collaborative interaction when they learn. According to the company, within six months of launch, the workshops had attracted 40,000 women participants across the coun-try, and by the end of the first two years, 200,000. Home-based par-ties are another learning-based, collaborative marketing program. Women who host Tupperware, Pampered Chef, Tomboy Tool, and even Passion Parties love helping other women by listening, laugh-ing, sharing, and selling to them.

This leads to our next key aspect of fulfillment in PrimeTime Women's lives—Girlfriends.

The Secret to PrimeTime: Girlfriends

Intimate friendships have always been important to women, but they become even more so in PrimeTime.

Friends are the most important elements in my life. Since I have retired, friends have become much more important to me. They give me support, companionship, and laughter.

Anne, 65

I have been on the planet for 67 years so I have to make time to check in with friends. You really have to . . . You have to make time for people . . . I think we are blessed as women. Look, here we are, sharing experiences, it's really wonderful. Unfortunately, men don't have that.

Willia, 67

PrimeTime Women now have time to get together with their girl-friends more often than when they were younger. From a casual glass of wine after work to "girlfriend get-away" weekend trips, from book clubs to exercise buddies, PrimeTime Women love to get together and talk.

One of my friends went to a women-only fly-fishing school in Montana and enjoyed the company of 20 other outdoorsy women who were there not only to learn to fish but also to drink wine, escape their husbands, and hang out with like-minded female trout-slayers. Molly Semenik, a wonderful river guide and founder of Tie the Knot, revealed why her classes are filled with PrimeTime Women: "It's their time. They finally have time to relax and enjoy themselves. They like to fish with their husbands, who usually are the ones who got them into the sport. But they would rather fish with their girlfriends. It's so much more fun."

Lots of research studies have established that friendship is one of the keys to a long and happy life. Successful agers from the Mac-Arthur Foundation Study cite friendship as the *key* factor in keeping them active and emotionally secure.[33] In fact, women's relationships and social support have always been a strength and a survival strategy in adversity.[34]

"Tend and Befriend"

Interestingly, researchers have discovered a hormonal basis for friendship! Up until 2000, it had long been established that in times of stress, the human body triggers a surge of adrenaline that preps the body for the classic "fight or flight" options. But a couple of women researchers at UCLA, Dr. Laura Klein and Dr. Shelley Taylor, were musing one day that when they feel under stress, their natural reaction was quite different: talk to a girlfriend.[35]

When they looked a little more deeply into the studies that "established" the adrenaline response, they were amused to see that 90 percent of the respondents were men, and only 10 percent were women.[36] So they did their own study, this time with women only. What they learned was that, in women, stress triggers the production of oxytocin, the hormone produced during childbirth that stimulates the emotions of nurturing and closeness to another person. So instead of a "fight or flight" reaction, women experience what these researchers named the "tend and befriend" response.

Mammogram Parties?

If you want to talk about calling on girlfriends to help cope with a stressful time . . . Not long ago, I read a story about six 40-year-old Dallas women getting together for a mammogram party! No one wanted to go alone, so these creative ladies decided to have a Girls' Day Out at the doctor and go as a group. Now their mammogram appointments are annual "Girlfriends" parties, and the typical trepidation of this unpleasant medical occasion is turned into, well, a party. As one woman said, "You're taking instant support with you."

The Red Hat Society

And then there's the Red Hat Society. It's not a women's movement, exactly, although it has spread like wildfire.

It all started when artist Sue Ellen Cooper bought a red hat in 1997 to give to a good friend turning 55, along with a copy of Jenny Joseph's poem "Warning." The poem opens with the lines, "When I am an old woman I shall wear purple / With a red hat which doesn't go and doesn't suit me" . . . pretty much the perfect expression of Prime-Time Women's newfound inclination to defy societal conventions!

Friends saw the hat and the poem and wanted their own. The ladies started going out together for tea from time to time, and each wore her red hat. They informally called themselves the Red Hat Society, and they must have been a pretty fun bunch, because other women kept asking to join the group.

Word spread, and soon women from other cities began contacting Cooper to find out how they could start their own Red Hat chapters. The chapter names are crazy ("High Fashion, Hot Flashin'" and "Red Hot Mamas" are two); the official regalia is red and purple; their "Hatquarters" is in Southern California; their last international convention, "Rhythm and Rhinestones," was big enough to fill the Opryland Grand Resort; and—my favorite—one of their "officers" is the "Mistress of Anxiety," whose job is to worry about other members' problems so they don't have to.

The Red Hat Society is mostly social—its motto is "Fun and Friendship over Fifty"—but Cooper says she's pleased that the society is focusing positive attention on older women, who all too often get ignored. As she says, "Red Hatters Matter."

In fact, women younger than 50 wanted in on the fun. But hey, ya gotta have standards, so Exalted Queen Mother Sue Ellen (yes, that's her official title) decreed that women under 50 could join—as Pink Hatters. Their regalia is pink and lavender, until they reach their 50th birthday and graduate to the "official" membership.

Nine short years later, the Red Hat Society is a worldwide sisterhood *one million* strong, with more than 41,000 chapters across the United States and in 29 foreign countries. You see what I mean about "wildfire!"[37]

One company that "gets" the relevance of "girlfriends" is Revlon. When launching its new Vital Radiance makeup line targeted to PrimeTime Women, Revlon didn't rely on the usual solo model talking straight to camera. The Vital Radiance TV ad features two of its attractive genuine PrimeTime spokeswomen talking to each other while relaxing on a sofa. They are discussing their changing skin care needs and sharing common insights. "She looks like herself, only better," one of them says about the other. That's the kind of thing a company couldn't credibly say. It only rings true coming from a girlfriend. (Too bad Revlon's financial woes—stock value tanked 80 percent in the past five years—brought Vital Radiance down. I'm waiting for a well-funded launch from P&G or Unilever to pick up the potential of this idea whose time has come.)

PrimeTime Women: Leaving a Legacy

According to developmental psychologists, one of the central tasks of aging is the search for meaning. PrimeTime Women find the answer by looking outside themselves to the greater needs of the world. It's about leaving a legacy.

Older people have long been America's most responsible citizens. Driven by their need for vital involvement, they volunteer more hours; give more money to community, church, and other causes; and vote at more than twice the rate of people in their mid-30s and younger.[38]

The Search for Significance

PrimeTime Women's search for meaning in life is a bit different than their male colleagues' quest because women have always been a bit more spiritual and more "others-oriented." Barbara Payne-Stancil notes in *The Handbook on Women and Aging,* "women's search for the meaning of their lives begins long before they become 'older women' . . . [it] is reflected in their involvement in religious activities and practices. Women are more religious than men—at every age."

In addition, because women are wired to be more other-oriented and inclusive, their worldview is "We're all in this together. Might as well help each other out." Therefore, their search for a meaning in life, for a way to give back to the world and leave a lasting contribution, has always been on their minds.

It comes to the forefront in PrimeTime. Social responsibility rises to new highs among women in middle age, a pattern that does not emerge among men; fully three-fourths of women over 50 say contributing to their communities is of central importance in their lives.[39]

Among high net worth individuals, the desire to give back is always stronger among women than men, as the statistics below show:

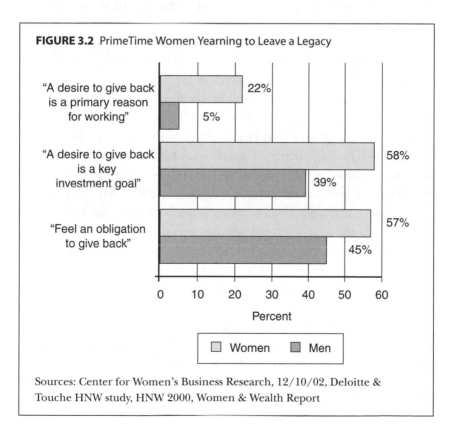

FIGURE 3.2 PrimeTime Women Yearning to Leave a Legacy

Sources: Center for Women's Business Research, 12/10/02, Deloitte & Touche HNW study, HNW 2000, Women & Wealth Report

When I worked with private asset management firm Neuberger Berman, they created a series of networking events targeted to very high-end women investors called "Beyond Success to Significance." The topic was one with extraordinary resonance among these women, so the invitations were successful in attracting a high level of attendance in each of five cities. All participants had achieved substantial professional success and were at that phase of wondering, "What's the meaning of all this? Isn't there some way to contribute more?" The events were headlined by panels of three well-known women executives, who discussed ways in which they had been able to leverage their position, rank, visibility, and influence into opportunities to make a higher-order difference.

Neuberger Berman took a very restrained role in the events they created. Their highest-ranking woman partner introduced the panelists and led the discussion; they had some discreet signage and materials in the room; and, most important, several of the firm's women advisors mingled in to make new connections with these very successful women.

The post-event evaluation forms were a powerful indicator of the positive effect these events had on the women attendees, and the positive halo it created for Neuberger Berman. Thirty-five percent of the women had checked the box "I would like to receive more information about Neuberger Berman." To give you an idea of how remarkable that is, a "normal" response for an inquiry like that would be on the order of 10 or 15 percent. As further confirmation of how effective these events were in engaging women: numerous attendees had written in "if you ever have another event like this, please make sure I am invited again."

Neuberger Berman also leveraged the legacy principle in one of their ads. It shows a beautiful portrait of a PrimeTime Woman, her daughter, and her granddaughter. The headline reads: "Money management is what we do." The copy continues below the photo with: "But we also know some dividends have nothing to do with numbers." (See Figure 3.3.)

Mutual of Omaha takes a more emotional, personal tack and approaches the topic from a different angle: *honoring* a legacy. It shows a PrimeTime Woman in a restaurant, and the copy is written as a compelling story. The headline reads: "What's your dream?" and the ad continues: "'Brian and I had some of the best times getting our

FIGURE 3.3 Neuberger Berman: Leave a Legacy

restaurant up and running. It was hard work, but just watching so many people have such a good time made it all worthwhile. Even though Brian is not here, his spirit always will be.' When her husband died, his Mutual of Omaha insurance provided the security Liz needed to keep their restaurant going. And allowed her to look toward the future. At Mutual of Omaha, it's our mission to help you plan ahead." (See Figure 3.4.)

FIGURE 3.4 Mutual of Omaha: Leave a Legacy

What's your dream?

Brian and I had some of our best times together getting our
restaurant up and running. It was hard work, but just watching
so many people have such a good time made it all worthwhile.

Even though Brian's not here, his spirit always will be.

When her husband died, his Mutual of Omaha insurance provided the security
Liz needed to keep their restaurant going. And allowed her to look toward the
future. At Mutual of Omaha, it's our mission to help you plan ahead. A mission
that for over 90 years has let millions of people take care of today, and tomorrow.

Begin today.

www.mutualofomaha.com
MLM3310

Mutual of Omaha

© 2001 Mutual of Omaha Insurance Company, Omaha, NE 68175

Portrait of PrimeTime Women

PrimeTime Women are happier, more satisfied, and more fulfilled in their 50s and 60s than they have ever been before. They aren't having midlife crises, they're having PrimeTime parties. They have freedom, passions, and purpose, lifelong learning and lots of girlfriends to share it all with. PrimeTime Women feel energized, liberated, and excited about the possibilities for the future.

And why wouldn't they be?

1. **PrimeTime Means More Experiences.** PrimeTime Women have traveled to more places, gone to more concerts, tasted more treats, kissed more lovers, seen more technological advances, laughed more, cried more, *lived* more.

2. **PrimeTime Means Better Perspective.** PrimeTime Women have experienced more of the bumps and bounces in life, more good days and bad days, more wins and losses. They know that life is about balance and that every cloud has a silver (how appropriate!) lining.

3. **PrimeTime Means More Confidence.** PrimeTime Women are comfortable with themselves and finally feel settled into their skins. They have learned more. They know more. They are not constantly doubting, questioning, wondering. They feel good about themselves and about their place in the world.

4. **PrimeTime Means Greater Love of Life.** PrimeTime Women have loved and lost. They have encountered many obstacles in life and can more fully appreciate the good times. Their smiles are broader and their hearts are bigger.

Aging has always been equated with the exhaustion of life; with the loss of vigor and vitality; with decline, despair, and depression. Get real. Getting older is good. It's fulfilling. It's productive. It's invigorating. It makes sense of the rest of your life.

Well. That should have shaken out a few dusty stereotypes. The PrimeTime Woman's midlife mind is ready and eager for new experiences, new possibilities, and certainly some new marketing approaches. Most marketers have a very distorted picture of the PrimeTime Woman. As you decide to reach out to this most productive and untapped of all markets, make sure you are working off of a more accurate portrait.

CHAPTER FOUR

PrimeTime Mental and Physical Changes

When most of us think of aging, we think of mental and physical decline, decay, debility, degeneration, deterioration . . . Good heavens, enough of that! There's no question that we give up some swiftness, some strength, and some reaction time. But most of that hits after PrimeTime. And believe it or not, recent research has revealed some noteworthy *advantages* of age. Besides, PrimeTimers are adept at adapting their brains and bodies in order to make the most of their increased longevity.

The PrimeTime Mind

Let's start with a look at the PrimeTime mind.

- The older brain—is it all bad news?

- Male and female brains—do they age the same way?

- The mind of PrimeTime Women—how do we refine our communications?

The (Not So) Bad News

The brain function declines that may start happening in Prime-Time are limited to a decrease in the raw speed of learning and problem solving, a more limited capacity for short-term memory storage, and very slight losses in cognitive performance.

Processing Speed. As we get older, the one thing that scientists can say for sure is that the brain receives and processes information at a slower rate. In fact, many gerontologists accept this slower processing speed as the only universal behavioral change yet discovered.[1] New learning takes longer, new information is processed more superficially, and details tend to slip a bit.[2] Information processing in the older brain requires neurological "detours" and these add to the time required to react. However, because most activities of daily life don't require rapid reactions, this doesn't usually cause any real problems with everyday brain work.[3] (But now I can be more understanding of why, as people move into the 70+ ranges, many tend to drive more slowly. It's the right and rational way to behave when an individual recognizes slowed reaction times.)

Leading author Malcolm Gladwell has some thoughts on older drivers as well. In an interview with Nerve.com, he states, "Someone who's sixty has a fraction of the physical abilities of an eighteen year old, but their unconscious knowledge of the driving experience is extraordinarily rich. Without even thinking, they look at the drivers around them and make very accurate judgements about what's going to happen next, what the range of possibilities are. And I think that's true in any number of settings. We've fallen in love with all the great attributes of youth—enthusiasm and energy—but I'd like to reclaim a space for experience."[4] He's not the only one, as we'll see in the next section on "The Good News" about the PrimeTime mind.

Short-Term Memory. Okay, I'll admit it. Every time I forgot where I left my keys, or what time my conference call was, I used to worry about the onset of so-called "senior moments." And sure enough, it is typical for people in their fifties and sixties to begin experiencing lapses in short-term memory. The good news here is that's typical, normal, natural. Not, as most people immediately start fearing, a sign of early-onset Alzheimer's! So, next time you find yourself wandering around the living room thinking, "I know I came in this room for a reason . . . ," just relax. It's no big deal. And although short-term recall worsens with age, long-term memory remains well preserved. It's very common to have repeated problems with where you put your keys, while long-term memories from your younger days remain clear and intact. Moreover, working memory, the learned routines on which all of us rely in our daily lives, shows little decline with age.[5]

Cognitive Performance. In a nutshell, most of the cognitive losses people experience come late in life (mid 70s and beyond), and many older people are not significantly affected by even minor losses of mental ability.[6]

Everyone knows we have five physical senses. (More on those in a few moments.) Interestingly enough, it turns out there are five primary cognitive abilities as well: verbal meaning, spatial orientation, inductive reasoning, number, and word fluency ("My mind is like a steel whatchamacallit"). According to a leading study, by age 60, nearly everybody shows a little erosion in one ability, and some people take a little off the top on two or three, but hardly anyone loses their edge on four or five. In fact, by age 88, only a tiny percentage of adults shows significant decline in all five abilities.[7]

The Good News

While there's a good deal of dread about the *declines* of Prime-Time (which, as we've just seen, aren't really too bad), there's precious little awareness and appreciation of the *advances* that come with middle-age mentality:

- The Wisdom of the (Middle) Ages
- Peak Brain Performance: Connecting the Dots

The Wisdom of the (Middle) Ages

The most important difference between older brains and younger brains is also the easiest to overlook: older brains have learned more than young ones.[8] They've been around the block a lot more times, seen the world, made mistakes, made discoveries, managed recoveries, and made amends. Says George Bartzokis, UCLA neurologist: "In midlife, you're beginning to maximize the ability to use the entirety of information in your brain on an everyday, ongoing, second-to-second basis. Biologically, that's what wisdom is."[9]

According to Dr. Gene Cohen, founding director of the Center on Aging, Health & Humanities at George Washington University Medical Center, throughout our entire lifetime, our brains encode thoughts and memories by forming new connections among neurons. The neurons themselves may lose some processing *speed* with age, but they become ever more richly networked. Magnified, the brain of a mentally active 50-year-old looks like a thick forest of interlocking branches—the "tanglier" the better, as this density reflects both deeper knowledge and better judgment.[10] Independent of IQ or speedy thinking, there is simply no substitute for the decades of learning and experience that PrimeTimers have acquired; in careers such as law, science, medicine, management, and almost any knowledge-based practice you can think of, older is truly better.[11]

Studies have shown that years of experience and practice enable older adults to build up a rich library of alternative ways to solve problems or make decisions that allows them to bypass steps needed by younger adults. We get better at sizing up a situation and problem-solving. We have more confidence in our opinions, feelings, and decisions and don't need validation from anyone else. We are more pragmatic. We develop a richer vocabulary and a better understanding of how to use these words effectively. The abilities we learned earlier in life and gained proficiency with over the years—like playing the stock market or playing tennis—are now smoothly polished and almost second nature. Our memory for factual and conceptual information, which we use to analyze situations and solve problems, remains well preserved. As the T-shirt says, "age and experience *can* defeat youth and skill."[12]

To illustrate, Dr. Cohen shared a story about one of his patients: A 51-year-old man remembers how he agonized over decisions during his 20s, searching in vain for the most logical choice. As he moved through his 40s and into his 50s, he found himself trusting his gut. "My decisions are more subjective," he said during one session, 'but I'm more comfortable with many of the choices that follow.'"[13] Spoken like a true PrimeTimer.

Peak Brain Performance: Connecting the Dots

Sigmund Freud once claimed that at "about the age of 50, the elasticity of the mental processes on which treatment depends is, as a rule, lacking. Old people are no longer educable." Ironically, Freud was 51 when he wrote those words and he went on to produce some of his best work after 65.[14]

In recent years, scientists have discovered that despite the few glitches with processing speed and short-term memory mentioned above, our mental capacity doesn't even reach its full potential until midlife. They are learning that, contrary to earlier assumptions, the brain continues to change and grow throughout life, and one key area of growth is the accumulation of white matter in the sophisticated thinking centers of the brain (which peaks at around 50). Because of these two factors, PrimeTime men and women can manage information better, analyze facts better, and generate meanings that were entirely beyond them when they were younger.

Thanks to newly developed brain-imaging techniques, researchers are realizing that the brain at midlife is a much more adaptable and resilient structure than anyone ever realized. We now know that the brain is ever changing and evolving—that it constantly repairs and remodels itself in response to everyday events or stimuli. This adaptability or malleability of the brain—*neuroplasticity,* or brain plasticity— promotes the formation of new neurons as well as new connections between those neurons, and continues throughout life. Far from powering down, the brain as it ages begins bringing new cognitive systems on line and cross-indexing existing ones in ways it never did before.[15]

Agatha Christie's famous detective character, Hercule Poirot, frequently credits "the little gray cells" for his superior intellect and analytic abilities. Turns out he's only half right. The truth of the matter (gray and white matter, that is) is that the brain is made up of two different kinds of tissue, closely interwoven and constantly interacting, but each with its own function. "Gray matter," which comprises about half the mass of the brain, refers to the surface of the brain, and is more formally known as the cerebral cortex. This is the "thinking" center of the brain where memory and cognitive functions reside. Believe it or not, gray matter is greatest among teenagers and steadily declines thereafter. Go figure.

The other half of the brain is "white matter," which refers to the nerve cells under or inside the gray matter, made up of long filaments that extend from the cell bodies. These are the "telephone wires" of the neural network, transmitting the electrical signals that carry the messages between neurons, between different gray-matter regions, and between the brain and the body. Covering each fine wire is a white sheath of myelin, which acts as an insulator and keeps nerve signals from sputtering out or cross-firing during transmission. White matter also governs the speed with which signals travel in the brain.

I'm no brain surgeon, but here's the way I'm visualizing the gray matter/white matter interface: the gray matter is like an internationally dispersed group of scientists in the 1950s, each really smart, each working on his own part of a problem, meeting and exchanging insights with other scientists through letters, phone calls, and conference interactions. White matter is like the Internet, which connects the scientists and allows them to exchange information via e-mail, Web sites, blogs, and instant messaging. The net effect is that, while the scientists themselves haven't gotten any smarter, the problems they're working on get solved faster because of the greater numbers of connections and communications exchanged among the scientists.

Interestingly, the brain continues to lay down fresh coats of myelin sheathing throughout life, actually *accelerating* in midlife.[16] Up to age 10 or so, this process is concentrated in regions that control essential primary functions, such as vision, hearing, and motor skills, as well as basic thinking and very basic impulse control. Then, in the 20s, 30s, and beyond, it moves on to portions of the brain responsible for more cerebral and abstract functions, such as reasoned thought.

In the 40s and 50s, the brain is still building up white matter, adding an impressive 33 percent and 55 percent respectively during each of those decades, according to researchers at Harvard University's McLean Hospital.[17] It's the location of this myelin growth that is interesting. Mature healthy adults have the most myelin in the frontal and temporal lobes, where the big thoughts live.[18] The brain is essentially getting into "the zone," similar to elite athletes at the peak of their training and careers. Think about Lance Armstrong training for his seventh Tour de France; he trained for months and years in order to optimize his performance at just the right time. His body—and mind—had achieved peak conditioning, and he was able to get in "the zone" and pedal to victory.

The Differences (and Similarities) between Men's and Women's Brains

In *Marketing to Women,* we used research on the differences between men's brains and women's brains to demonstrate the differences between men and women when it comes to responding to marketing. It has become common knowledge that women and men have different cognitive strengths:

Women

- Better at language/verbal tasks (more articulate, better reading)

- Better people skills (more empathetic, better at remembering faces)

- More perceptive and intuitive abilities

- More networked, contextual thinking

- More acute senses

- More in touch with emotions

- Pay attention to key issues and details

Men

- Better at spatial tasks (ability to perceive, visualize, and act in three dimensions)

- Greater mechanical aptitude

- More linear, focused thinking

- Greater strength and speed

- More in line with abstract principles, rules

- Pay attention to key issues, not details

- Stronger reasoning and problem solving talents

In Chapter 1, I discussed how the population is becoming more female (i.e., greater ratio of women to men). It turns out, on top of that, *each person* in the population is becoming more female; basically, everyone's brains become more female as they age. I'm not a neuroscientist, but the intriguing evidence suggests that male brains become more female with age, and female brains become even more female. As we grow older:

- Our brain hemispheres become more integrated as we age, just as women's right and left hemispheres are more connected.[19]

- Our limbic system puts us more in touch with our feelings as we age, which lines up with the fact that a woman's brain is hardwired to be naturally more empathetic.[20]

- The hormonal shift that takes place at midlife among both women and men creates a dominance of estrogen and a swing toward female personality traits.[21]

As a result of this, as we grow older, the cognitive characteristics that women of all ages possess become even more pronounced in both men and women over 50.

Hemispheres in Harmony

Women's brains show more connections between the hemispheres than men's brains;[22] MRI studies conducted by a team at Indiana University School of Medicine showed that women have four times as many connections as men do between the left and right hemispheres of the brain.[23] Researchers believe that this connectivity makes women more perceptive, articulate, and verbally fluent.

This hemispheric connection may also account for women's in-clination to think holistically, preferring to view individual elements and interactions in context as part of a bigger picture. Women are bet-ter equipped to move data from one side of the brain to the other. With this "crossover" brain capability, a woman cross-pollinates all kinds of information from her surroundings. She is unconsciously accessing those file drawers of the right brain, tapping into emotional memories and feelings, sorting and looking for similarities and rela-tionships to what she is presently encountering. Researchers believe this capability to know something without knowing how they know is the basis for what has long been recognized as women's intuition.

Here's what happens in the mature mind. Neuroscientist Rob-erto Cabeza's recent work shows that unlike young adults, who han-dle most tasks on one side of the brain or the other, older adults tend to use both hemispheres. Why this is so is still unclear. Cabeza takes a compensation view of these age differences. To compensate for the decline in any one processing center, older brains seem to bring in reinforcements, activating more processing centers to accomplish a given task.[24]

As they bring together and integrate more thoughts and feelings from different parts of the brain, PrimeTimers—women and men—are looking more at the big picture, and allowing themselves to trust their gut instinct more.

Priming the Emotional Pump in PrimeTime

Emotions, our most basic cerebral reactions, evolved when mam-mals did, about 100 million years ago, and are generated in the middle layer of our three-tiered brain, the limbic system. Here's where we gen-erate the value judgments we make, often unconsciously, that exert such a strong influence on our behavior. When I say "value judgments," by the way, I don't mean anything high-falutin' like right or wrong, good or bad. What I'm talking about are basic reactions: "I like it. I hate it. It's nice. It's horrid. Can I have more? Get that away from me!"

It is commonly assumed that women are more connected to their emotions than men are. Simon Baron-Cohen, author of the wonderfully insightful book, *The Essential Difference: The Truth about the Male and Female,* theorizes that the male brain is predominantly hardwired for understanding and building systems, and that the female brain is predominantly hardwired for understanding and empathizing with people. He calls it the empathising-systemising (E-S) theory.

Baron-Cohen believes that men's brains have evolved to analyze and explore systems, to extract underlying rules that govern their behavior, and to construct them. Women's brains, on the other hand, are designed to identify another person's emotions and thoughts, and to respond to these with an appropriate emotion. The empathizer has a knack for knowing how people are feeling, and how to treat people with care and sensitivity.

Similarly, the brain of an older person is mellower and more in touch with its emotional side—especially the positive feelings, I'm happy to say. One consequence of the increased neural and hemispheric connectivity discussed above is a greater facility in integrating thoughts with feelings. According to Dr. Gene Cohen, the brain's emotional circuitry matures and becomes more balanced with age; the limbic system appears to grow calmer. Current research suggests that the *amygdalae*, two almond-shaped structures that generate some of our most intense emotions, show decreased reactivity to negative information while maintaining or increasing their reactivity to positive information.[25] Psychological studies back up this finding and show that midlife is a time when adults have less anxiety and higher self-esteem than before.[26]

So, forget the stereotypes of grumpy old men and cranky old ladies. PrimeTime men and women mellow with age. According to a study reported in the *Journal of Personality and Social Psychology*, researchers found that as people get older, they become happier, not sadder. The older the respondent was, the more he or she reported experiencing positive emotions in the past 30 days, like cheerfulness, life satisfaction, and overall happiness. In contrast, younger participants reported more negative emotions, like sadness, worthlessness, and hopelessness.[27] All good news, and certainly counter to the conventional assumptions of older people as "sadder but wiser." Wiser, yes. Sadder, no.

Women have always responded more to emotional relevance in their marketing communications because of their social values of empathy, warmth, commonality, and so on. Similarly, studies show that older adults pay attention to, seek out, and perform cognitive tasks better when they involve more emotional material.[28] In other words, marketing messages that include or focus on a positive emotional dimension will do a better job seizing PrimeTimers' attention, holding their interest, locking in recall, and motivating a reaction.

Hormones: Estrogen Rules

Hormones are chemical messengers that course through our bloodstream and turn on switches that regulate everything that happens in our bodies. Different glands and organs throughout the body produce hormones. It is the hypothalamus that controls how much estrogen and testosterone are produced.[29]

In *Marketing to Women,* I coined the term *biological jujitsu* to describe the switch in ratios of testosterone and estrogen experienced by men and women in midlife. Men and women become more alike in their hormonal make-up as they age—men lose testosterone and women lose estrogen. As a result, they undergo a bit of a personality flip; men become more relaxed about having things their way and more interested in strengthening family ties while women become more assertive about their likes and dislikes and self-confident in pursuing them. Psychological theory supports this conclusion as well, led by Carl Jung who said that one of the central tasks of aging is coming to terms with the "contrasexual other."[30] Basically, he meant that men need to come to terms with their feminine side, and women need to come to terms with their masculine side.

Upon further research, I've come to clarify the personality shift concept a bit. There is indeed a convergence, but it's not in the middle, halfway between men and women. Instead, there's a decided lean toward the female.

The Preponderance of Estrogen. The scientific community is debating the impact of hormones on the brain right now. It's a relatively new area of study, and therefore without a lot of conclusive, firmly agreed-upon findings. For instance, Dr. Louann Brizendine recently published a well-researched book (she reviewed 1,008 studies on men's and women's brains) called *The Female Brain* in which she makes the argument that low oxytocin, which ensues after estrogen declines at menopause, may lead women to feel "less interested in the nuances of emotions" and "less concerned about keeping the peace;" this is why more divorces are initiated by women than men in PrimeTime. Furthermore, she says that the PrimeTime Woman is "much less concerned about the problems and needs of her family, friends, and children."[31] This is one point of view, and I have to tell you, I find it very surprising. Most women would probably disagree with her oxytocin notion. And scientists are disagreeing too; they are debating the amount of credit, responsibility, and blame that Brizendine gives to hormones, as opposed to other environmental factors, in the nature vs. nurture debate on gender differences. Others point out that her descriptions of how hormonal swings can result in unbalanced behavior and irrational emotions reinforce already negative stereotypes about women, menopausal PrimeTime Women especially. However, I am encouraged that there is starting to be much more in-depth research on the topic of women, aging, hormones, and the brain. I look forward to more studies in this area in the near future.

There *are* certain verifiable facts about hormone changes in PrimeTime. And they are intriguing. Let's start with men. Between the ages of 40 and 80, men's T-levels (levels of testosterone in their blood) drop dramatically, by as much as 50 to 60 percent.[32] Furthermore, their estrogen levels actually increase. In young men, a normal estrogen to testosterone ratio is about 1:50. By the time they are in their 70s or 80s, the ratio is more like 1:8—still heavy on the testosterone, but with the estrogen ratio dialed up by 600 percent compared to what it was in their youth.[33] At menopause, women's production of estrogen also drops significantly—so much that by age 72 they actually have less estrogen in their blood than men do. In fact, men's estrogen levels at that age *are three times* as high as women's.

Channeling of Testosterone. One function of estrogen is to dampen the effects of testosterone. Researchers have shown that the drop in older women's estrogen levels during menopause results in an "unmasking" of their testosterone, releasing it to manifest itself in feelings and behavior.[34] However, young men and older women channel their testosterone drive differently. Whereas high-testosterone young men display greater aggressiveness and a drive for dominance, older women experience a milder effect, expressed as greater assertiveness and self-confidence. This additional biologically based

assertiveness reinforces PrimeTime Women's determination, deci-
siveness, and forward-looking goal of seeking their destiny.

Legacy. While PrimeTime Women are finding new confidence,
they are using it to benefit not just themselves, but others. Some
researchers have found that both men and women describe themselves as more nurturing, intimate, and tender with increasing age,
trends that are related to "generativity," meaning concern for the
next generation.[35] This increase in generativity among both men
and women simply amplifies many of the social values that women
hold dear: warmer not winner, empathy, commonality, people
power, the need to give back, and so on. Therefore, women's values
are driving this shift in personality traits in PrimeTime.

In essence, we are coming full circle. We are all conceived female
and, later in life, we all return to the female state. The human fetus
(both XX and XY fetuses) starts out female. Then, about six weeks
after conception, the little Y guy triggers a prenatal testosterone womb
"wash" that changes everything. Presto! The XY fetus becomes a boy!
Then at around age 70, the human male shuts down a good deal of
his testosterone production and dials up his estrogen to about three
times the level of his female counterparts. Not surprisingly, then, the
brain structure and personality characteristics of both genders reflect
these hormonal changes and become predominantly more female in
midlife and thereafter. The circle of life is alive and well and female!

In summary, older brains are becoming more female—using
both hemispheres for greater connectivity, becoming more mellow
and linked to emotions. And hormone levels are moving both genders toward more female personality traits. Therefore, we can expect
men to think more like women (rather than the other way around,
Henry Higgins!). PrimeTimers (both male and female) will exhibit
more linkage between thoughts and feelings, a greater incidence of
going with gut instinct, less impulsive behavior, more big picture
thinking, and a recognition of greater context. The built-in Prime-
Time bonuses of greater experience and wisdom and peak brain performance will also change the way PrimeTimers think, feel, behave,
and decide. Later I will show you how these changes to the Prime-
Time mind impact the way to market to PrimeTime Women, who are
not only at their financial peak but also their at intellectual peak.

Moral of the story: with two or three exceptions, all the Gender-Trends marketing principles outlined in my first book, *Marketing to Women,* and later in this book, apply even more to older women than to younger women . . . and *also* resonate with older men. This is extraordinarily good news for marketers. Far from having to choose which of the two major demographics trends you want to hitch your fortunes to—women as the majority of the population and the primary buyers of almost everything; or the massive shift of the population toward older lifestyles at the peak of their spending power—it turns out that practicing the principles of marketing to PrimeTime Women is the best way to reach *both* of them.

What's With This Body?

Like the mental changes, most physical changes happen gradually and don't substantially affect people until they are in their 70s, post-PrimeTime. In the meanwhile, most of the physical adjustments are relatively minor; PrimeTime Women accept them, adjust to them, figure out how to deal with them, and move on with their lives.

Proactively Protecting Her Health

Boomer women have always taken responsibility for their health. They launched Jane Fonda into the fitness craze of the 1980s and are driving the growth of Pilates and yoga today. They have managed their own health as well as that of their families by demanding better nutrition options from food manufacturers nationwide. According to a new study just released by AARP, 91 percent feel "confident they are doing all they can" to keep themselves as healthy as possible. And it seems to be working: 81 percent would consider their health "good" or better; more than half (56 percent) say it is "very good" or "excellent."[36]

PrimeTime Women are much more proactive about taking care of themselves than most Americans are. They are careful to eat a balanced, low-fat diet, believe in getting an annual physical, and actively seek information on how to stay in good health, as shown in the following table.[37]

PrimeTimeWomen: Proactively Protecting Their Health

Activity	Percent PTW	Index vs. Total U.S.
Went online in past month for medical info 1–5x	24	155
Describe themselves as very active health managers	23	149
Look into healthcare treatment	22	145
Actively seek nutrition information	22	143
Have regular medical check-ups	62	136
Frequently take preventive medicine	38	136
Research online, ask Dr. about health	40	135
Usually snack healthy	31	132
Ask friends advice on health	22	129
Try to eat balanced diet	20	128
Heavy user of vitamins /supplements	28	203

Source: Simmons Spring 2005 NHCS Adult Full Year Unified Study, 2005 MRI Doublebase, provided by DDB Worldwide

The ad in Figure 4.1 for Fiber One Honey Clusters cereal recognizes PrimeTime Women as proactive health managers, vital, active, and leading life on their own terms. It shows a beautiful but "real" PrimeTime businesswoman and the copy reads: "My schedule is always full, so I know it's important to start the day with a healthy breakfast of Fiber One Honey Clusters cereal." It also offers a promotion to win one-on-one yoga classes with a personal instructor in one's own home, a well thought-out appeal to this health-motivated audience.

PrimeTime Women's higher education levels have created a desire for primary health knowledge so they can make informed decisions. Their growing affluence has allowed them greater access to better health care and activities that advance their wellness agenda. And their growing assertiveness means that they are confident challenging doctors and the medical establishment when they receive insufficient attention, careless treatment, or an incomplete diagnosis. And believe me, they still do. Studies show that medical professionals who can't make a diagnosis tend to dismiss their PrimeTime Women patients' complaints as "normal aging," or "probably psychological," without the extent of testing they give to their male patients. It is

FIGURE 4.1 Fiber One: Proactively Protecting Her Health

Reprinted with the permission of General Mills, Inc.

only very recently, for example, that researchers discovered women's symptoms of a heart attack are often very different from the classic symptoms in men.

In this chapter, we're going to start by looking at the physical changes you can't see—the ones that cause the aches and pains—and move on to the ones that you can—the ones that affect PrimeTime Women's appearance.

The Changes You Can't See

Almost all PrimeTimers experience a moderate amount of hearing loss, vision impairment, body temperature adaptation, and bone and joint changes. Most of these changes begin slowly, develop slowly, and sometimes aren't noticed for decades. Some, such as shifts in vision, can begin as early as the 20s but don't require correction until the 40s or 50s. Others, like variations in touch, generally don't start until after 50. Men usually experience the physical changes before women. But most of these modest PrimeTime physical changes are dealt with fairly quickly and easily through simple medical solutions or innovative offerings from smart marketers.

Experiencing the World—The Five Senses

Hearing. Hearing loss begins gradually during your 40s and accelerates over the next two decades; by the time we reach 65, 60 percent of us are hearing-impaired to one degree or another.[38] The most common age-related hearing problem is reduced sensitivity to high-pitched tones, which occurs in your 40s or 50s.[39] In fact, savvy teens today are trying to take advantage of their teachers' (and parents') slightly impaired hearing by downloading a new ring tone on their cell phones: only teens can hear it, so they won't get in trouble for having their cell phones on and getting text messages in class![40]

Hearing loss generally hits midlife men harder than women. Female mammals across the board have better hearing than males, and human beings are no exception.[41] One of life's ironies is that women have spent most of their lives perceiving something to be twice as loud at half the volume of men . . . and now it will get even worse, because men lose their hearing before women. Personally, I plan to keep a set of earplugs in the glove compartment of my husband's car.

A decade ago, the first saxophone-playing president of the United States found he could no longer hear clearly at receptions. President Clinton grew up as many Boomers did, listening to loud music, driving in loud cars, and hearing loud city noises. So in 1997, at age 51, he got two hearing aids. The First Boomer did not let hearing loss slow him down, and neither do the rest of his cohorts.[42]

Vision. There are several age-related changes to the eye. In their 40s, more people experience presbyopia, difficulty in seeing close objects clearly, necessitating either longer arms or corrective lenses.[43]

In addition, the size of the pupil diminishes with age, so less light comes into the retina. Older people need 100 watt bulbs, where in their younger days, 75 watts would do. Paradoxically, the eye gets more sensitive to glare, interference from reflections off shiny surfaces. The lens of the eye yellows a bit, causing poorer color distinction, particularly at the green-blue-violet end of the spectrum, which is one reason most medicine capsules come in yellow and red. And finally, the ability to transition between light and dark declines, making it more difficult to walk from daylight into a dimly lit restaurant or theater.[44]

Given the virtual universality of these sight changes among Prime-Time Women, it's not surprising that over-the-counter reading glasses have become popular; the surprising development is that they have ventured into the realm of fun-to-wear fashion accessories. Prime-Time Women are into frames in bright colors and unusual patterns like leopard prints. For convenience, I have 12 pairs, scattered all over the house, so I can always find one nearby.

Incidentally, this is a perfect example of two key take-aways from this chapter. First, PrimeTime Women are dealing with these minor changes of aging good-humoredly and without a terrible amount of angst. Second, some savvy businessperson—I warrant it was a woman—recognized it as a business opportunity. Five years ago, reading glasses were black and brown and round and dull and available only in the old folks' section of the drugstore. Now they're colorful and cool and carried on cash register counters everywhere as an impulse item.

Taste and Smell. Both taste and smell diminish as we age, though, as with all senses, the decline is slow.[45] The decline in smell is much greater than it is for taste, which is a shame, because studies show that smell is even more important than taste in discriminating among foods.[46] Once again, men are generally affected sooner and to a greater degree than women.[47]

Touch. Women have a highly tuned sense of touch. In fact, in an average group, the *least* sensitive woman can feel a lighter touch than the *most* sensitive man.[48] When they're perusing clothes or entering a new environment, it is almost instinctive for women to raise a hand to experience what it feels like. To compensate for the fact that the other senses are dimming a little, the PrimeTime Woman may appreciate some extra thought on helping her enjoy her sense of touch.

Temperature. This can be a big one for PrimeTime Women. One of the first signs that a woman is peri-menopausal (approaching menopause) is the proverbial hot flash. You don't recognize them at first and can easily endure them for several months before you even recognize what's going on. They're not dangerous, of course, but they are a *major* annoyance.

There you are in the middle of a presentation, a cocktail party, a quiet reading session, and with no warning and for no reason, the gods give you your own personal sauna—and no way to leave it. Once again, PrimeTime humor steps in to help cope: "They're not hot flashes. They're power surges." Well, PrimeTime Women don't care what you call them, when they're standing there literally dripping, they certainly don't feel powerful. Anybody that can come to the rescue is going to make a fortune.

On the other side of the equation, late in PrimeTime, as people approach their 70s, they may start to experience some circulation problems, and hands and feet get chilled. Moreover, as people age they begin to have difficulty telling that their core body temperature is low.[49] In other words—they get cold more easily!

The Body Infrastructure

After decades of jogging, tennis, hiking, and biking, PrimeTimers are wearing out their body parts. Muscles shrink a little and lose some mass; endurance and strength wane a bit; and handgrip strength decreases, making it a tad more difficult to accomplish routine activities such as turning a lid or a jammed key.[50] Joints don't move as easily, and unless you work on it, flexibility can decrease. Changes in finger joints, more common in women than men (and maybe hereditary), make precise tasks like pressing small buttons something you have to focus on.[51]

But here's an area where we really do get some miracles of modern medicine. Procedures to replace knees and repair rotator cuffs have become almost routine.[52]

One of today's most successful housewares companies came about due to one man's desire to address his wife's difficulties with holding ordinary kitchen utensils because of arthritis. Sam Farber put together a group of researchers that included a gerontologist and developed a line of 15 products using "universal design." The line, now known as OXO, has grown to include more than 500 items, including utensils with broad, cushy handles and angled measuring cups that can be read from the top. OXO has won international design awards and has devotees across every age group. Although originally developed for older consumers, the design and functionality makes their products appealing to everyone.[53]

Ford's Third Age Suit

One company that has taken steps to address all of these physical changes is Ford. Back in 1999 executives at the Ford Motor Company had an epiphany: Their engineers were sometimes 30 years younger than the fast-approaching PrimeTime market. How were these engineers, who had great eyesight and fine mobility, who were smart but limited by personal experience, supposed to understand the restrictions of the older generation?

Ford's Third Age Suit (see Figure 4.2) looks like a cross between a beekeeper's protective gear and a high-tech astronaut suit. It's made of stiffened fabric that simulates reduced flexibility in the elbows, stomach, back, hands, wrists, upper and lower torso, knees, and ankles. Because it's harder to manipulate small switches and buttons as we age, gloves reduce the sense of touch. Engineers wear goggles that replicate older eyes, yellowing the lens and increasing sensitivity to glare.

FIGURE 4.2 Ford's Third Age Suit

The Ford Motor Company

"When you're young and fit enough to leap out of a car without effort, it's hard to appreciate why an older person may need to lever themselves out of the driver's seat by pushing on the seat back and the door frame," said Mike Bradley, Ergonomics Supervisor at Ford's Dunton Engineering Centre in Essex, England, where the suit was first utilized. "But try leaping out while you are wearing this suit and you really understand the challenges we face."

The first Ford car to be designed with input from the Third Age Suit was the Focus, and results were so positive that the suit is now a standard design tool (or, as the company calls it, an "empathy tool"). Ford has also shared its Third Age Suit with Boeing, with whom it has a research partnership, and the aircraft manufacturer is now using it in the design of its passenger planes.[54]

"Sense"-ible Marketing Solutions

With each physical change, PrimeTimers will be encountering new, albeit minor, irritations—and for marketers, that spells opportunity. Look for ways to adapt your products, services, and environments to PrimeTimers' pleasure. And remember, very often it is the seemingly small detail that will differentiate your product from your competitors' and be the deciding factor in the PrimeTime Women's purchase choice.

Hearing:

- Include self-adjustable volume control on timers for ovens, microwaves, and other appliances with beeping indicators.

- Make cell phones with more volume range in the ring-tone so she can adjust it for a noisy environment.

Vision:

- On those cell phones above, be the first to add a flashing light option so she can find it quickly when it's buried in the bottom of her purse.

- At retail, design a "transition area" in the entrance so people can stand there for half a tick while their eyes adjust without being in the way of your other customers. In restaurants and other moodily lit establishments, dial up the light levels. Lighting can be dramatic without being dim. Use music and color to create mood and romance.

- Store and product design—Lots of articles have covered the do's and don'ts of visual design for older people but, for completeness, here are the top five:

  - Use more color differentiation in your color-coded store schemes and labels—apparel size tags, for example. Instead of peach and petal pink, pick colors that are easier to tell apart. Use more contrast. Stay away from blue/green adjacencies.

- Print menus, brochures, price tags, etc. on dull stock to minimize glare.

- Use dark type on a light-colored background, not light type reversed out of a dark background. Don't print over pictures or images.

- Don't use complicated or even sans-serif fonts. Use at least 12-point type—at least for copy you really want your consumer to read.

- Even for nonselling copy, since women always want more information than men, find a way to make the information legible or available somewhere else, for example, in a package insert or on your Web site. This goes for packaged goods nutrition labels, operating instructions for consumer electronics, apparel washing instruction labels, and more. (And how about those beauty products that come in small bottles? It's really hard to read that wrinkle-reduction guarantee in teeny tiny mouse print. Coincidence? I think not.)

Taste and Smell:

- Push aromatherapy in more categories than just soaps and candles.

- Offer customizable packages of seasonings, herbs, and spices in take-along packets. Include them in packaged foods like microwave meals and sell them separately at the checkout aisle. Restaurateurs can offer a platter of condiments on tables so customers can season to their liking—not just ketchup or salt and pepper, but horseradish, garlic powder, tarragon, fresh lemongrass, vinegar, fresh cilantro, chili peppers. Even try new and exotic flavorings, like sriracha, a spicy Thai sauce.

Touch:

- Consider interesting shapes and textures in food, apparel, packaging, and other products. Try velvet, beading, silks, satins, pebbled grains, ridging; or in environmental design add elements that are warm, cool, water, pulsing, etc.

Temperature:

- Consider heat lamps in waiting areas such as valet parking outside of restaurants and taxi lines outside hotel vestibules.

- Restaurants—You know how high-end restaurants have coats and ties available for men who weren't prepared for the dress code? Why not have pretty wraps available for women who get chilled while dining on your outdoor patio? When I was on a girlfriends' getaway in Cabo San Lucas, our first meal was dinner at an outdoor restaurant. When we sat down in the early evening, it was warm; by the time we left, it was freezing. In our inexperience, we hadn't realized how much the temperature would drop at this seaside resort. Fortunately, the proprietor was used to novices like us and was prepared to offer a colorful poncho to each of his late-dining patrons. An added thought: Change the styles every couple of months, feature new designs or local designers, have an ethnic theme or a color theme, and it could be the deciding factor that gets the girlfriends to choose your place just to see what's new.

Balance and Dexterity:

- Make sure your floors aren't slippery, your stairs are edged in a contrasting color, and you have handrails to help with balance, especially in areas where your customer has just emerged from a more dimly lit environment into a bright one.

- Make lids easier to open. Tylenol has it all over the competition with their E-Z Open Cap, which has no carton, and a "sail plane" handle which is simple to twist.

- Manufacturers of BlackBerries, cell phones, portable calculators, and car radios need to make their heavily button-laden devices easier for PrimeTimers to operate.

- Forward-thinking Bic markets a pen that lets writers customize the pen shape to fit the contours of their own hands.

Menopause: Not What It Used to Be

While most of the physical changes discussed affect both midlife men and women, albeit to a greater or lesser degree, there is one major physical transformation that is all female, and that's menopause, or "the change of life." As I discussed in the last chapter, the psychological impact of menopause is not really that big a deal.

So, what about from a physical point of view?

Hot Flashes. The fact of the matter is that for most women, hot flashes are a bothersome nuisance, but usually for only a few months, while they're trying to figure out what's going on. These days there are lots of ways to reduce, if not eliminate, most of the physical symptoms. Sixty-two percent of women over 50 are on hormone replacement therapy.[55] And for women who choose not to avail themselves of that, there's calcium, soy, and various herbal supplements to help.

Smart, new products on the market are also making a difference. A company called HotCool Wear began making menopause pajamas in 2000 from the same polyester fabric used in workout clothes. The material, which feels like soft cotton, wicks away sweat and allows the body to cool, thus lessening the impact of nighttime hot flashes. Then there's the Bedfan®, which sounds kind of wild. You install it under the covers at the foot of the bed, where it delivers a soft breeze that flows between the sheets and along the body—allegedly without disturbing your partner on the other side of the bed.

When researchers for the MacArthur Foundation Study on Aging, the most extensive, comprehensive study on aging in America, asked women their feelings about menopause, the majority, 62 percent, said they felt "only relief."[56] Kind of makes sense—no more dealing with menstrual periods every month, and for those who don't practice birth control, the substantially more significant end of worry about getting pregnant.

Hot Sex

An analysis of data on more than 3,100 women aged 42–52 reported there was no difference between post-menopausal and pre-menopausal women in frequency, desire, arousal, or physical or emotional satisfaction from sex.[57] But there is a big difference in what younger and PrimeTime women want to wear underneath it all, and it's not Victoria's Secret.

So let me think—we have all these women, they have lots of money, they have lots of sex, and there's almost nowhere they can buy some pretty lingerie? Well, leave it to Chico's, the company whose amazing results over the past several years have been built on understanding PrimeTime Women. Soma, a sister company to Chico's, sells lingerie that is beautiful, comfortable, and sexy, but not so skimpy and not so revealing in all the wrong places.

Keeping Up Appearances

Self-Image

In the movie *Something's Gotta Give*, 57-year-old Diane Keaton is cast as a playwright at the height of her career, deliciously perplexed by the dilemma of choosing between two admirers played by Jack Nicholson and the much-younger Keanu Reeves. When an interviewer asked this PrimeTime Woman if she'd done anything special to get in shape for her nude scene, Keaton replied, "No, I did nothing. I thought, 'It's going to be a woman's body, and that's the way it is.'"

As Boomer women slide gracefully, even gleefully, into their PrimeTime years, they are rejecting society's attempts to define them as frumpy and unattractive. Sure, they have their bad hair days, but they've been working out, staying active, and eating right for decades and will continue to do so. They're comfortable in their skin, accept themselves, gray hair, wrinkles, and all, and are too busy working and having a good time to be standing in front of a mirror bemoaning their lost youth.

Incidentally, neither are they dashing off to the plastic surgeon the minute they turn 50. You may be surprised to learn that, in fact, 72 percent of all cosmetic surgical and nonsurgical procedures are performed on patients under 50.[58] Not that there's anything wrong with plastic surgery. What's wrong with lifting a jowl here and an eyelid there? I'm just pointing out that the strong majority of people who are doing this are women in their fearful 40s, not PrimeTime Women.

Why do PrimeTime Women account for so few of the procedures? The answer is in the last chapter: because their self-images are rooted in reality. Actress Jamie Lee Curtis gave a new definition to the term "self-acceptance" when she posed in the September 2002 issue of *More* magazine wearing a black two-piece workout outfit, revealing love handles and a less-than-hourglass waist. "I don't have great thighs," she said. "I have very big breasts and a soft, fatty little tummy. Glam Jamie, the perfect Jamie . . . it's such a fraud." And then she added, "The more I like me, the less I want to be other people."[59]

Speaking for so many PrimeTime women, she identified the fact that at midlife, women stop worrying about impressing others and redirect their energies toward being the best, truest person they can be. Other PrimeTime Women role models are: Susan Sarandon, Emmylou Harris, Sigourney Weaver, Goldie Hawn, Katie Couric, Meredith Vieira, Oprah, Linda Ronstadt, Martina Navratilova, Dianne Feinstein, and Condoleezza Rice.

Defying Gravity

Gravity is a wicked, evil force, but it keeps us on the planet, so we deal with it. Mostly through exercise.

PrimeTime Women have known for years that aerobic exercise, strength training or weight-bearing exercise (walking, stair-climbing), plus eating a low-fat, high-fiber diet, can do wonders to stave off thickening waists and drooping and dropping breasts, knees, and glutes. As the character Elphaba (the Wicked Witch) sings in the Broadway musical hit "Wicked," "I think I'll try defying gravity. And you can't pull me down." PrimeTime Women are singing the same tune when they are working up a sweat in gyms, on roads, on bikes, in kayaks, on the tennis courts, and on ski slopes across America.

Exercise: The Perfect Answer. Lori Bitter and the JWT Mature Market Group have been leaders in addressing the marketing opportunity in the 45+ arena with their annual Beyond the Numbers Summit and regular "Live Wire" newsletters. They assert that two-thirds of all Boomers exercise, and more than half of the 33 million health club members in the U.S. are over 40. Leading edge Boomers (55+) are the fastest growing segment of health club members. And PrimeTime women are leading the charge. They are more active than midlife men AND younger women who "exercise regularly":

- 39 percent of women 50–69
  - versus 36 percent of women 35–49
  - versus 34 percent of women 25–34
  - versus 33 percent of men 50–59[60]

The comments from our PrimeTime Women research make it clear that they consider exercise both important and enjoyable.

I do the same things I did before. I walk, I ski, I go rollerblading.
Ellen, 55

I walk and do tai chi. If I don't do those every week, I feel something is missing.
Gretchen, 67

I either go to the Y or run 5 to 6 days a week at 5 AM. I began training for and running marathons 2 years ago. I have run 3 marathons and 2 half-marathons.
Melody, 50

Health clubs, spas, personal trainers, masseuses, clothing manufacturers, yoga mat-makers, marketers of sweatbands, home exercise equipment, protein bars, energy drinks, bottled water, MP3 players, walking shoes, bicycles, volleyballs—all of these products and services will be booming, thanks to PrimeTime Women.

Thirty years ago, Boomer women bonded with Jane Fonda and tried to "feel the burn." Now, they've discovered exercise doesn't have to be painful. It can be social and fun, offering an opportunity to connect with friends in a way that doesn't depend upon food (calorie-wise, lunch can be a very expensive chit-chat). One company, the women's-only Curves International, has addressed all these issues—and in doing so has become the world's fastest-growing franchise of any kind in history.[61] Their strategy: Make exercise easy, fun, quick, supportive, and social. (By the way, Curves is featured in Chapter 9 as an extraordinary example of marketing to PrimeTime Women.)

As PrimeTime Women look for good ways to make use of their newly freed time, they intensify their search for ways to blend physical activity and sociability.

I was recently invited to speak at the annual conference of Golf 20/20, the marketing arm of the golfing industry. The industry was looking at ways to grow the game of golf given that there were more courses to fill and the core target (middle-aged white men) was pretty much tapped out. The industry was highly motivated to attract more people to the game, but was stumbling over the "who" and the "how." My immediate thought was, *where are the women?* Male golfers outnumber women three to one. Only six percent of women in the United States golf, compared to about 20 percent of men.[62]

Attracting the women's market was not a new concept to Golf 20/20. They had determined that women were a viable target and were targeting young professional women, urging them to include the game as part of their business networking strategies. That's one of the main reasons men play, and with more women working, they assumed women would too.

I asked why they didn't target PrimeTime Women who have both the time and the money to immerse themselves in the game. Their reasoning was that if a PrimeTime Woman hadn't taken up golf before age 50, she would never do so. Another case of the "get 'em while they're young" fallacy.

The reality is that, of all the consumer segments you could pick, young women professionals are probably the least likely to be able to take up golf. Interested? Yes. Able to? No. They are mired in the "establish yourself" phase of their careers, and many or them also have young families at home. When you've just bought a house, and you have to replace the baby clothes and paraphernalia every three months, money is tight, and time even more so.

My recommendation was for them to take a totally different tack. Golf is a perfect PrimeTime Women vehicle because it combines fresh air, exercise, relaxation, sociability, girlfriends, and fun. Talk about multitasking! When you look at it that way—and talk to PrimeTime Women about it that way—it has everything. As I detailed in my first book, just what women are looking for, The Perfect Answer! It's a new way to connect with three of their best friends (or make new friends).

But they need to know they're welcome, and that's where the industry needed some "lessons from the pro," so to speak. Here's what I suggested to the Golf 20/20 executives:

- Market the game to PrimeTime Women. They have the money, the time, and, with the right positioning from you, the motivation.

- Focus on having a good time, not beating your partner. Highlight fun and sociability. The game of golf—and to women it is a game, as opposed to most men, who think of it as a competition—is about connecting with friends old and new, getting out and doing something good for body and soul.

- Forget "product as hero" and focus on the golfer herself, not the equipment or the course.

- Market to high-end PrimeTime Women's groups looking for annual events, like chapters of the Women Presidents Organization, the Committee of 200, the National Association of Women Business Owners, and so on.

- Sponsor golf clinics, which remove the competitive aspect and confidence issues.

- Look for ways to lessen the time commitment for time-starved women. Even those who are retired or semi-retired are busy with commitments—but they are commitments of choice. Make golf fun, and they'll choose you. Promote three-, six-, and nine-hole games. Offer the golf clinics during the lunch hour.

- Be creative and inventive and think way outside the box. Most country clubs have catering facilities. What about offering take-out dinners their golfers can bring home? (And let's face it, most of the golfers who think about bringing home dinner are going to be women.) A roasted chicken, a gourmet pizza—if supermarkets can do it, surely the golf industry can make It happen.

- Don't neglect your pro shop. Both Dior and Chanel have added golf lines to their collections. And only 38 percent of women who buy golf apparel actually play in it, so nongolfing women members will be interested in it too.

A Little Help Here and There

PrimeTime women are not stressing over their weight and body changes, but they are certainly not averse to a little help here and there. The body shaper, hair color, and cosmetics industries are all moving fast to serve the PrimeTime Woman's needs and open her wallet. But the fashion industry? Not so much.

Body Shapers—Spanx You Very Much

Sales trainer and stand-up comedian Sara Blakely cut the feet out of her pantyhose in order to wear them with any shoe style, including open-toed shoes and sandals. Believing other women would want them—but from a material that smoothed leg "imperfections" while being ultra-comfortable—she designed a product with no binding cords in waistbands or leg bands and a light but strong material designed to be worn even in warm weather.[63]

With no professional backing Sara wrote the patent herself and finally found a mill owner willing to give it a shot. She named her brand Spanx, designed a bold, red wrap unlike any other pantyhose packaging, and set up meetings with department store buyers. After success with Neiman Marcus and ultimately Bloomingdales, Saks, and Nordstrom, Spanx had found its market.

The body-smoothing pantyhose, designed for practicality and comfort, is now an international hit. And the Spanx brand has grown to include an entire "Hide and Sleek" collection of body shaping undergarments, the "Bod-A-Bing" collection of body-shaping pants and tops, leg-supporting maternity wear, and a plus-size collection.

Does She, or Doesn't She?

Hair color is one beauty secret that PrimeTime Women are not giving up—but that's because hair color is really a fashion accessory these days. Remember the 1955 campaign for Miss Clairol? "Does she . . . or doesn't she? Hair color so natural, only her hairdresser knows for sure." In the 1950s "nice girls" didn't color their hair. After struggling to get the slogan approved (some male executives felt the line was "too suggestive"), the campaign finally went forward and the number of U.S. women using the product shot from seven percent to more than 50 percent.[64] Sales skyrocketed 413 percent in six years.[65] The key to the campaign was that, while women were still coloring their hair in the privacy of their own bathrooms, after those ads, if someone suspected her of dyeing her hair, it elicited a sly wink from other women, instead of a disapproving frown. Today if you were to ask, "Does she or doesn't she?" the offhand answer would be, "Who cares?"

A PrimeTime Woman knows how she looks. She doesn't want magical solutions. But she does want to look her personal best, because if you ask her, that's pretty darn good!

PrimeTime Women—A Passion for Fashion

Fashion industry, listen up. Do you know that the average clothing size of an American woman is size 14?[66] "Average" means that fully half the female population is *larger* than a size 14, and because of the childbirth thing, and the gravity thing, I guarantee you *more* than half of PrimeTime Women are larger than a size 14. If *I* know that, how come *you* don't know that?

At least, it doesn't look like you know that, because most of your mannequins and models look to be about size 4. Can the average woman, who couldn't be more different from Heidi Klum if she were a fish, identify with that? (Rhetorical question.)

Most PrimeTime Women *love* clothes. They love fabrics, textures, embroidery, elegance, lines, shape, drape, and color. They want to *buy* clothes. And it appears that very few of you want to sell to them.

There are a few exceptions. Chico's, of course. Did I mention how phenomenally successful they have been? Coldwater Creek, whose customers send them glowing fan mail. Nordstrom, of course, because they always "get" what's going on with women. L.L.Bean, because they're one of the most "authentic" companies out there. But beyond those . . . hmmm.

I have a dear friend who works with a major department store chain. A huge part of their business is women's apparel. I was talking with him about this size 14 thing, and he said, "Yeah, Marti, we tried that, but the problem was, with larger models, it's hard to make the merchandise look as good." Well, there's your problem right there, I thought. It's not about the models making the merchandise look good. It's about the merchandise making the *models* look good.

Here's a secret that will make you a million dollars: to make PrimeTime Women love your clothes, you need to make clothes that love PrimeTime Women. It's that simple.

About 15 years ago, a woman I know who's a little on the heavy side was shopping in the New York garment district and happened upon a store with gorgeous Joan Vass cotton knit skirts and sweaters.

They felt like cashmere, and they even came in her size. Of course, she would never buy knits because when you're on the heavy side, the last thing you want is fabric that clings to your bumps and bulges. A saleswoman invited her to try on something, and of course she declined, and told her why. "Nonsense," said the saleswoman, "That's because you don't know how to wear knits."

They went into the dressing room and the saleswoman showed her how to wear the sweaters bloused up to give them drape, instead of pulled down over the hips; how shoulder pads and pushing up the sleeves to just below the elbow raise the visual center of gravity, guided her away from the mid-calf skirts and sold her on the knee length (at the time, conventional wisdom said otherwise) because she had slim, shapely legs.

In other words, the saleswoman didn't focus on the clothes. She focused on the woman who would be wearing them. She provided useful information and helped her feel good about herself. This woman walked out of there with three garment bags stuffed with out-fits, and for years, wore Joan Vass for work, socializing, and special occasions. Later she said to me, "That advice made all the difference in the world. Why didn't I know this stuff before? Where the hell is the fashion industry?"

The PrimeTime Woman wants a different product than her younger cohorts do. She wants fashion that flatters the figure she has, not the figure the fashion designers *wish* she had. She knows mini-skirts may not make her look her best, but cropped pants and capris can cover many flaws and still show a shapely ankle. She isn't looking for bustiers or belly-baring t-shirts. She knows princess seams, a deep V-neck, three-quarter length sleeves, and a little light shoulder pad-ding can slenderize her waist and pull the center of gravity up off her hips.

She knows black is slimming only if you live in a world with dark walls. Boxy cuts make her look solid and blocky—generally not the look she's going for! Unstructured garments and linen fabrics that look casual and nonchalant on the model make her look like a rum-pled mess. Tiny dressing rooms cramp her style, literally.

PrimeTime Women have a passion for fashion. They want to look fabulous and your job is to help them. They want to give you their money. Where are you?

The Health and Beauty Care Industry: Making "Real" Progress

When I wrote the first draft of this chapter, I had pretty much the same comments for the cosmetics industry as I had for the fashion industry above. But there's late-breaking news, I'm happy to say. With respect to PrimeTime Women, both the cosmetics industry (makeup) and health and beauty care industry (lotions, creams, cleansers, shampoos, styling gels, etc.) have had some significant breakthroughs recently.

Cosmetics

The problem for the cosmetics industry was that the marketers figured out what products women needed before they figured out how to sell to them. For several years there was this rather bizarre phenomenon where you saw advertising for "age-defying" this or "rejuvenating" that, featuring models who looked . . . oh, about 22. It was as if nobody had told the casting director and photographer what product the shoot was for.

All right, I know that's not what happened. What happened is somebody read all the articles about Boomer women going kicking and screaming into old age, in denial, mourning their lost youth. Somebody picked up the finding that Boomers think they look 15 years younger than they really are and concluded you should always use models that are 15 years younger than your target customer. I guess it never occurred to "somebody" to check and see if just because Boomers were that way when they were in their 40s, it meant they would be that way in their fifties and sixties.

Well, they aren't. And you know why, right? All that stuff in the chapter about midlife transition and changing attitudes, authenticity, and the "real self."

The sad part is, once PrimeTime Women "crossed over" into their new reality, the "fountain of youth" message backfired big time. It left PrimeTime Women feeling not just neutral, but negative. Did they buy the products? Yeah. Did they love the brands? No.

Did "somebody" really believe PrimeTime Women would think a lovely, barely legal model's silky skin was a result of using the product pictured? Were they supposed to think, "Hey, if I use that product, my skin will look just like that?" In fact, it's much more likely they were thinking "If they can't show a real woman who has used the product and benefited from it, does it really work?" Or even more directly, "It must *not* work."

Women in general don't relate to perfect, "aspirational" women to begin with. They are more likely to respond to advertising featuring people who look like they could be the next-door neighbor—the good-looking next door neighbor, maybe, but definitely not someone who would make it on the catwalks.

This goes double for PrimeTime Women, who add to that general feeling a strong inclination toward authenticity. They're going to respond to women who look great at the PrimeTime age they are. And now they have some. L'Oreal gets credit for being the first, because they stuck with the gorgeous and quirky (read "authentic") Andie McDowell and let her move the brand with her, as she developed her first fine lines and little skin sags. Next out of the gate was Revlon, with Susan Sarandon, 60, and Julianne Moore, 46. And that was it for a while. For all the other brands, drugstore and department store, it was business as usual and it was all about youth. Recently, however, there's been a veritable flurry of activity: Christie Brinkley came back to Cover Girl, Catherine Deneuve signed on with MAC, and L'Oreal recruited Diane Keaton. Another company took the plunge and launched a brand that owned up to being for older women: Vital Radiance.

So it looks like "somebody" woke up. Good news for the stockholders, because there is no doubt in my mind that the cosmetics industry has taken the first step toward making itself relevant to the largest, most prosperous market in the world—PrimeTime Women.

Health and Beauty Care

Actually, I'm not going to talk about the whole category. I'm going to talk about one brand, the brand that broke the mold in marketing to women of all ages: Dove.

Dove has always stood for authenticity. For years, their TV and print ads have featured real women telling their skin care stories in their own words. They were likeable, they were believable, and they did a great job connecting with women. But health and beauty care is a tough category—too many choices, making too many claims, too hard to tell apart. Dove needed something to help them stand out, to differentiate them from the hundreds of other choices on the shelves, to give women a reason to choose Dove, to build affinity and loyalty with their customers.

Lots of companies would have gone to the research lab at this point and asked the R&D folks to come up with a big breakthrough. Instead, Dove went to their consumers.

They commissioned a global study to learn more about women's images of themselves and their thoughts about and experiences with beauty products. They found that just two percent of women around the world describe themselves as beautiful, and 75% rate their looks as "average."

The core insight is that millions and millions of women of real, genuine beauty had bowed to the stereotypes and had been taught to define themselves as "average." So Dove launched the Campaign for Real Beauty. Some people think the campaign has been so successful because it tells women to let go of the belief in their poor self-image and the belief that they are inadequate, to redefine the definition of beauty on their own terms. Dove tells them they are beautiful after all, and the campaign response was an outpouring of gratitude.

I think the dynamic was quite different; and understanding this subtle difference is the real key to this campaign's phenomenal success. I believe, in their heart of hearts, women across the world thought that a lot of women, including themselves, actually looked pretty good, even if they didn't look like supermodels and even if the stylesetters didn't recognize them. They defined themselves as "average" because they had been taught what conventional beauty standards are and they knew they didn't conform. But when they get dressed up on a Saturday night to go out with a guy or the girlfriends, they think they look *great!* Not that they're allowed to say so, mind you, because that would be boasting and nice girls don't do that.

That's a huge distinction, actually, and absolutely key to the power of the campaign. To me, women's explosive reaction to the campaign feels more like "Finally! Someone understands!" than like "Really? You think I'm pretty? Honest?" If I'm right, it reveals that women's underlying attitudes about their appearance may be quite different from what they generally tell market researchers.

Dove sensed and saw this pent-up demand for a company to understand and acknowledge what women all over the world were feeling. And they recognized there is no stronger way to build an intimate connection with a woman than to see into her real self, know her secret thoughts, show that you understand, and tell her that you love her "anyway." And that's exactly what Dove did with the Campaign for Real Beauty.

The campaign launched in the UK in 2004 with an ad for firming lotion. Print ads and billboards feature six real women of various shapes, colors, and sizes confidently posing in their skivvies.

"We wanted to debunk the beauty stereotype that exists. We are recognizing that beauty comes in different sizes, shapes, and ages," said Philippe Harousseau, Dove's marketing director. Besides, he added, "A size 2 supermodel would have been a real challenge in highlighting the benefits of our products."[67] (Remember, the initial ad was for firming lotion.)

After the campaign's debut, three things happened. The billboard drew immediate media attention; it sparked intense debate about society's narrow definition of beauty; and within six months, sales of Dove's firming products had increased 700 percent.[68]

Dove then expanded the concept to a global campaign spotlighting everyday, "girl next door" women, including five print ads that asked readers to make a judgment about the "model's" looks. An ad featuring a voluptuous woman smiling radiantly at the camera, asked "Oversized? Outstanding?" followed by "Does true beauty only squeeze into a size 6?" Another ad pictured a 96-year-old African-American woman who looks a little like Mother Theresa and the words "Wrinkled? Wonderful? Will society ever accept old can be beautiful?"

Although I believe the strength of the campaign is driven by the brand's emotional connection with women, it also delivers a lot of credibility at the product level as well. One ad, for shampoo, has a single line of copy bordered by pictures of sixteen women of various ages, races, and sizes. It says, "None of these women are hair models. After all, neither are you."

The ads direct viewers to campaignforrealbeauty.com, where they'll find Dove's original global research study, a subsequent U.S.

research study, information about the campaign, a real women photo gallery, discussion boards, and other material for, by, and about real women.

The Web site also highlights the newest phase of the campaign, the Dove Self-Esteem Fund, aimed at changing, educating, and inspiring girls to accept themselves based on a wider definition of beauty. This newest phase of the campaign was launched with an ad during the 2006 Super Bowl in an effort to reach fathers as well as mothers. It suggests ways in which adults can make a difference in how girls feel about themselves. The self-esteem effort includes outreach programs, events throughout the United States, downloadable workbooks for mothers and daughters, and a host of other activities such as the recent "Free Our Girls From Beauty Stereotypes" tote bag promotion in conjunction with the Girl Scouts of the USA.

Throughout its campaign, which the company says will last indefinitely, Dove is talking to women in a way they can relate to. Instead of molding women into one conformist view of beauty, Dove is affirming each and every woman's secret suspicion that even if she's no runway model, she is genuinely beautiful anyway. In fact, Dove is collecting one million online photos of women from around the world in order to achieve its goal of showing a new, broader definition of beauty. There is no need to be anything other than what you are, they are saying. Because what you are is beautiful.

Women everywhere responded with a sigh—no, a cry—of relief. Finally! A company that gets it. A company that gets *me*. Anybody can make a 19-year-old supermodel look fabulous. But only this company meets the needs of women "like *me*."

This stereotype-breaking, history-making campaign absolutely defines what I mean by authentically communicating with women. Although its appeal is certainly not limited only to PrimeTime Women, there is no question that it is a gold-standard example of a communication that resonates, motivates, and generates a powerful business response.

So. We've talked about her mind, and her body. Now let's talk about the life of PrimeTime Women.

CHAPTER FIVE

PrimeTime Life-Stage Changes

Award-winning journalist and acclaimed best-selling author Malcolm Gladwell focuses on rapid cognition, the thinking that happens in a "blink of an eye" in his new book, *Blink*. He says that we all have the powerful ability to "thin slice"—that is, to make sense of situations based on the thinnest slice of experience, or to be able to filter the very few factors that matter from an overwhelming number of variables. His core hypothesis is that snap judgments, the instant conclusions that we reach in the "blink of an eye," are not only immensely important but also occasionally and surprisingly right. But Gladwell goes on to acknowledge the dark side of "thin slicing" or rapid cognition. People carry with them unconscious prejudices that cause them to leap to erroneous conclusions. This is how society creates and perpetuates stereotypes. But we can alter the way we "thin slice" by changing the experiences that comprise our impressions, according to Gladwell. By making positive associations, we can manage and control our impressions, our snap judgments, our stereotypes. That's what this book is all about. Negative stereotypes about aging are everywhere. By focusing on the positive attributes, behavior, attitudes, and power of PrimeTime Women, I hope to shatter the stereotypes that have made marketers blind to this enormous business opportunity.

Stereotypes abound about the desperate, depressive life-stages that women must "get through" in midlife. The big three for Prime-Time Women are the empty nest syndrome, caregiving, and grandparenting. Let's say you were a PrimeTime Woman and got to pick which stereotype you get labeled with. Which one would you pick?

- **Door Number One: The Empty Nester**—Abandoned mother, sneaking back into the rooms of her children who have left the nest and throwing herself on the bedcovers in a fit of tears and grief

- **Door Number Two: Caregiver**—Dutiful daughter crushed by the unending drudgery of caring for a parent who doesn't even know who she is anymore

- **Door Number Three: Grandparent**—Plump, doddering old grandma making homemade streusel and wearing stockings rolled down to her knees

You win! Because as a PrimeTime Woman, you get stereotyped as all three! All someone has to do is mention "women over 50" in a marketing conference room or planning meeting, and the ghost of Whistler's Mother rises in the room. Or maybe that farm woman with the pitchfork from American Gothic.

This chapter is dedicated to shattering these stereotypes. The truth is . . .

- The "empty nest" actually turns into the "next quest."

- Caregiving, not as prevalent or devastating as the press would make it, creates resources and resilience.

- Today's PrimeTime Women grandmothers are engaged, empowered, and energetic.

"Empty Nest" Becomes the "Next Quest"

Who's Crying Now?

Every autumn, psychologist Dr. Karen L. Fingerman at Purdue asks her students how they think their parents are dealing with their newly emptied nests. And every year, students say that their parents are doing worse now that they're gone. It comes as quite a shock to most of them when they learn that, in fact, their parents are coping quite well, thank you, and are actually enjoying increased satisfaction and improved relationships with remaining family members.[1]

Students aren't the only ones who believe in the so-called empty-nest syndrome. Sociologists popularized the term in the 1970s (right around the same time as Erickson's "incomplete woman" theory), and ever since then, the media have helped make it an expected life-stage that everyone must go through. This is so much the case that parents these days feel a little embarrassed if they *aren't* despondent once the kids fly the coop.

Now research has been done to show that while parents do feel a sense of loss when they launch their children into their own lives, they are also enjoying their newfound freedom. Consider the results of this 2004 survey of Baby Boomers by the adult home developer Del Webb:

- 71 percent say parenting was a wonderful experience, but it wasn't easy.

- 58 percent are emotionally prepared for the kids to leave the house.

- 57 percent feel an increased freedom to be themselves.[2]

Studies are also debunking the myth that the so-called empty nest syndrome affects women more than men. In fact, research shows that there is no increase in depressive illness among women at this stage of life. More mothers work these days and, therefore, have less of a feeling of emptiness when their children leave home.[3] PrimeTime Women have always led multiple lives, balancing parenting, career, friendship, volunteer jobs, and marriage while most men have concentrated on their careers. So, relatively speaking, it's not that big an adjustment when one role disappears or changes, because there are other roles already in place to take up the slack.

Actually, researchers have found that the so-called empty nest may be harder on men than on women. In an as-yet-unpublished study of mothers and fathers of high school graduates, Dr. Helen DeVries found that the moms were prepared for the separation and were actually looking forward to their kids leaving home. They had started planning and preparing for the next stage, their "my time," whether that meant going back to school, going to work, or exploring new interests. In contrast, the men in DeVries' sample didn't seem to focus on it as a major transition and therefore were not prepared for it. As a result, the dads were more likely to express regrets over lost opportunities to be involved in their children's lives before they left home.[4]

While Boomer moms and dads both are notoriously workaholic, it is still the moms who manage the home front. Consequently, relative to fathers, mothers often have had closer relationships with their children as they were growing up. Instead of this resulting in greater grief at the separation, it actually makes it easier, because they know they will remain close. In contrast, the classic irony is that just as midlife men mellow and feel ready to turn more attention to family and relationships, the kids are ready to go off on their own, leaving many dads with a sense of loss and missed opportunity.

Next Quest Bonus

Aging expert Ken Dychtwald calls the decades in midlife *middlescence*. He sees it as a time when, as in adolescence, PrimeTimers experience high-spirited growth and ascension, not retreat and decline.[5] PrimeTime Women are gifted with more than just freedom and opportunity during these midlife years; they have both more time and more money on their side as well. Eighty-five percent of empty-nest parents saw a boost in discretionary income; about one-third reported a rise of $10,000 or more.[6] Just in time for PrimeTime Women to rediscover those old passions, explore new possibilities, spend more time with girlfriends, and find opportunities to give back.

So, say goodbye to the so-called empty nest syndrome and hello to the "Next Quest" life-stage.

The Boomerang Effect

Although PrimeTimers are looking forward to their Next Quest time and money bonus, many of them are still going to have to wait a while. According to the Del Webb survey, 25 percent anticipate their adult children will move back in with them! Of the Boomers polled, 15 percent are already experiencing what experts are calling the "Boomerang syndrome," when Boomers' grown children return to the nest.[7]

According to U.S. Census figures, among today's 18- to 24-year-olds, 56 percent of men and 43 percent of women live with one or both parents. Presumably a significant percentage of these are off at college and are reported as "living with parents" because they are still dependents. But get this: according to a job search Web site, 62 percent of college students say they expect to live at home after graduation.[8]

On "Boomeranging," the Del Webb survey among Boomers shows that

- 25 percent expect their adult children to move back in with them at some point; of those, 28 percent plan to make those kids pay rent.

- 65 percent would "be happy" to help if their grown kids needed to move back in.

- almost one-fourth (23 percent) would "feel obligated" to help.

- of parents eager to find other living arrangements for their adult children, fathers (33 percent) were more likely to do so than mothers (14 percent).

There are many reasons behind the Boomerang syndrome, but most revolve around simple economics. In the tight labor market of recent years, many young adults find themselves loaded up on college loans and jobless or making very little money at lower-end jobs.

In the meantime, the cost of living, especially housing, is skyrocketing, so they can't afford to live on their own.

Some return for personal reasons, too, to recover from a divorce or an illness. And let's face it, life is sweet and easy at good old mom and dad's house—meals served, laundry done, and a comfortable place to find stability amidst the insecurity of the young adult years.[9] In the old days, parents might not have put up with the young free-loaders, but today's parents have become more indulgent.

Marketing to Next Questers

A few marketers have tapped into the Next Quest syndrome as a way of creating "that's me" moments, the self-recognition dynamic that drives women's humor. Toyota recently ran ads for its High-lander SUV that clearly capture the point that PrimeTime Women have flown the coop too. In one, a college kid stands outside a dorm building among suitcases and boxes while a Toyota Highlander drives away in the background. The copy reads: "5:15 PM. Dropping the kid off at college. 5:17 PM. What kid?"

Launching kids out of the house means that PrimeTime Women will be launching themselves into new territory as well, which means new needs requiring new products and services.

Staying in Touch. Although PrimeTime Women relish their new-found freedom, enjoying their "my" time and missing their children are not mutually exclusive. These days, with the miracles of modern telecommunications, the apron strings may stretch, but they never really snap. She'll always be "the mom," and just because she's practicing her craft long-distance doesn't mean she can't reach out and touch someone. E-mail, cell phones, instant messaging, Web cams, video cameras, and more consumer electronics products and services can help parents stay in touch.

Launching Themselves. This life-stage has particular implications for the travel industry. The Del Webb study reported that half of the Boomers reporting more disposable income intend to spend it on travel. The world has opened its doors, and the PrimeTime Woman is barreling through.

In the past, she may have limited her travel to family vacations. Now, experts are noting that PrimeTime Women are the drivers behind the fastest growing trend in the travel industry, "soft adventure" travel.[10] Whether it's climbing Mt. Hood or sea kayaking in the Mediterranean, it's all about exciting activities, exploration, and discovery, but without broken bones, leeches, and rustic latrines.

Among the service providers targeting this group are

- Journeywoman, which is an online travel resource and magazine;

- Gutsy Women Travel, which runs by the motto "It's Your Life . . . Live it";

- Las Olas Surf Safaris for Women, which purports to "make girls out of women" (they get the whole Jungian "return to true self" thing);

- Women Traveling Together, which provides the perfect solution for women who want to travel but don't like the idea of traveling alone;

- Adventure Divas, which is the online companion to the popular PBS program of the same name and provides stories and information from women travelers on the fringe;

- "Grannies on Safari," which was developed as an adventure travel TV show and is expanding to actual programs, geared toward women over 60;

- and let's not forget adventurewomen.com, the grand dame of them all. It was founded almost 25 years ago by Susan Eckert and is geared toward active women over 30. It is truly a PrimeTime Woman's company, as evidenced by the quote of one traveler: "It is impossible to explain just how this experience has made me feel, except to say that I found the true "me" again." Its advertising and marketing showcase PrimeTime Women having fun together. (See Figure 5.1.)

Before we move on—don't go thinking that you can start calling your products "Granny's Digital Camera" or "Luggage for Grannies." This falls in line with one of the warnings I give to marketers in my

FIGURE 5.1 Adventure Women: Launching Themselves

© Susan L. Eckert, AdventureWomen, Inc.

first book about trying to market to women by "painting the brand pink." In virtually every category, overtly characterizing a marketing program as "for women" will backfire with both genders. There's one big exception to the rule, which are products and services "for women," *from* women. It's one thing when the gesture says "we women" and quite another when it says "you women." The same holds true for PrimeTime Women. Only "grannies" can call themselves and their products "grannies;" you can call them "ma'am."

PrimeTime Women—How Much Do They Care?

Family caregiving is nothing new to American culture. Yet, it has received a lot of press lately, specifically focused on what I call the "poor" story, about how Boomers are going to be burdened by their long-living parents and how this devastating financial and emotional weight will ruin their lives and make the second half of adulthood a nightmare. The "poor" story spotlights PrimeTime Women especially, who supposedly will find themselves shackled to their caregiving role for their entire lives, caring first for their children and then for their parents and elderly relatives.

The caregiving phenomenon has even given rise to a new term for PrimeTime caregivers, the Sandwich Generation—those who are squeezed in the middle taking care of *both* the younger *and* the older generations at the same time. While there is some truth to the rumors about this new life-stage, the reality is that most PrimeTime Women will *not* be saddled with the role of caregiver, and if they are, it is often not as devastating as most accounts have thus far painted it to be.

There are many advocates of the "poor" story who want to create a reason for the government and health care behemoths to do something to help the aging, and their caregivers, in America. The rapid growth in the elderly population has come at a time when families are less equipped than in previous decades to provide such care. Families today are smaller and more geographically dispersed, and more women—traditionally the family caregivers—are managing their caregiving chores on top of juggling work and their immediate family care duties. There is a shortage of trained caregiving professionals and inadequate pricing and funding for such services.

All that being said, it's not unusual for the more provocative "poor" story on any issue to get a disproportionate amount of press. Sometimes the impression you get from reading the papers is that a problem is a good deal more widespread than it is.

What's the Real Scoop?

What percentage of women, specifically of PrimeTime Women, are currently caught up in caregiving? And how is that likely to change in the next 20 years?

These are not simple questions to answer. First off—and this is not academic—what do you count as "caregiving?" Some studies only count people who do the "hard-core" chores, like helping to feed, bathe, walk, and so on. Others also include people whom I would characterize as helping out—they bring groceries, run errands, pay bills from time to time. Still others add in people who help their parents only via financial assistance; that is, they send a check either every month, or now and then.

Now if you add all three groups together and define them as "caregivers" and divide that number by the U.S adult population, you're going to see a very high incidence of caregiving in the United States ("everybody's doing it"); and when you instead divide it by the population of PrimeTime Women, that percentage will go higher still.

But among the three levels of caregiving involvement, there is a *huge* difference in how they impact the caregiver's time, money, energy, and stress levels. So when we're trying to figure out how caregiving affects the lives of PrimeTime Women, we need to know what percent of them are involved, and at what level.

The most up-to-date and comprehensive study on caregiving that I could find was published by The National Alliance for Caregiving and AARP in April 2004. Let me pull out for you a few of the stats that make me wonder if maybe straits aren't as dire as they seem.

To qualify as a caregiver in the National Alliance study, a person must perform at least one lighter weight task, like grocery shopping, driving, housework, laundry, doing dishes, paying bills, filling out insurance claims; or one harder chore, like bathing, toileting, feeding, dressing, getting in and out of a bed or chair. Using this definition, 100 percent of caregivers report performing at least one lighter weight task for their care recipients; 80 percent of caregivers provide help with three or more lighter weight tasks; and 50 percent of care-givers perform harder chores. Almost half (48 percent) of caregivers report spending 8 hours or less per week helping out; 23 percent spend 9–20 hours per week providing care; 8 percent spend 21–39 hours; and 17 percent report providing 40+ hours a week.

Now let's take a closer look at the National Alliance study:

- 21 percent of the U.S. population 18 and older provides un-paid care, as defined above, to adult friends or relatives.

  – Now hold it right there: Are they trying to tell me one out of every five persons from the age of college freshmen on up are caregivers? I don't believe it.

- Level 5 (the highest level) caregivers are those with the heavi-est burden. They help with at least two harder chores and pro-vide more than 40 hours per week of care. 10 percent of all caregivers are Level 5 caregivers.

  – OK, these are the people I always think we're talking about whenever anyone says *caregiver.* It's a very tough job, but there really aren't too many people in this situation: Even if 21 percent were a good number rather than the overstate-ment I think it is, 10 percent of that is only 2 percent of the adult population.

- The majority of caregivers (62 percent) say they feel little or no financial hardship as a result of providing care, which pre-sumably means that caregiving does not impair their own spend-ing plans/needs/wants.

- Nearly half (46 percent) of caregivers helping someone 50 or older not in a nursing home receive some type of paid help.

Some Good News

PrimeTimers' parents are living longer *and healthier* lives. A poll conducted by the Pew Research Center in December 2005 found that 71 percent of today's Boomers (42–60 years old) have at least one living parent. This is up dramatically from the results of a 1989

Gallup survey, which found that just 60 percent of people ages 41 to 59 had at least one living parent.[11]

According to John W. Rowe, MD, and Robert L. Kahn, PhD, authors of *Successful Aging,* when you compare 65- to 74-year-old individuals in 1960 with those similarly aged in 1990, you find a dramatic reduction in the prevalence of three important precursors to chronic *disease:* high blood pressure, high cholesterol levels, and smoking. There has also been a significant decline in the prevalence of arthritis, arteriosclerosis, dementia, hypertension, stroke and emphysema, as well as a dramatic decrease in the average number of diseases an older person has. The one exception is Alzheimer's, whose prevalence among the older population is growing. Alzheimer's afflicts one in ten individuals over 65 (remember, that's not "10 percent of 65-year-olds," but "10 percent of everyone 65–110+"), and nearly half of those over 85.

Furthermore, most midlife and older Americans are free of *disabilities* as well as disease. Seventy-three percent of 75- to 84-year-olds report no disability at all,[12] and even those over 85 are still going strong, with only 20 percent needing assistance even with lighter-weight tasks.[13] Moreover, this reduction in disability among older people appears to be accelerating.

Consequently, only 5 percent of people over 65 live in nursing homes, and that percentage has been falling for at least 10 years.[14]

PrimeTime Women's Caregiving Perspective

Caregiving came up spontaneously in our PrimeTime Women's research, indicating that it was indeed a fact of life for many of our participants. The most important thing in life both to care recipients and their caregivers is a sense of control, of being able to live independently without relying on family members or anyone else for assistance. Nobody wants to give up their freedom and independence, and most people fear becoming a burden on others in old age. So, care recipients want to stay in their own homes as long as possible and would appreciate help every now and then with groceries, home improvements, driving, housework, and so on. But that's not the same as moving into a daughter's house and requiring full-time care. There are many other options.

No matter what level of care they are giving, most PrimeTime Women in our Girlfriend Groups and 50/50/50 panel said they don't feel additional stress from caregiving because they have balanced this role with the other priorities in their lives. They have that reserve of resilience to draw on, and they're able to balance their lives to include plenty of "my time." In addition to their caregiving stories, all of our PrimeTime Women caregivers also told stories of traveling, of being very involved with children and grandchildren, and making time for their girlfriends. They did not portray caregiving as any sort of overwhelming burden. It obviously impacts their lives, but they plan and deal with it accordingly.

My husband and I also make frequent trips about once a month to New Jersey to visit my mother-in-law. She will be 89 this year and is in a continuing care facility. She cherishes her independence and it is beginning to slip away . . . and I have so much empathy for her. For both my Dad and my mother-in-law we have tried to ensure that they made decisions for themselves as long as possible.

Dee Dee, 54

[My mother-in-law] has recently entered a nursing home following spinal surgery. We hope to move her shortly to an assisted living facility and hopefully back to her house. She lives 2 days away by car. We had been visiting her about 4–5 times a year but in the last month and a half we have been there 4 times. In order for her to go home, we will have to install a chair lift on her stairs, she will have to wear a Medic Alert bracelet and we will have to hire a health care worker to help her several times a day. Even so, we hope she can return to the comfort of her home. She does not want to move close to us as she has a large network of friends where she lives.

Susan, 58

I worked part time until about 10 years ago. I have been taking care of elderly relatives since then. My mother-in-law had Alzheimer's and I had to intervene to make sure she was taken care of. I'd have to go to San Diego to make sure all was well. Overlapping that with an elderly aunt who had no children so I took care of her, she had a stroke in 2000 and I took care of her here. Now I have an 82-year-old cousin living with us. She was in Arrowhead and that was an undertaking. However, physically I feel good. My husband and I are happy. He retires next month. He has been patient with people living in our house, but now I don't know how that will be once he is home. She was so good to us when we first moved out here. She made us feel special, so I owe her. It's going to be difficult to make a decision when my husband retires.

Tomi, 62

PrimeTime Women's Caregiving Influence

Being caregivers means that PrimeTime Women will be making decisions not just for themselves but for their care recipient(s). From finances to housing to health care to food, a lot of money will be passing through caregivers' hands and marketers have the opportunity to establish long-term relationships with these important decision-makers. They will be looking for products and services that make both their lives, and their care recipients' lives, easier. If you provide these, you will earn not only their deep and immediate appreciation, but also a longer-term loyalty payoff because they may ultimately provide caregiving help of some sort to two or three more recipients, such as their husband's parents and eventually their own husbands.

Furthermore, PrimeTime Women caregivers will also be looking ahead to their own needs for care. They are making decisions not only for this generation of caregiving, but for future generations as well.

PrimeTime Women will be a caregiving marketing channel in and of themselves. They will use word of mouth to learn about and spread the good (and bad) word about any and all developments in caregiving that make their lives, and the lives of their care recipients, better.

Helping PrimeTime Caregivers

PrimeTime Women are ready, willing, and able to be caregivers. But they would love some help retaining control of their lives while providing care for their loved ones. Here are a few ideas that some smart marketers have dreamed up that would be helpful to have on hand:

- "Driving Miss Daisy" in Canada provides a cab and companion service that takes seniors shopping, to doctors' appointments, lunches, and other social events. The company markets itself by emphasizing extra care and security for their customers. What a break—and what a boon—for the caretaker!

- Parent Care, a new national Internet-based resource service for Baby Boomers faced with taking care of their elderly parents while living a long distance away. For about a dime a day, each Parent Care subscriber receives a personalized home page with one-click access to services in the county where the senior parent resides. An 8- to 10-page report also provides a detailed summary of local services, supplemented by national and state senior services. The service provides links to free prescription medication programs, rebate forms, checklists to enhance parents' future safety and independence, seasonal information, monthly articles on eldercare topics, weekly chats with peers, daily eldercare tips, and 24/7 senior news. The Web site, launched in May 2005, posted about 20 percent of its first-year subscription orders from clients in Europe and Asia.

- Embedded sensors in chairs and beds measure vital signs. When embedded in the floor, the sensors determine if someone has fallen.

- A memory-assisting caller ID system shows the user a picture of the caller and offers details of the last conversation.

- Resistance Chair Exercise System, an innovative approach to helping older adults or anyone with a physical limitation, helps to achieve optimum exercise benefits at home and without the stress that often accompanies other commercial exercise products. Maintaining balance and stability from a seated position, the Resistance Chair System helps users tone and strengthen their arms, chest, shoulders, abdomen, back, and legs.

- Other ways to help the PrimeTime Woman caregiver by providing services and products to assist her in making her older care recipient's lives easier could include: housecleaning services, grocery delivery, personal chefs, pill boxes that beep to indicate when it's time to give medication, extra-warm, nonskid slippers, and clothing that fastens with Velcro.

While only a small portion of PrimeTime Women will be caregivers, according to the statistics, those who are and whose families are impacted will welcome a revolution in products and services that make caregiving a more integrated and positive life-stage.

Grandparenting—Ain't Life Grand?!

The average age of a first-time grandparent is 47.[15] Believe it or not, that's *average*, not *youngest*. Average means "intermediate, not highest, not lowest"; so that means there are a lot of grandparents *younger* than 47. With today's life expectancy of 77.9 years, PrimeTimers may have as many as 30 years of grandparenting ahead of them. There are 72 million grandparents in the United States today. That's 34 percent of the entire adult population. By 2010 it is estimated that number will grow to 80 million, an increase of 33 percent over a decade ago.[16]

Because of the higher mortality rate for men, grandparents are disproportionately female. And today's grandmothers are different from any generation of grandmothers that have come before them. Jean Giles-Sims, a sociologist at Texas Christian University and the founder of www.grandmotherconnections.com, is working on a new book, *Becoming Grammy: Today's Grandmothers Redefining the Old Stereotypes,* to address the impact of this transformation. "I call them 'empowered,'" she says. "And they've got much more money."

The PrimeTime Woman of today has changed the face of grandmothering. At 48—and 58 and 68—she is no longer the ever-available babysitter, watching *Laugh-In* reruns with her knitting on her lap. She's too busy working, hanging out with friends, hiking and biking, taking computer classes, and going to the latest Eric Clapton or Paul McCartney concert. She enjoys having the little ones around—and enjoys having the little ones go home. And she's unapologetic about it all.

The PrimeTime grandmother of today is just as likely to be like Christine Crosby, founder of *GRAND* magazine, who skates, does yoga, and videoconferences with her grandchildren. *GRAND* has featured celebrity grandparents on the cover such as Martin Sheen, Cokie Roberts, Goldie Hawn, and Paul McCartney and is a great resource for learning about the intergenerational issues of today, with toy and book reviews, fun and games, vitality and wellness, fiscal fitness and financial insights, and so on. In just two short years, its circulation has increased to 100,000, signaling a definite interest in the new definition of grandparenthood in the 21st century.

Today's grandparents are going all out in terms of developing lasting relationships with their grandchildren because they are looking back at their busy workaholic Boomer lives and realizing some of the things they gave up. Their need to leave a legacy comes on strong with their own children's children.

The Power of Grandmother's Purse

Grandparents spend a median of $500 per year[17] on grandchildren, an impressive $30 billion annually. Believe it or not, that's twice the amount spent just 10 years ago. According to AARP's 2002 "Grandparent Study" and *American Demographics:*

- 87 percent of grandparents buy clothing for their grandchildren.

- 80 percent purchase books.

- 78 percent purchase "fun foods."

- 52 percent help pay for the grandchildren's education.

- 45 percent help pay for living expenses.

- 45 percent purchase DVDs or videos for their grandkids.

- 37 percent purchase jewelry.

- 31 percent buy video games.

- 25 percent contribute to medical and dental costs.

Seventy-six percent of grandparents buy toys, accounting for one out of every four toys sold in America each year[18] or approximately $3.4 billion annually.[19] In fact, contrary to what you might expect, data shows the 55–64 age group spends more per capita on toys than the 25–44 age group;[20] they tend to buy high ticket items.[21] American Girl or Lego Mindstorms, anyone?

It's not just toys and gifts that grandparents lavish on their descendants. Today's PrimeTime Woman helps with piano lessons, takes the kids to Disneyworld, introduces them to theater, and takes them out to eat. She travels to see them. She contributes mightily to their college funds. One PrimeTime Woman I know bought her newborn grandchild 100 shares of General Electric stock and has purchased shares as gifts for every birthday and Christmas.

This speaks to the exponential influence that PrimeTime Women will continue to have on their families, immediate and extended. We heard echoes of this in our own PrimeTime Women research as well:

I do a lot for my kids. My oldest granddaughter is going to school, and I am going to help pay for that.

Willia, age 67

Daily Grandparenting

Furthermore, grandparents today are exerting a lot more daily influence on their grandchildren by assuming some of the child-rearing responsibilities. According to the U.S. Census Bureau, more than 5 million grandparents are raising grandchildren (but experts suspect the number may be as high as 8 million). In an AARP national survey of 800 grandparents over age 50, 11 percent of grandparents identified themselves as caregivers, with 8 percent providing day care on a regular basis and 3 percent raising a grandchild by themselves.[22]

It's Time to Play: Grandparent and Grandkid Activities Together

It's not just money that grandparents give to their grandkids; it's also time. AARP reports that 70 percent of Boomer grandparents take their grandkids to a playground; 57 percent have played sports or exercised with them in the last six months; and 27 percent of grandparents aged 50–59 vacation with their grandkids. According to Peter Yesawich, author of *Leisure Travel Monitor*, 4 out of 10 active travelers are grandparents going with their grandchildren or extended family on vacation.[23]

Several companies are dedicated to the burgeoning intergenerational travel industry. Grandtravel has been providing such tours for 20 years and offers everything from digging for dinosaur fossils in western Colorado to lunching with a cosmonaut in Moscow. In 2000, Loews Hotels introduced "Generation G" and suggested, "Something magical happens when grandparents and grandchildren travel." For prices starting between $135 and $250 per day, depending on location and options, guests get a room, photo album, in-room movie and popcorn, postcard, phone card, disposable camera, and other vacation items. Hotel Wales on Manhattan's Upper East Side has the "Young at Heart" package, which includes milk and cookies at bedtime and tickets to the Metropolitan Museum of Art. Boston's Seaport Hotel has its "Grandparents' Great Getaway" package, which offers admission to the Children's Museum and a children's movie in the guest room.[24]

Marketing to Grandparents

Other marketers are also tapping into the grandparenting market. A Norwegian company called Mormor.nu is an online store that sells baby and children's wear from the time when grandma herself was a wee lass. ("Mormor" is Danish for "Grandma"). In fact, the company's employees stem from an era when everything was made by hand, the youngest employee being 68 years old. All products are handmade, from pure wool, alpaca wool, or cotton. Old knitting and crocheting techniques and patterns have been revived, and colors and materials updated, making the products meet modern demands for fashionable children's clothing, as well as for old-fashioned quality and honest materials. Cool little touch: clothes come with a small nametag signed by the grandmother that made the item.[25]

One charming product I just came across is "my granny's purse"—a cross between a pop-up book and a grab-bag, with lots of compartments, each with an intriguing item inside. Filled with colors, textures, shiny objects, and sounds, "my granny's purse" helps the grandmother share times of discovery and delight with her infant or toddler grandchild.

AIG SunAmerica Mutual Funds offers grandparents a program to help educate their grandchildren about such critical matters as saving, planning, and investing for their financial future. The company developed the much acclaimed K.I.D.S. (Kids Investing for Dollars and Sense) program to help educators, parents, and grandparents teach young children the fundamentals of saving and investing— including the origins of money and the importance of setting goals, budgeting, and managing their own finances. In short, it helps teach them how to manage their own spending power and take control of their own financial future.

MasterCard recently ran a wonderful grandparents ad in its "price-less" campaign. It shows a little boy leaning over a fence, and the copy reads: "Gap hoodie for grandson: $29.50 (knowing you're not the one who has to wash it: priceless.)" MasterCard clearly gets this new age of grandparenthood, which is a bit more complicated, thanks to PrimeTime Women's more active lives and adventuresome outlooks.

* * *

This chapter has explored opportunities that arise from three newly emerging need states that most PrimeTime Women encounter in midlife: the Next Quest syndrome, caregiving, and grandparenting. Now let's look ahead to what PrimeTimers are planning for retirement, which reveals a new set of product and service opportunities, partic-ularly for the housing, real estate, and home furnishings industries.

CHAPTER SIX

Looking Ahead

Now that we have uncovered the attitudinal, mental and physical, and life-stage changes that PrimeTime Women will experience during their 50s and 60s, let's gaze out to the future, to their PrimeTime Plus years, once they start moving into their 70s. That's only 10 years from now; PrimeTime Women are already planning toward it, and the major economic sectors that will be most affected are going to need the lead time.

As can be expected, PrimeTime Women will revolutionize this next phase of life as much as they did midlife. (Being the healthiest, wealthiest, and the most educated, active, and independent generation of women in history has its privileges, you know.) This chapter will tune you into the major changes you can expect as they create radically new answers to the following two questions:

1. What will they do when they reach retirement age?

2. Where will they want to live once they retire?

The two major sectors that will be especially affected by the impact of PrimeTime Women? Only two of the most important drivers of the U.S. economy—the American workplace and the housing and real estate industry.

Still Working

So that you can appreciate how dramatic the forthcoming workplace changes will be, let's first establish a baseline. Who's in the workforce today?

According to Brigitte Madrian, a professor of financial gerontology at the University of Pennsylvania's Wharton School, the average American today retires at the age of 62.[1] That means that among the cohort of men and women who are currently PrimeTimers, (recall that the 50- to 60-year-olds are Boomers, but the 60- to 70-year-olds are the so-called Silent Generation), the majority, those 50–62 years old, are still working. Though as usual we don't have data broken out to pinpoint PrimeTime Women, as an indicator we can look at the data broken out for the subset of PrimeTimers aged 55–64 years old. As would be expected, most of them (62 percent) are currently in the workforce, with a slight skew toward men.

- Sixty-nine percent of men that age are working.

- Fifty-seven percent of women are as well.[2]

The big news here, as you will see in a moment, is that 80 percent of Boomers, men and especially women, intend to continue working for many more years. Remember, there are no longer any mandatory retirement rules in corporate America. That average age of retirement is about to soar.

The Myth of the Brain Drain

Building on the whole "Boomers are turning 60" theme, the U.S. business press has been giving a fair amount of "red flag" coverage to predictions of an imminent doomsday scenario where corporate America suffers a major labor shortage and brain drain due to the mass exodus of Boomers as they retire. For example, in March 2005, *Fortune* magazine ran an article called "How to Battle the Coming Brain

Drain." Ken Dychtwald, expert on aging and author of *Age Power,* has even published a book on the topic called *Workforce Crisis: How to Beat the Coming Shortage of Skills And Talent.*

A lot of companies think that they will be impacted by this "brain drain" and are taking steps to address it. Procter & Gamble wants to make sure that its R&D department is not decimated as the corps of smart, experienced PrimeTimers retires *en masse.* Therefore, it has joined forces with Eli Lilly and created Yourencore.com, an online network of retired and semiretired research scientists and engineers that matches available brains with short-term R&D projects.[3] Similarly, IBM has set up a network of alumni to recruit retired people for particular projects.

Frankly, I think this is another one of those "everybody's saying there's a trend . . ." things. At first glance, I can see how the stats in my first paragraph above could lead someone to the expectation of a Boomer exodus. But you only have to look one level deeper, or ask the AARP what they think, and based on the research I'll share with you in a moment, they'll tell you to settle down, the Boomers aren't going anywhere.

No one really knows one way or the other, of course, since the first Boomers haven't even reached the ripe old age of 62 yet. Boomer guru Matt Thornhill, founder of the Boomer Project, has been saying this all along. He often points out in his informative and insightful e-newsletter that nobody can possibly know how the heck Boomers are behaving in retirement because, as Matt says, "What Boomers are already in retirement? Only the very rich, or very lucky, we suspect, as there isn't yet a Boomer on the planet older than 60. Those early Boomer retirees aren't indicative of how 78 million Boomers will behave later in life."

All in all, it seems unlikely that a Boomer brain drain is about to crash our economy:

- First, let's look at what Boomers are saying. According to the AARP study, over 80 percent of Baby Boomers plan to work well into their 70s.[4] They've got their reasons:
  - Boomers identify themselves with work and career more than previous generations did.

– Life expectancy is increasing. A 65-year-old man today can expect to live another 17 years, and a 65-year-old woman another 20.[5]

– Rising health care costs increase their motivation to retain insurance benefits.

– Savings and stock portfolios have recently plummeted.[6]

• Second, even though Boomers outnumber Gen Xers overall, younger generations are graduating from college at a higher rate and will supply plenty of skilled workers for entry level positions. According to Peter Capelli, management professor at Wharton, "some 930,000 bachelor's degrees a year were conferred at the height of the Boomers' run through college— while the *smallest* graduating class for Busters (another moniker for Gen X, so named because they "busted" the boom with a sudden decline in birth rates) produced 1.16 million grads. Now college-educated members of the 'Echo Boom,' a group close in size to the Boomers themselves, are starting to enter the workforce. No evidence there of a shrinking skilled labor pool."[7]

  (On a side note: Most of those Echo Boom college graduates are women—58 percent. Add that, on average, college graduates' lifetime earnings are roughly twice the earnings of someone who has completed only high school, and you've got a pretty picture of accelerating earning power among young women.)

• Finally, there are other labor sources, admittedly not at all popular among American workers, but available nonetheless: offshoring, outsourcing, immigrant workers, and so on.

The Myth of the Crushing Burden

You've heard this one: The sheer demographics of the enormous Boomer population will crush Social Security and flatten Medicare. Because they haven't saved enough, Boomers will all be on the dole, soaking up money from government entitlement programs funded insufficiently by the sweat and tears of the smaller generation that follows them, eventually bankrupting the system. Damn them.

Hang on a minute. First of all, they will not all be on the dole because as of right now, they're planning to keep working. As noted in Chapter 1, Peter Francese, esteemed analyst with *American Demographics,* estimates that these additional PrimeTime workers will add at least $400 billion a year to consumer spending. So that's a pretty penny not only in incremental consumer demand, but also in taxes paid.

Second, given the midlife emergence of the urge to give back noted earlier, we can expect a substantial surge in volunteerism. The Boomers will be an enormous economic resource contributing economic value for *free* (not unlike the generations of women who have provided unpaid labor inside the home!). Read Marc Freedman's book, *Prime Time: How Baby Boomers Will Revolutionize Retirement & Transform America.* (Yes, I thought "Prime Time" was my idea, but it looks like Mr. Freedman got there first.)

Freedman wrote the book as a refutation of the excessively narrow—and overwhelmingly negative—portrayal of America's aging population, focused almost entirely on fiscal issues and the solvency of federal entitlement programs, and numerous articles in the popular press portraying Boomers as greedy geezers destroying the nation. He believes that, on the contrary, the PrimeTime population will turn their golden years into a time of intense social activism, volunteerism, and lifelong learning—an immense social resource that will contribute much more economic value than it consumes.

Redefining "Retirement"

As noted above, most PrimeTime men and women are not planning on retiring, anytime soon or anytime at all. Actually, these days, it's unclear what Boomers even mean by the word *retirement,* at least the way the survey results are worded. I thought "retirement" meant "not working any more." In fact, the thesaurus says synonyms for retirement are "departure, leaving, giving up work, withdrawal."[8]

But when asked what they planned to do "after retirement," respondents to the 2003 AARP study of Baby Boomers' expectations of retirement were given a choice of options that included working part time, leaving current job but working somewhere else full time for pay, and starting their own business. Call me crazy, but to me those sound like extended career strategies, not retirement. Never mind—let's just go with the assumption that what Boomers were thinking when they said "after retirement" was "after the usual age of retirement, about 62."

Percentage of Baby Boomers who say that the following statements best describe what they think they will be doing during retirement

	2003
Not working at all	20%
Working (net)	79
Working part time for enjoyment's sake	30
Working part time for needed income	25
Starting own business	15
Retiring from current job but work full time for pay doing something else	15
Other	3
Don't Know	1

Source: AARP, 2003, "Baby Boomers Envision Retirement II," May 2004

So it looks like "retiring" will mean doing just about anything except *nothing*.

PrimeTime Women in the Workforce

PrimeTime Women workers will lead the surge in older employment. Over the past decade or two, the labor force participation rate of older men has fallen, while that of older women has risen. Between 2003 and 2012, the ranks of women workers over 55 are projected to grow substantially more than those of older men:

- Working women aged 60–64 will jump by 61 percent

  – Men that age by 51 percent

- Women workers aged 55–59 will increase 41 percent

  – Men the same age just 30 percent[9]

In 2002 the National Center on Women and Aging conducted a national poll of women over 50 who were currently working, and found that 29 percent planned *never* to retire. The PrimeTime Women in our 50-50-50 Panel echoed this sentiment. The majority of them are still working, sometimes by necessity, but usually by choice:

> *My work is my passion. It's fun, stimulating and part of my life journey. 'Retire' based on my parents' definition would be totally boring.*
> Dori, 50

> *[I don't plan to retire for] . . . a few more years because of the enjoyment and intellectual stimulation that I continue to get from it and because we still have twins in college!*
> Debra, 56

> *Right now I enjoy my job and will continue to stay here as long as I enjoy what I do, enjoy the people I work with, and feel that I am making a meaningful contribution. If I retire from this position, I would get another full or part-time job. I would not be happy not working.*
> Melody, 50

> *I don't see myself stopping work, certainly slowing down, but I did this as a retirement business. I like the constant flow of money; I don't like the idea of using my assets up, so I like the idea of refilling the leaking barrel.*
> Nan, 52

PrimeTime and PrimeTime Plus Women will be at the front of the line in terms of earning power in their "retirement" years. That's because they have higher educations that lead to better paying jobs, and they are more motivated to succeed in midlife, thanks to their increased confidence and assertiveness. Multiply their numbers by paychecks that grow with knowledge and experience, and you're looking at billions of dollars of PrimeTime Women spending power.

The New Retirement

The AARP study referenced above reveals how Boomers plan to spend their impending retirement years. Whatever choice they make, PrimeTime Women will be putting their experience and energy to good use.

Part Time in PrimeTime

Part-time work offers a key benefit to PrimeTimers and that is flexibility. Older workers want more flexible schedules to spend time on new hobbies and old friends, with aging parents and young grandchildren, or volunteering.

One forward-thinking company that has taken advantage of this new PrimeTime part-time workforce is CVS. The pharmacy chain actively recruits "older snowbirds," those workers over 50 who live in cooler climates in the summer and travel south for the winter. CVS gives them the opportunity to transfer employment according to their migration plans. The company's percentage of employees over 50 has risen from less than 7 percent in the early 1990s to 17 percent in 2006.[10]

Another company who has seen the PrimeTime part-time light is The Home Depot, who is partnering with AARP to recruit older workers. "At The Home Depot, we believe knowledge, experience, and passion never retire," said Bob Nardelli, chairman, president, and CEO of The Home Depot. Through its partnership with AARP, The Home Depot seeks to attract skilled part-time or full-time associates to a variety of positions including plumbers, electricians, landscapers, design, sales, and customer service representatives. The Home Depot offers medical and dental insurance, tuition reimbursement, a discounted stock purchase plan, the opportunity to share in the company's growth through its Success Sharing program, and other benefits. (See Figure 6.1.)

Other companies have since joined The Home Depot in collaboration with AARP to open doors for older job seekers: Cendant Car Rental Group (Avis/Budget), Cingular Wireless, Comcast Cable Communications Inc., Right at Home In-Home Care & Assistance, News America Marketing, New York Life Insurance Company, Quest Diagnostics Inc., Schneider National Inc., SunTrust Banks, and Verizon.

Third Age Entrepreneurs

Many people who have been in conventional jobs all their lives have carried with them the dream of opening their own business when

FIGURE 6.1 Home Depot: Saying "No" to Retirement

The Home Depot

they retire. And many of them have acted on that dream, as reflected in the fact that, at present, 22 percent of men and 14 percent of women over 65 are self-employed, compared to just 7 percent for other age groups.[11] New research shows 5.6 million workers age 50 and older are now self-employed, a 23 percent jump from 1990.[12] A report released by Barclays Bank entitled "Third Age Entrepreneurs—Profiting from

Experience" shows that older entrepreneurs are responsible for 50 percent more business startups than 10 years ago. This amounts to around 60,000 business startups last year alone.

As they retire, this new generation of Boomer women is likely to be more interested than previous generations in starting their own businesses. According to the Center for Women's Business Research, for approximately the past 20 years, women in general have accounted for almost 70 percent of all small business startups.[13] And the strong majority (73 percent) of women business owners (WBOs) in nontraditional industries are over 45, suggesting it is generally older women with some workplace experience who are starting these businesses.

Today's female entrepreneurs and women business owners are more likely than previous generations or their male counterparts to have above-average educations. Many have risen through the ranks in corporate jobs, then exited to start their own consultancies.

The two ads in Figures 6.2 and 6.3, for New York Life and the Southern Company (an energy company in the southern states), show how companies understand that PrimeTime women are an entrepreneurial force to be reckoned with. New York Life's ad shows three professional business women, including a PrimeTime Woman or two, and is a recruitment ad for women who want to be their own bosses. The Southern Company ad features an image of four Prime-Time Women business leaders in nontraditional fields who work with Southern Company as suppliers. The headline reads: "You Might be Surprised What They Consider Women's Work," and the body copy supports the Southern Company's Supplier Mentor Program which helps female-owned companies grow and thrive.

Vital Volunteers

"Happy Birthday," said Dr. Jay A. Winsten. "What will you be doing for the rest of your life?"[14] Dr. Winsten is associate dean of the Harvard School of Public Health Communication and those are the words he used to launch an effort aimed at promoting volunteerism among retired Boomers.

Upon retiring, PrimeTimers will be searching for opportunities to take action on their urge to give back. They have a wealth of talent, experience, skill, good will, and brain power to offer, and they

FIGURE 6.2 New York Life: PrimeTime Women Starting Their Own Companies

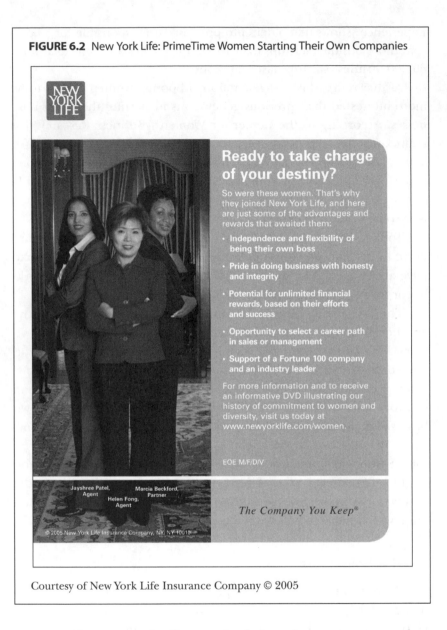

Courtesy of New York Life Insurance Company © 2005

are as anxious to put it all to use in their retirement years as when they were building careers. In fact, in the 2003 AARP study, among people 50–70 years old, 57 percent agreed that retirement meant performing volunteer or charity work.[15] Charities and community-based organizations provide an opportunity for them to contribute and connect with like-minded colleagues.

FIGURE 6.3 Southern Company: PrimeTime Women in Nontraditional Fields

Southern Company 2005, EW Productions

PrimeTime Women are more deeply committed to finding opportunities to give back—more deeply than men, as we touched on earlier; and as it turns out, more deeply than younger women as well. Four-fifths of women age 50 and over cite helping others as a core personal goal, several percentage points higher than women in any other age group, including girls in the typically idealistic stage of adolescence.[16] We heard from the PrimeTime Women in our own research that this desire to give back and volunteer is coming on strong.

I never want to not work. I want to do something . . . ideally, I'd like to be in a position where I could go somewhere and help with the Red Cross.
Rachel, 60

I started an education group when I moved here. I wanted to take classes at the U, but they didn't have such a thing for folks who didn't need any more degrees or units. So, I volunteered to start an adult education program. I started a program called "Wonderlust"— Journeys for the Mind. Building a Community of Lifelong Learners in the Gallatin Valley."
Sally, 65

This is the generation that grew up with the Peace Corps. Those who joined up, or those who thought about joining, will find there are now national organizations that help catalyze volunteerism among PrimeTimers, including the Senior Corps and the Experience Corps. It's no coincidence that they call themselves "corps" as they seek to evoke those associations among their Boomer target audience.

The Senior Corps-sponsored RSVP program matches people over 55 with organizations in their community looking for volunteers. Opportunities for involvement include everything from tutoring children to building houses. RSVP even provides volunteers with on-the-job training and, surprisingly, supplemental insurance.

Another prominent national group is Experience Corps, which provides "new adventures in service for Americans over 55." Experience Corps is the signature program of Civic Ventures, a national think tank and incubator founded by visionary Marc Freedman. His pioneering mission is to generate ideas and invent programs to help society leverage the vast and untapped experience of the older generations. The organization showcases older adults as a national resource that can and should be engaged to help solve serious social problems, specifically illiteracy. Today more than 1,800 Experience Corps members serve as tutors and mentors to children in urban public schools and after-school programs where they help teach children to read and to develop the confidence and skills to succeed in school and in life.

Civic Ventures just launched another worthy program, the Purpose Prizes, which are annual awards of $100,000 each to five people (or teams) who are role models for PrimeTimers because they are using their midlife experiences in innovative ways for a greater purpose. The first winners include several PrimeTime Women:

- Dr. Marilyn Gaston and Dr. Gayle Porter, who have dedicated themselves to lowering the rate of preventable deaths among African-American women through a support network they created called Prime Time Sister Circles.

- Conchy Bretos helped create assisted-living services in Miami for low-income adults who need help to stay in their homes.

Why Not Retire?

Why do 80 percent of Boomers plan to continue to work? Well, six out of ten of them need the money. Boomers have a long way to go to fund any unemployed "retirement." And many want to keep their health benefits. However, there are other reasons as well. They want to be mentally engaged, they want to feel appreciated, they want to continue to feel they are making a contribution, and they like the camaraderie and enjoy teamwork.

Need the money	61%
Need the health benefits	52%
Desire to stay physically active	49%
Desire to remain productive or useful	47%
Desire to do something fun or enjoyable	37%
Desire to help other people	29%
Desire to be around other people	24%
Desire to learn new things	17%
Desire to pursue a dream	14%

Source: AARP Report, "Baby Boomers Envision Their Retirement: II," May 2004

Energized and Engaged

According to the PrimeTime Women in our Girlfriend Groups and 50/50/50 panel, being busy, engaged, and energized are the keys to feeling and looking younger. They *love* having a lot to do. The time starvation of their 30s and 40s, when they prayed for more than 24 hours in a day to get everything done, has been replaced with a new-found appreciation for how rich their days are—filled with activities chosen rather than prescribed by their obligations. PrimeTime Women love being active, thrive on it, and look forward to it. Being busy has gone from being a burden to being a blessing.

> *I have always been a high energy person. I try to be realistic with my time, but I could be busy five days a week . . . Now I spend three days religiously in the studio. The thing is it is like a job, but it's not a job. I think when you are retired you have to have a program or you don't do anything.*
>
> Pat, 61

> *I'm a mom. I help my husband do the book work for his business. I have a lot of free time, I enjoy it. There is always something going on.*
>
> Joanne, 52

> *Work is my most important source of joy; for everyday social life, stimulation, travel, learning, and challenge . . . I also enjoy drawing, singing lessons with my husband and a varying cast of gospel singers, movie club, book club, etc.*
>
> Colleen, 56

To be candid, one reason PrimeTime Women like to be so busy is simply to get out of the house. We heard from several women on our 50/50/50 panel that retired couples can often find their new status creates friction:

> *The biggest challenges have come since we have "retired." We spend a lot of time together. I am away from home more than he is and sometimes I am dying for him to be gone a day or two. I traveled often when I worked so I had a lot of alone time. I miss that. . . . the truth is he does not help you with your problems—you take his on along with yours!*
>
> Susan, 59

The change in status came when we both retired and moved.
It was a difficult transition and we fought like cats and dogs.
But we figured it out.

Sally, 65

In fact, in Japan, when wives of retired men developed stomach ulcers, rashes, throat polyps, slurred speech, and other stress-related illnesses, you know what the Japanese doctors called it? "Retired Husband Syndrome."[17] (I'm not kidding!)

People Power

PrimeTime women like to continue working because they enjoy the built-in network of friends that comes with the job. According to the MetLife Mature Market Institute, many current workers ages 55–70 cite "social interaction with colleagues" as one of the main reasons why they work (after the need to make more money and the desire to stay active).

As viewed by the PrimeTime women in our 50/50/50 research panel:

People aspects are a priority I have always set for myself as I believed that by taking care of the needs of people, beginning with family and friends and then branching out to those outside my circle (whether they are personal needs or taking on a project like education or the state through chairing United Way's Success By 6 program or serving on the Governor's Commission on Quality Education) the other things would fall into place—and they did.

Debra, 53

I was semiretired and returned to work full time. I like to get up in the morning and have a place to go. I also missed the personal work "relationships."

Susan, 62

The Marketing Opportunity

The Boomer "retirement" revolution means that as they keep moving into PrimeTime, marketers can expect to see continued activity, increased income, more and different spending, and new opportunities. Whether they are working full time or part time, volunteering, or starting their own businesses, PrimeTime women will be busy and they will be buying.

For marketers, this means they will want time-saving products and services in PrimeTime as much as they needed them when they were younger. In other words, if you're marketing products or services developed and positioned to offer convenience or time-saving benefits, don't make the mistake of assuming that PrimeTimers won't be interested because they're "retired." They may be just as interested as moms and other younger women are, and twice as able to pay for them.

Corporations that serve small business can expect to see growth in the PrimeTime and the PrimeTime Plus market (depending on when she decides to leave her corporate job) for the next two decades. In fact, some of the market leaders already have initiatives targeting women business owners, including IBM, the United States Postal Service, American Express, Wells Fargo, and UPS.

Financial services companies are already lining up to help Boomers plan for PrimeTime, including Oppenheimer, Lincoln Financial, and Mass Mutual. Boomers will also be changing their spending patterns in the travel, education, and health care and housing categories, to name just a few.

For local businesses, companies that help with home office design and setup, computer hardware/software networking and upgrading, postage and shipping, Web site development, online marketing and sales, and so on will find demand for their products and services accelerating as well. And if they're looking for prospects they need look no further than the local chapters of NAWBO (National Association of Women Business Owners) and ABWA (American Business Women's Association).

Moreover, don't think just *office*. Think about adding or emphasizing personal services such as home delivery of drug store prescriptions, personal trainers, massages, catering, at-home manicures and pedicures, and more.

One thing small business owners almost always find is that they're working twice as many hours as they were on the corporate side (not that they mind), and the personal stuff that needs to get done gets put aside. A little help in that arena would be much appreciated. In fact, someone could start a nice business as a personal assistant, perhaps serving a different client each day of the week, who handles grocery shopping, home service sourcing and supervision, bill paying, dinner preparation, and more. Take my idea—please! (And call me when you expand to Chicago!)

Home Is Where the Heart—and the Money—Is

How Much Money?

The other sector that can expect to feel the enormous impact of PrimeTime Women is housing and real estate. That's because home is not only where the heart is; it's where the biggest investment of time and money is! PrimeTime Women will make dramatic housing changes when retirement approaches. Look at the facts:

- The National Association of Home Builders says the fastest-growing part of the housing market is the segment of buyers over 50.

- According to the Del Webb 2005 Baby Boomer Survey, 41 percent of older Boomers (50–59) indicate that they plan to buy a new home for their retirement.[18]

- Women are involved in more than 80 percent of home purchase decisions.

  - In the United States, married couples account for 62 percent of home purchases.

  - Single women own 22 percent of homes and are one of the fastest-growing segments.

  - Single men account for only 12 percent of home purchases.[19]

- Women initiate 80 percent of all home improvement decisions, especially big-ticket items like kitchens, flooring, and bathrooms.[20]

- Both Lowe's and Home Depot report that half their customers are women.[21]

- A 2004 survey of affluent women (median HHI $150,000) showed that a whopping 93 percent of the respondents expect to decorate and redecorate their homes indefinitely.[22]

- According to a study conducted by Ace Hardware, women spend 50 percent more per average purchase than men.[23]

PrimeTime households put their money where their homes are and spend at a much greater rate on most home furnishings and services than their younger counterparts. The table below compares spending among 55- to 64-year-old householders to that of 25- to 34-year-old householders. And it also looks at how fast that spending is growing.

FIGURE 6.4 PrimeTimers Put Their Money Where Their Homes Are

Household Spending: Households 55–64

	Index vs. HH 25–34	Percent Change vs. 1997
Purchases		
Owned dwelling	119	+23%
Vacation homes	358	N/A
Services		
Maintenance/repairs	227	+28%
Utilities	118	No chg
Yardwork	523	N/A
Housekeeping	215	+44%
Furnishing		
Furnishings	123	-6%
Furniture	103	+11%
Major Appliances	149	-20%

Source: *New Strategist* 2004 and 2005

What Kind of Housing?

As they approach retirement, PrimeTime Women are exploring many options, each of which has its own particular needs and offers its own particular opportunities to companies in the housing and real estate industries. Options they're considering include

- staying put—upgrading and repurposing their primary residences once the flock has flown;

- moving on to vacation/second homes, college communities, or unconventional destinations;

- getting together by joining forces and exploring group living with old and new friends; and

- getting care by making the move to assisted living facilities.

Staying Put, Upgrading, Repurposing

The remodeling industry has exploded in recent years. According to trendwatching.com, home remodeling is a $125 billion industry. PrimeTime Women are getting busy and are repurposing the kids' rooms into upstairs entertainment centers, home offices, workout rooms, and yoga/meditation retreats. They're screening in areas to create indoor/outdoor living spaces. They're welcoming back their boomerang kids with separate living quarters. And for those who bring aging parents into their homes, they are adding "mother-in-law" suites (or even wings, additions, and small carriage houses) as well as adding banisters, elevators, inclines for wheelchairs, intercoms, and so forth.

Here's an interesting development in elder care housing: ECHO (Elder Cottage Housing Opportunities) is a separate, small, manufactured home added right on the property of a single-family house. Older parents can then live "with" their children without actually moving into the same house. These ECHO houses are modular homes built in a factory and trucked to their destination and can easily be moved if the family is relocating or no longer needs it. And they're outfitted with Universal Design features that make the homes accessible for people of all ages, sizes, and abilities.[24]

High-end luxury appliance manufacturers like Wolf Sub Zero are tuning into this upgrading/remodeling market. One of their ads (see Figure 6.5) shows a PrimeTime couple cooking together in their gourmet kitchen—very much the sort of activity that would seize a PrimeTime Woman's imagination.

Now PrimeTime Women can even have a designer in their kitchens (other than Martha Stewart!), with the new line of kitchen fixtures just launched by Giorgio Armani. Called "Bridge" because the cupboards form a wooden arch over the cooking and washing areas, Armani's kitchen fixtures feature his signature dark-brown sukupira wood, woven bronze cabinets, and fabric-covered drawers.

FIGURE 6.5 Wolf Sub Zero: Staying Put and Upgrading

Photography by Hans Gissinger

The fact that PrimeTime Women want to remodel their homes doesn't necessarily mean that they want to do it themselves. So the company that for years heartily endorsed the "do-it-yourself" approach to sprucing up the home has now diversified to embrace the "do-it-for-you" service mode as well. The Home Depot has opened in-store service desks that offer installation home improvement services in more than 20 different product areas including roofing, boilers and other heating devices, air conditioning, decking, fencing and garage doors, windows, siding, floor covering, and kitchens.

The Home Depot's new strategy appears to be working as the company reports that it does approximately 11,000 installation projects per *day;* it reported revenues from installation services of $2.8 billion in 2003, growing at a rate of 25 percent year-on-year.

Moving On

Home Sweet Second Home. The great financier Bernard Baruch is supposed to have said, "The way to make money is with your butt:

Buy land and sit on it." Boomers listened. An unpredictable stock market, once thought to be the brass ring for investors, made many of them turn to real estate. Subsequently, the purchase of second homes for both investment and as a retirement residence has made this one of the largest segments of the real estate market.

While ownership of second homes was once considered a perk of the rich, today it is a huge and growing reality for many Prime-Timers.[25] Look at these statistics from a May 2006 survey of Boomers, conducted by the National Association of Realtors (NAR):[26]

- There are 6.8 million vacation homes and 37.4 investment homes in the United States.[27]

- Boomers own 57 percent of all vacation homes and 58 percent of all investment homes.

- Of those who own vacation homes or seasonally occupied property, 13 percent said they own two or more vacation or seasonal homes.

- Four out of ten respondents who own a vacation home or seasonal property intend to eventually make that property a primary residence, double the rate of the previous survey results from vacation-home buyers.[28]

Clearly, there is a large and growing opportunity for marketers of home products and services. Owners of second homes need lawn care, pest control, security, and housecleaning, as well as kitchen appliances, organization systems, and furnishings. In essence, they need everything they need for their first home, and sometimes more!

Getting Together: Groovy Kind of Living

In a 2001 survey conducted by Harris Interactive for AIG Sun-America, 1,000 adults over 55 were asked what they believe contributes most to living a long life. The greatest percentage of those polled (47 percent) responded "Supportive friends and family." Skeptical of being able to find that in conventional retirement homes, they're making sure they get it by creating their own communities. Remember the communes of the '60s? They've been resurrected by Prime-Timers who are returning to the ideals and connections of their youth. Their "communes" have taken a decidedly 21st century turn, and PrimeTimers are revolutionizing the concept of retirement housing.

PrimeTime Co-housing Communes. One such PrimeTime commune is a co-housing community called Silver Sage, located in Boulder, Colorado. Co-housing communities are small-scale neighborhoods that provide a balance between personal privacy and living amidst people who know and care about each other. Silver Sage offers this kind of participatory community where residents are over 50, neighbors become friends, amenities are close at hand, and you can, as Oprah says, "Live your best life."

Sounds fantastic—16 duplexes and attached homes, a common green, an outdoor sitting area, raised beds for gardening, an outdoor kitchen for community cookouts, and the hub of the wheel, the community center, which will include a gourmet kitchen, a large dining area, intimate parlors, guest rooms, crafts and performance areas, as well as a spacious deck with exceptional views of the Flatirons. It's the perfect place for "Creative Aging," a concept promoted by Silver Sage that entails moving forward in life, taking on new adventures, and delving deeper into passions through physical and emotional wellness, inward reflection, and outward service.

PrimeTime Women Power Properties. I predict we will soon see the emergence of another type of community, one comprised solely of PrimeTime Women. With 67 being the average age of widowhood, most women are outliving their husbands by 15 to 18 years.[29] Recognizing the likelihood that they'll be alone for this substantial period, "the girlfriends" across the country are starting to think ahead. They'll build their own communities.

AARP's Women's Leadership Circle recently did a study among women over 45 and found strong desire for "alternative" living arrangements; fully 39 percent of respondents liked the idea of living with women friends. Girlfriend get-away weekends will turn into permanent PrimeTime Women Properties, where women of a certain age will live together, grow older together, and share the experience with women they care about and who care about them. I can't believe I'm putting myself in this frame of reference, but I think it will actually be a lot like The Golden Girls!

Active Adult Communities: Not Your Mother's Retirement Home. What used to be called retirement homes has transformed itself into "active adult housing," and it's the fastest-growing segment of the U.S. housing market. These are communities geared toward adults over 50 that combine friends, fun, and purpose.

The Sun City of yesteryear, focused on endless canasta, golf, and bridge, is no longer the only retirement reality. The current batch of active adult communities are not just about living the good life, but about actively participating in *making life good*. Some active adult communities have clubs that members can join to explore the great outdoors, everything from astronomy to butterflies to rocks and minerals to fishing. There are also chartered clubs for traveling, RVs, motorcycles, cruises, and hiking. Volunteerism is an important element of active adult communities as well. Residents are often organizing charity events, raising funds for communities in need, or contributing mentoring skills to students. Most communities adopt a local school to assist and support.

The active adult complexes provide as many activities as there are interests, including classes in things like yoga and Chinese meditation. And increasingly they are providing luxury for those who want to experience an upscale PrimeTime lifestyle. After having worked for so many years, with so many years in front of them, PrimeTimers are settling into retirement communities with gourmet food on the premises, apartments with every convenience, concierge services, Olympic-sized swimming pools, and private golf courses and tennis courts. When they travel, their homes are looked after. When they return, there are fresh flowers in the living room. They have a coterie of like-minded, active friends with whom to shop, travel, play, and dine.

"Who can afford all that," you ask? The National Investment Center for the Senior Housing & Care Industries reports the top 12 percent of independent living communities charge residents 54 percent more than median-priced facilities, yet they have almost identical occupancy rates. Somebody's got some money.

Getting Care: Assisted Living

When PrimeTime Women do need more assistance or just want more peace of mind in case of a health emergency, there are "continuing care" facilities. They offer a wide range of housing, usually on one campus. Residents start in an apartment where they manage on their own, though meals are available in a common dining room. As residents age or need additional help, they move to the assisted-living or nursing care buildings. Most offer wellness centers (which can include fitness centers, health classes, or physicians and nurses on staff), educational opportunities, and Internet access. Woodworking shops, crafts and hobby studios, and greenhouses can be found in many places. Some are near country clubs with golf and tennis facilities. All have shuttles to take residents to whatever activities interest them, such as concerts, sporting events, and shopping.

Continuing care is an appealing option that includes housing, services, and health care as well as the security of having one place to live for you and your friends, for the rest of your days, no matter what your health condition. In fact, there is usually a contractual agreement that the facility will guarantee these services for a lifetime.

Even hotel companies have gotten into the new continued care game. Classic Residence by Hyatt has 18 retirement communities throughout the United States, and more being developed each year. Hyatt offers two distinct types of luxury senior living communities: Rental retirement communities where residents sign an annual lease and pay a monthly fee; and Continuing Care Retirement Communities (CCRC), with on-site care centers featuring assisted living, Alzheimer's care/memory support, and skilled nursing care. Classic Residence by Hyatt also offers club-style dining in thematic restaurants with menus and meals prepared by classically trained chefs. Each community features a computer center with Internet and e-mail access, and offers health and fitness programs such as tai chi, aqua aerobics, strengthening and flexibility exercises, and health screenings.

Moving Away: Heading South? It Might Just Be for the Birds

Don't deny it; when you think "retirement," you think "south." Don't you? For decades, that's been the traditional retirement migration: Go down to Florida, sit by the pool, play golf, have the early bird special. (In fact, there used to be an old joke: "What's the state bird of Florida?" "The early bird.")

However, PrimeTimers are not necessarily moving south—they are more scattered across the country. Charles Longino, a sociology professor at Wake Forest University and author of *Retirement Migration in America,* has identified shifts in retiree migration patterns. Although Florida remains a popular destination, Longino notes mountainous areas in the West and smaller states of the South are becoming increasingly popular, as are metropolitan areas like Washington, D.C., Minneapolis, Atlanta, and Dallas.

In addition, Baby Boomers show greater propensity to "age in place"—continuing to live in the same geographic area. PrimeTimers have built a network of friends and want to maintain these bonds throughout their PrimeTime and beyond. Developers are responding to these changing preferences and shifts in population concentrations. For example, Pulte Homes is planning 22 active adult communities, half of them in cold-weather states, including Illinois, Michigan, New Jersey, and Ohio.[30]

College Communities. Some PrimeTimers will want to stay near family and friends, but get just a little closer to the action. Many will be moving back from the suburbs where they raised their kids to the city where they whiled away their family-free youthful days. Another growing trend is that affluent retirees are moving to adult housing developments in college towns. Located on or near college campuses, these communities offer residents access to classes, cultural events, sports facilities, and professors. At some, such as The Village at Penn State, residents can teach classes and participate in research. Prime-Time volunteers are welcomed as assistants at on-campus day care facilities for the children of students or campus employees. In 2005 there were at least 50 such developments near campuses around the country such as Notre Dame, Duke, the University of Michigan, and Stanford; 10 to 15 others are in the midst of feasibility studies.[31]

Reverse Urban Flight. PrimeTime Women looking for city life want a relaxed, maintenance-free lifestyle with plenty to do—both intellectual pursuits and physical recreation (walking, biking, and water sports as well as tennis and golf). They can find it all at places like The Clare, a new luxury retirement high-rise community in Chicago. According to a recent survey they conducted, only 3 percent of Chicago seniors plan to move away after selling their homes. They want to continue a lifestyle of opera and symphony subscriptions, lectures, classes, movies (lots of choices), and shopping. They don't want to lose their important social networks. The Clare selected a site just off the Magnificent Mile of Michigan Avenue, within walking distance of museums, theaters, and shops. It incorporated a cinema, day spa, bank, classes, and valet parking into its building. It's attracting non-migrators—Boomers from the suburbs who want someone else to take care of garbage pickup, change burnt-out light bulbs, and prepare their meals.

Another new housing prospect for Chicago's PrimeTime Women is the new Canyon Ranch Living—Chicago, which is a 67-story glass elliptical tower, home to 256 lavish residential condominiums, a 65,000-square-foot wellness center, a café and dining room focused on healthy choices, and five-star hotel with 128 hotel condominiums. Now you can live the Canyon Ranch experience every day in your own home! The wellness center has an integrative team of physicians, behaviorists, therapists, nutritionists, exercise physiologists, and nurses to help Prime-Time Women take charge of their health and well-being. Everything is geared toward "being at home with the happiest healthiest you." As the tagline says, "At Canyon Ranch Living—Chicago, make the rest of your life the best of your life." Sounds like heaven.

Boomer Big Spenders Welcome Here

States that have historically *not* attracted many retirees are now going out of their way to attract Boomers and their big bucks. Florida, Arizona, and South Carolina don't get all of the PrimeTime Women largess. The moral of the story is that there is plenty of opportunity for everyone, everywhere.

- Mississippi established the Hometown Mississippi Retirement project in 1998 to support the efforts of small towns to prepare for relocating PrimeTimers. The state helps local officials market their communities and provides a state seal of approval for towns that meet certain criteria, such as having excellent health care facilities and cultural opportunities. Louisiana and Texas have similar programs.[32]

- Alabama and Tennessee have spent billions of dollars developing golf courses and other facilities desired by retirees.[33]

- Wyoming has created the Wyoming Boomers and Business Initiative to provide resources for those retirees who want to enter Wyoming's workforce. The governor has attended workshops throughout the state to hear what Boomers want in Wyoming's small towns, and what the state needs to do to meet their needs.[34]

- Communities in Colorado, Idaho, Washington, Wyoming, and other Western states are working with telecommunications providers to deliver Internet services throughout the wide open spaces, thus eliminating problems for retirees seeking connectivity.[35]

This chapter is called Looking Ahead because retirement and retirement housing are really more PrimeTime Plus than Prime-Time issues. Still, I can promise you that, as the family researchers, PrimeTime Women are the ones who will be thinking ahead and starting to plan for the next phase of their lives. Not only do they make the majority of the decisions when it comes to home purchasing, remodeling, investing, moving, upgrading, transitioning, and building, but they will outlive their mates and will significantly influence their immediate and extended families.

Now that you've gotten a pretty good portrait of the PrimeTime Woman—her attitudes, her key concerns and her midlife transitions—it's time to start thinking about how you will reach out to her effectively, earn her attention, and compel her response. Let's go to the GenderTrends™ Marketing Model and polish it up a little with what you've learned, so it's customized specifically for PrimeTime Women.

PART TWO

THE FIELD GUIDE
FOR MARKETING TO
PRIMETIME WOMEN

In this second half of the book, we turn our attention away from PrimeTime Women and focus on you, the marketer. Now that we understand the hearts and minds of these Boomer Big Spenders, it's time to talk about how to win their business. The following chapters are a terrific "how to" guide to help you

- identify relevant insights about PrimeTime Women;

- apply these insights to many different marketing vehicles to reach PrimeTime Women more effectively;

- generate ideas that will make PrimeTime Women sit up and take notice of your brand;

- develop more impactful communications materials that speak PrimeTime Women's language;

- create word of mouth that will translate into greater awareness and loyalty;

- learn and be inspired from real-life examples and best practices of marketing to PrimeTime Women;

- understand how fully integrated marketing programs targeted
  to PrimeTime Women can deliver outstanding results; and

- get in front of the CEO with a powerful opportunity to grow
  your business.

CHAPTER SEVEN

The GenderTrends™ Marketing Model Applied to PrimeTime Women

The GenderTrends Marketing Model

In *Marketing to Women,* I introduced the GenderTrends Marketing Model, which is a systematic and simple tool designed to do three things:

1. structure the complexities of gender differences into an organized view of female gender culture;

2. show how to use the principles of female gender culture to enhance each element in your marketing mix; and

3. apply the resulting insights to the five stages of the consumer's purchase path.

The model organizes complex concepts and is intended to help you better understand your consumer, focus on what motivates her, choose and use tactics effectively, and create communications that persuade.

The key to the GenderTrends model is that it brings together both gender expertise and marketing experience. To create an effective program, you need both. Without gender expertise, you can't

163

have the in-depth understanding of your consumer that you need to create communications that motivate. Your programs will end up looking just like everything you've done before, just like everyone else's—and you won't be any farther ahead in capturing your share of the large, growing, and profitable women's market. Without marketing experience, you won't have the practical knowledge necessary to develop programs that are not only motivating to women consumers but also executable in the marketplace.

And now with this book, we add another element to the equation—age expertise. By customizing the GenderTrends model to PrimeTime Women's emerging attitudes, physical and mental states, and life-stage developments, we can sharpen its ability to help you develop programs and communications that will reach and motivate your target prospects.

The model, and the strategies and tactics that flow from it, spans countries and continents, ages and generations. The key learnings and insights can and should be customized across the spectrum of women's segments, from young to old, from mainstream to multicultural, from America to Armenia. This chapter details how to customize the Gender-Trends Marketing Model and principles for PrimeTime Women.

The Star

The first component of the model is the GenderTrends Star. The four points of the GenderTrends Star—Social Values, Life/Time Factors, Decision Styles, and Communication Keys—signify four dimensions in which women's gender culture differs materially and relevantly from men's. As we go through each of the Star Points, we will highlight not only the gender differences but also the age-related changes that merit additional attention. The core premise of this book is that each of these Star Points exerts a considerable influence on how a PrimeTime Woman makes her purchase decision.

The four points of the GenderTrends Star are:

1. **Social Values:** different beliefs and attitudes about how people should relate to each other

2. **Life/Time Factors:** implications of the ways in which women's roles differ from men's.

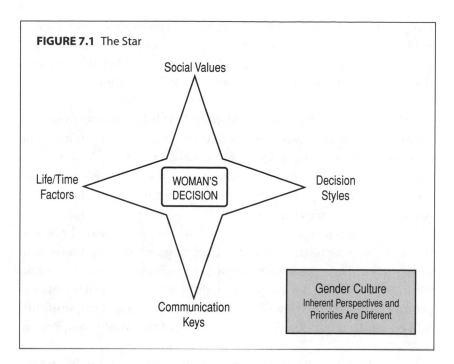

FIGURE 7.1 The Star

Social Values

Life/Time Factors

WOMAN'S DECISION

Decision Styles

Communication Keys

Gender Culture
Inherent Perspectives and Priorities Are Different

3. **Decision Styles:** consistent differences in how women perceive and process.

4. **Communication Keys:** different patterns and rituals of expression.

Star Point One: Social Values

The Differences Between Men and Women

Men Pay Less Attention to People; Women Are People Powered. Men hold the view that people are important, but no more so than current events, new ideas, or cool gadgets. Women think that people are the most important and interesting element in life, and they are oriented this way from birth.

Men Are Soloists; Women Are Ensemble Players ("We" Not "Me"). Men look at the world from the perspective of the individual. Their core unit is "me." Freedom—that is, autonomy, independence—

is one of men's highest values. Women see themselves—and everybody, really—as part of an ensemble company. Their core unit is "we" (sometimes "we two," sometimes a larger group). They take pride in their caring, consideration, and loyalty to and for others.

Men Do Unto Themselves; Women Do Unto Others. Men view themselves first as individuals, then as citizens of a community. The most desirable outcome is for "me" to get what "I" want. Women view themselves first as members of a community, then as individuals. They feel responsible for people who need help, and they open their wallets to support companies that care too.

One extension of this principle is a marketing implication I call "corporate halo," which is a bigger idea than cause marketing. Cause marketing is a marketing partnership between a business and nonprofit entity for mutual benefit. But corporate halo is more than just a business partnership—it is the sum of a company's acts of social responsibility and community citizenship for the benefit of the whole community.

Men Aspire to Be "Winners;" Women Prefer to Be "Warmer." Men think competition is fun. It's built into how they work, how they play, and how they communicate. Every encounter in a man's professional and personal life is seen as a contest. Because of this, men's mentality is rooted in concealing; any imperfection could be construed as a sign of weakness. To women, interaction is fun, conflict is not. Playing is fun, but losing isn't—somebody's feelings are going to get hurt. Compared to men, women test equally high on internal competitiveness or the drive to achieve their personal best, but the drive to conquer someone else is not nearly as strong. Instead, the female focus is on teamwork. Women's first instincts are to trust and share, and their mentality is rooted in revealing, not concealing.

Men Occupy a Pyramid; Women Occupy a Peer Group. In a man's worldview, groups naturally fall into hierarchies, with some people "naturally" ahead of others. He relates to other people in comparative terms: higher/lower, faster/slower, bigger/smaller, and so on. The goal is to be looked up to or admired as superior, to be at the top of the pyramid. A woman's view is that all people are equal— no one person's interest comes ahead of anyone else's. Her outlook is relational without being comparative: similar to/different from, know her/don't know her, and so on. Combined with the Social Values of people power, others orientation, and warmth, a place at the top of a pyramid is going to look pretty unappealing to a woman. Women don't particularly want to be looked up to, any more than they want to be looked down on.

Men Are Driven by Envy; Women Are Driven by Empathy. Men are motivated by the operating principle of aspiration. They are evolutionarily programmed to aspire up, to seek alpha status, to win. And when they do win, they will be admired by envious peers. The operative emotion with women is empathy. Women want to belong and to be understood. They think making other people jealous is sort of petty and small minded. They're more likely to relate to the premise, "Yep—that looks like my life. If that product works for her, it'll probably work for me as well." Whereas men want to be admired, women want to be appreciated.

Men Respond to Idealized Scenarios; Women Are into Keeping It Real. Men want products and services that will make them stand out from the crowd and they respond to scenarios that let them imagine themselves as the best, the first, the top dog. When women see idealized scenarios, they don't identify with them; in fact, they may conclude that the company's products and services are for "someone else." Instead, women are looking for "that's me moments," that flash of recognition between her and the real people, real situations, real product usage, and real reactions that tell her you get who she really is.

Men Like Buddies to Do Stuff With; Women Can't Live Without Talking to Girlfriends. Men are inclined to think of other people as a *drain* on their energy. True male bonding can occur without a word being spoken. They bond through activities, like going to a ballgame together or going fishing. Women see others as a *source* of energy. They bond through talking and can't understand how men can spend hours together and never exchange a personal word. Women's relationships with their close women friends are some of the most cherished elements in their lives.

Men Can Be Offended by Advice; Women Welcome It. Men don't like asking for advice or seeking out help—they feel it frames them as "one down" versus the other guy, and, worse, he's going to try to tell you what to do. Women see advice as valuable and are more likely to seek and welcome assistance from other people, including financial advisors and salespeople.

Degrees of Difference

From the descriptions above, it should be evident we're talking about some pretty significant differences of opinion here—men's and women's opinions, that is. The thing to keep in mind is that not only does each gender identify itself with a given set of characteristics, but depending on the context, each may be indifferent to, or sometimes even repelled by, the other gender's traits. Women may see what men call self-sufficiency as a nicer name for selfishness and wonder how men can be proud of an outlook that seems sort of aloof and thoughtless. Men may see women's attention to others as foolish, wondering why anyone would want to spend so much time meddling and interfering in things that don't concern them—let alone why others would allow themselves to be interfered with.

Of course, neither is right—and both are right. As far as marketers are concerned, the important thing is to understand that we're talking about core beliefs and values here—the building blocks of motivation. Sometimes a word choice or the wrong visual is all it takes to transform a difference into a deficit. What male advertisers see as an image of autonomy and freedom (e.g., an investment company ad visualizing financial independence as a PrimeTime Woman paddling a canoe in the wilderness, free to go wherever she wants) may have overtones of isolation and loneliness to women: a woman all alone in the middle of nowhere.

The Differences Between PrimeTime Women and Younger Women

What happens to women's Social Values in PrimeTime? How do they change? How are they different, relative to younger women?

"My" Time

For perhaps the first time since their 20s, PrimeTime Women have a newfound ability to spend more time and money on "me." With fewer people to support, the PrimeTime Woman has less chauffeuring, shopping, and laundry to get through each week, not to mention fewer games and concerts to attend, fewer minor emergencies to deal with, and fewer fracases to mediate.

To be clear, it's not that she cares any less about her family and loved ones, it's that now there is room for her as well. The kids are on their own so there's more time and money for things for "just me."

Interestingly, having the kids out of the house doesn't diminish PrimeTime Women's influence on spending. In fact, it expands it. One of the unexpected findings that came out of our PrimeTime Women Girlfriend Groups was the extent of their influence on the finances and spending of the "satellite" households of their immediate and extended families. They feel responsible and take a major role in determining the entire family's well being.

Yearning to Leave a Legacy

Expect cause marketing to be an even more productive tactic as women move into PrimeTime, when their thoughts turn more toward legacy and leaving the world a better place.

1. The faceoff with mortality during midlife human development leaves PrimeTime women yearning to leave a worthwhile legacy after they are gone.

2. As noted in Chapter 2, civic activism is increasing for this generation of PrimeTime Women in particular.

3. PrimeTime Women are at their peak years of income and have a significant amount of discretionary spending burning a hole in their pockets. They can afford to pay a little more in order to "do good." Witness the success of programs that promote "with purchase, we will donate a dollar to . . ." Not only can PrimeTime Women afford it themselves, but they seek out opportunities to support companies who help make the world a better place.

Craving Authenticity

As people get older, materialistic aspirations wane; a new awareness of "you only go 'round once" replaces them with the desire for experiences and the drive for personal fulfillment. It's about enjoying something for its own sake, not impressing others. PrimeTime Women are experiencing the midlife desire to "get real," both internally and externally. In the process, they stop caring about fitting in, being accepted, and conforming, and start craving authenticity. When a PrimeTime Woman finds her "real self," she achieves a state of integrity, or of wholeness, and she feels strong, complete, uncorrupted, powerful. This is "real," down to her core.

When it comes to marketing to a PrimeTime Woman's real self, both internal and external, authenticity is key. PrimeTime Women will not respond to fake flattery, dopey denials, and youth-driven dreams. They are seeking authenticity in themselves, their peers, and their products.

Love the Skin You're In

Take heed, marketers. Boomer women are not "in denial" about how old they are or what they look like. They accept their age, actually relish it, and can't wait to see what the second half of life brings them. Remember that women in their 50s and 60s report these as the happiest decades of life. Many PrimeTime Women say you couldn't pay them to be 20 again. They love the advantages that age brings: experience and wisdom, strength in the face of adversity, greater appreciation of life and time, wonderful "girlfriend" time, freedom to pursue passions, etc. Once they reach the Big 5-0, PrimeTime Women say "Bring it on!"

Most PrimeTime Women are no longer in the dating and mating mode. Physical perfection is no longer their primary source of female definition, and other things have been added into their priorities— family, career, community, and more. Good thing too, because childbirth and gravity have taken a toll. But PrimeTime Women recognize it and are reconciled to it.

The problem is with the media and advertisers who don't recognize what's going on. They persist obstinately in the belief that PrimeTime Women agonize about aging and will respond only to "aspirational" images that portray them as 25. Truth is, that approach is bound to backfire. PrimeTime Women are actually moving beyond a tolerant eye-roll to an adamant insistence on a portrayal more true to who they really are. This is happening for two reasons:

1. PrimeTime Women are going through the midlife human development stage where authenticity and integrity resonate more than social belonging and idealization.

2. The growing awareness of their economic power is triggering greater annoyance with advertisers who fail to acknowledge them. Big red flag here: They're losing patience.

One of our 50/50/50 panel participants put it this way:

> *I really resent the notion that you can't grow old comfortably.*
> *You must NOT have wrinkles. The truth is, they are a natural*
> *part of aging and we must accept them.*
>
> Susan, 59

PrimeTime Women are not denying their age but celebrating it. They're 50 or 60 or 65 years old, and their attitude is not "I'd do anything to be young again," but rather "I love being this age. This is what the *new* 55 looks like, and I'm fine with that." In other words, they love the skin they're in.

Appearance—PrimeTime Personal Best

Women of all ages have been telling advertisers for decades that they are more annoyed than enticed by the Stepford sameness of the size six beauties they see in all communications. PrimeTime Women are beyond annoyed: They're mad. As the darlings of marketers for the past thirty years, it never occurred to them that they'd be jilted just because they grew a little older. They're fully aware of their consumer clout, and they're getting cranky about being ignored and invisible. The bottom line is, PrimeTime Women have evolved a different concept of beauty.

A real PrimeTime Woman's beauty comes not only from her physical features. Because of her greater experience and confidence, her appearance also reflects her well-formed personality, her zest for life, and her sense of style—all qualities that enhance our perceptions of a person's attractiveness. PrimeTime Women carry themselves with more confidence and serenity. They like who they are, and it shows.

When it comes to beauty, PrimeTime Women believe in the concept of "personal best." When I say they don't mind looking older, it's not that they don't care about what they look like. They still want to look good when they walk out the door every day. But not as if they are walking the red carpet at the Oscars. They don't feel the need to look like Jennifer Aniston, Catherine Zeta-Jones, Halle Berry, or other Hollywood ideals of perfection and beauty. Nor have PrimeTime Women lowered their standards. They have simply redefined what looking good is all about, as one 50/50/50 panel member told us:

> As you mature, you have different needs and expectations.
> I don't need to fit into a size 6 and look like the hottest cutie on
> the street. I do need to know how to care for my health—and staying
> fit and lean and active is important. Both "needs" may end up
> looking pretty much the same (both may even result in buying a
> size 6) but the motivations are completely different.
>
> Mary Ann, 56

PrimeTime Women have achieved self-acceptance and always believe in looking their "personal best."

More Time for Girlfriends

Because girlfriends are even more important to PrimeTime Women than to younger women, this principle offers rich terrain for marketers. Here are some ways that marketers can use the growing relevance of girlfriends to reach PrimeTime Women:

- Develop specific "girlfriend-friendly" products (travel, telecommunications, spas)

- Execute girlfriend-themed promotions (Girlfriend Group prizes, Tell a Friend, Bring a Friend)

- Portray girlfriends in your advertising and other marketing communications. One marketer, Renuzit, has done just that. In a recent print ad for its air freshener line, four PrimeTime Women were featured gathering for tea and some conversation. The headline reads, "It's not just air. It's atmosphere." Here's basically a low-interest commodity product that has tapped the girlfriends principle to (1) catch her attention and (2) create a context with warmth that adds emotional resonance to the brand personality.

Star Point Two: Life/Time Factors

The Differences Between Men and Women

Men Live a Single Day; Women Live a Double Day. Men focus most of their energies on what they see as their primary responsibility: their jobs. Yes, these days many men have taken on some of the housekeeping and child care chores, but most view it as "helping out" rather than a primary responsibility. These days, most women also work outside of the home (60 percent), and still retain primary responsibility for the majority of work inside the home as well. Moreover, they tend to wear more "hats" than men. They generally handle the family social schedule, and even the community, church, and school functions. So, women are not just busy, they are time starved.

Men Prioritize; Women Maximize. Men like to structure their lives linearly: first things first, finish one thing before going on to the next. Prioritizing ensures they get the most important things done before tackling anything lower on the list. Women multitask, moving forward on several tasks simultaneously. In fact, if they aren't operating at that capacity, women feel a vague sense of unease and start looking around for something to add into the mix. This allows women to accomplish more, just less predictably.

Men Live Day to Day; Women Mark Milestones. Family milestones affect women substantially more than they do men. They mark the end of a journey, the beginning of a transition, or just a special event to be celebrated—the kind of event a woman looks forward to. Milestones just aren't that important to most men. Who never forgets the birthdays and anniversaries of every sibling on both sides? Who organizes the bar mitzvahs? Who knows? As far as men are concerned, these things just seem to get done somehow. Because of a woman's role in daily life, she's usually the one to handle all the logistics.

The Differences Between PrimeTime Women and Younger Women

How do Life/Time Factors change for PrimeTime Women, in relation to younger women?

No Time to Lose. Relative to younger women, time takes on ever-greater importance for PrimeTime Women. They weigh time with the end of it in sight and therefore value the time they have even more than when they were younger. In *Sex and the Seasoned Woman,* Gail Sheehy notes that "time is perceived differently after 50. People begin counting backward, thinking in terms of years left to live."[1] Life is short, and recognition of mortality can shift your priorities pretty dramatically. Dreams long postponed take on new urgency. For marketers, one way to tap into time that will resonate with her—because that's the way she's thinking herself—is to ask her "Why not now?" For added emphasis, you could overlay a promotion, an offer with an expiration date, to give her a reason to take action on that impulse.

Secondly, "not worth my time" takes on new meaning for Prime-Time Women, and a petty annoyance with your product or staff can pretty quickly sever a relationship. Her patience is at a premium, and long lines at the cash register or glitches online are going to cost you—so make sure you don't have any.

Finally, go beyond customer service to provide customer servi*ces* that literally save her time. If you're thinking that because she's retired, she's no longer busy, you're way off track.

Managing Major Milestones. All milestones have two qualities in common:

1. The incremental tasks and logistics are almost always handled by the woman.

2. There is usually a substantial emotional component.

Chances are that PrimeTime Women are more skillful than younger women at handling both the logistics and the emotions because they have more experience and are equipped with greater equanimity.

PrimeTime Women's milestones are different from younger women's. There are the difficult ones: the 3 D's—divorce, death, and diagnosis of disease. And the more positive but still challenging transitions to a new job, new home, new husband, daughter's wedding, first grandchild, and so forth. Milestones are the markers at the beginning of a new phase, characterized by high demands on time, money, and transitional skills. By their very nature, milestones create new and urgent spending needs. Therefore, marketers should anticipate these needs and be where PrimeTime Women will be looking for information to guide them through these transitions.

Milestone marketing can be a very efficient targeting strategy. Marketers seeking to reach PrimeTime Women at a time when they are particularly likely to be looking for help might consider focusing their product, services, and communications on one or more PrimeTime milestones. The media vehicles are easy to find because each milestone has its own vehicle. And you have the advantage of knowing what her most pressing problem at that moment is, so you know how to help right then and there.

Star Point Three: Decision Styles

The Differences Between Men and Women

Men Care about the Important Stuff; Women Care about the Important Stuff . . . and the Details. Men prefer to focus in on the important things when making a high-involvement purchase decision, namely, the top few items on their list of criteria. Once they find something that meets all the key criteria, they're ready to move ahead on a decision. Women pick up on things that men don't even register—either because they physically or perceptually can't, or because they can't be bothered. Although it's true that men care only about "the important stuff," the corollary is not that women care only about the details. The way it really works is that women want all the same things as men—and then some. They have a longer list. Details matter.

Men Extricate; Women Integrate. Men believe in peeling away the "extraneous detail." If it's not one of the top three to five factors, forget about it. Clarity comes from simplification, stripping away the small distinctions, discarding the data that clutter up the main points. With women, it's an entirely different story. In their view, a comprehensive grasp of how the details fit together is essential to understanding of the situation. How can you possibly grasp the big picture without a detailed knowledge of the specifics? Women look to add information, not cut it away. While men see this as complicating the situation, women see it as necessary for due diligence.

Men Find a Good Solution; Women Seek the Perfect Answer. Men see decisions as a problem to be solved, ideally as quickly as possible. The first option they find that meets all the criteria at the top of the list—bam; they're done. Men "shoot from the hip." Basically, women set the bar higher than men do. Women don't settle for "good enough." They want the "perfect answer"—the option that meets as many criteria as possible, with as few tradeoffs as necessary. It can take a while to find and assess all of the options, but it's worth it to know you made the best possible decision.

The Differences Between PrimeTime Women and Younger Women

What are the key changes for PrimeTime Women when it comes to the Decision Styles of Star Point Three? How do their decision styles differ from those of younger women?

Zeroing in on the Details That Matter. When it comes to Prime-Time Women, details still matter; they just don't register the same way. Both women's brains and older brains operate with a more comprehensive sense of context. PrimeTimers of both genders rely more on their gut instinct to make decisions, and less on sorting through the specific elements of a decision in the same systematic way they might have tackled the same choice in their younger days. For PrimeTime Women, that means that details still matter, but some details matter more than others. PrimeTime Women have had a lifetime of gathering details, so at this point they're able to move quickly and qualify what will work and what won't, which details matter and which don't.

Always Learning. As we have seen, learning for personal growth and for the sheer pleasure of learning is stronger for men and women in the second half of life. So, use learning as a draw for your events and traffic-building promotions: "Come to our July 4th event to learn what you need to pack to equip your son or daughter for college." Combine learning with fun ("have a glass of punch or wine") and socializing ("meet other moms and share college admission stories"), and be sure to invite her to bring a friend.

PrimeTime Women have more time on their hands and are excited about their newfound freedom to explore interests, old and new. And they are always gathering new data to add to their mental, physical, and electronic files of knowledge.

Companies with complex products—for example, financial services or hybrid cars—will find it effective to offer seminars to help PrimeTime Women get up to speed on what the key issues are and sort out for themselves the pros and cons of various alternatives. There is no better way to introduce your products and services and to build affinity.

The Perfect Answer *Now*. PrimeTime Women have been around the block enough times to know that sometimes The Perfect Answer turns out *not* to be The Perfect Answer after all. And that's okay. It's not the end of the world. They realize that their decisions are not irreversible. Time is more valuable to them now, and their greater experience has conferred a better sense of scope: some decisions just don't warrant a significant investment of time. So, relative to younger women, PrimeTime Women are willing to trade off The Perfect Answer ("I checked absolutely every single option and this is *it!*") for The Perfect Answer *Now* ("I checked the top, most likely, options and this decision isn't worth spending any more time on.").

This can be good news for marketers, because it means the PrimeTime Woman has learned to shortcut her decision process; she will be ready to say yes or no without quite the amount of due diligence she used to insist on. So for example, when I do Sales Coaching seminars about how to sell to women in general, I recommend that, instead of presenting her with a single "best" option, as one might for a man, present her with three options across a range ("small, medium, and large") and list the pros and cons of each. For PrimeTime Women, two good options would probably be enough for her to assess, based on her greater experience.

Star Point Four: Communication Keys

The Differences Between Men and Women

Men Want the Executive Summary; Women Want the Full Report. Men prefer to start with the main point and supply specific detail only if the listener asks for it. Conversely, women will often start with a lengthy background and build up to the summary conclusion—an approach consistent with their belief in context and richness of detail. A woman wants the full story—and "making a long story short" is not usually the best way to get and keep her attention.

Men Do "Report Talk"; Women Do "Rapport Talk." Sociolinguist Dr. Deborah Tannen characterizes men's conversation as "report talk," whose role is to transmit information, solve problems—and establish or defend individual status. She calls women's conversation "rapport talk," whose purpose is to transmit information, solve problems—and create connections among individuals.

Men Hide from Emotions; Women Seek Emotions. Men regard self-revelation as "indecent exposure." They're not comfortable revealing their innermost thoughts and feelings and squirm when someone tries to get touchy-feely with them. One of the ways women connect is through candid emotions. They look on emotional revelations and expressiveness as interesting, intimate, and to be encouraged. Showing that somebody cares one way or another is always going to be more powerful—and memorable—to women than a high-tech product presentation.

Men Connect Through Status; Women Connect Through Story-telling. Men see verbal jousting and challenging banter as a friendly way to size each other up and a good way to get to know one another. Women wonder how these guys are always one-upping one another and putting each other down. How rude. Women relate to each other by telling stories. When Jill tells Janet she likes her bracelet, Janet is unlikely to reply with a simple thank-you and move on. Instead, chances are she will launch into the story of how she got it with a good deal of detail for color commentary. The men in the conversation are bored to tears, but the other women in the conversation seize on the details to find something in common and build up the relationship.

Men Like to Laugh at the Other Guy; Women Like to Laugh at Themselves. Men's humor grows out of men's culture. For most men, humor is outer-directed, basically ridicule aimed at someone lower down the ladder. Just look at the language. Expressions like "the butt of the joke," "the joke's on him," and "he can't take a joke" capture the key dynamic of what's funny for men—humor is about losers. Not surprisingly, women's humor grows out of female gender culture. It operates on the dynamic of identifying with the person in the funny situation, the delighted recognition of commonality, the "that's me!" moment.

Men Like to Read; Women Like to Ask. Men like to get their information from impersonal sources such as written material, instructional videos, computer screens, and the like. Asking somebody else for information is uncomfortable because it frames them as "one down" relative to the more knowledgeable other person. Women prefer to get their information from people. Not only do they get the benefit of others' experience and opinions by doing so, but they also see the inquiry as a relationship-building gesture. Women are also more likely to volunteer both good and bad purchase experiences. In this respect, women are a medium unto themselves—I like to call it the word-of-mouth marketing multiplier. When you convert a female prospect, you get not only her own purchase power but also a lifelong string of referrals. One of the best ways to connect with women and to get their word of mouth motor running is to unexpectedly deliver something extra. "Surprise and delight" them, and you've created a cadre of brand ambassadors.

The Differences Between PrimeTime Women and Younger Women

So, how do Communication Keys change with age? How can they be customized for PrimeTime Women vs. younger women?

She Knows What She Likes. As we age, we come to rely more on our emotions or "gut feel" to speed our decision-making process. Research has indicated that older adults pay attention to and seek out emotionally relevant information more than younger people do, and they are especially in tune with positive feelings rather than negative ones. Therefore, don't focus on the product features, the functionality, the price value, or other technical information. Marketers should concentrate their messaging on how it will make PrimeTime Women feel when they use it, what the experience will be like, how it will allow them to connect with others, and so on.

I'm not talking about every moment has to be a Kodak moment, sappy and superficial. PrimeTime Women know what they like (and what they *don't* like) and are more attuned to products and messages that deliver on all of these PrimeTime Women principles. You know the old saying, "I don't know much about art, but I know what I like." That's the PrimeTime Women philosophy in a nutshell.

The Story of Her Life. For older people, stories take on a new importance: Storytelling helps us process our lives.

Dan McAdams, author of *The Stories We Live By: Personal Myths and the Making of the Self,* has studied how adults make narrative sense of their own lives. First, the stories we tell are part of the life review, part of the first phase of shucking off the "old" self. Second, our life stories, and how we tell them, help us generate our new identities in the second half of life. In fact, many people create "new" life stories or "revise" their own in order to make sense of particularly emotional or random times in their lives. As thought leader Rolf Jensen says in *The Dream Society,* "Storytelling has become an important part of market strategy; whoever tells the best story, and whoever tells it in the best way—will win."[2]

For PrimeTime Women, a storytelling format will always have more power to engage and interest her than any product description. Women's fundamental interest in people is so ingrained that they almost can't resist a story, whereas many men almost shy away from them if they're any longer than a paragraph or anecdote.

Humor Helps Her Handle Life's Hurdles. PrimeTime Women use humor to get them through some big transitions. They are experiencing emotional and life-stage changes like never before—some are dating again, some are dealing with hot flashes and mood swings, some are saying goodbye to children and hello to a whole new life. As Gail Sheehy says, a sense of humor, an appreciation of the absurd, allows us to hit the bumps of life with a little more bounce. One of the ways PrimeTime Women exercise their growing inclination to free themselves from social conventions is by giving themselves permission to laugh more often, and yes, more loudly. Their humor is more personal, more honest, and a lot more ribald. Sit next to a group of them next time you are at lunch or dinner in a restaurant, and you'll understand what I mean.

By its very nature, humor that's based on "that's me" moments is self-deprecating. And as with any self-deprecating humor, it only works if it's coming from "one of us." When a joke about hot flashes or gray hair comes from men, or a faceless marketing company, you may get a polite smile, but you'll know from the raised eyebrows that you should have kept your observation to yourself.

To marketers: not surprisingly, women *love* funny ads, funny brochures, funny labels, funny package inserts, funny hang-tags on the clothes they buy. The surprise here is not that women love funny stuff, it's that no one is doing it except for the T-shirt people and the companies that make cocktail napkins. Are you looking for a way to add some zest to your brand personality? To make sure your consumer never makes a buying decision in your category without at least looking at what your brand has to say? To give your prospect a little premium item that you know for sure she will keep in front of her on her desk or refrigerator? To give your buyer a little "surprise and delight" moment that she wants to tell her friend about? Sure you are! Try humor.

But here's the thing: it really needs to be the right humor. I'm not saying it's that hard—I see dozens of things that make me burst out laughing every day. But I am saying it's very different from male humor. For PrimeTime Women-targeted humor, don't let the young guys write it, or even the older guys, and don't let the young ladies approve it. Young women's humor is much closer to male humor. Things change when you've been in the world a while; sometimes things that crack up the young folk can seem a little mean-spirited or juvenile with fifty years' perspective.

PrimeTime Word of Mouth: The Marketing Mega Multiplier

Word of mouth, this media vehicle unto itself, becomes even more important in PrimeTime for two reasons. First, PrimeTime Women have had a lot more experience in life, with shopping, buying, using, and comparing products. So, they have a lot more information to share with their friends.

Second, PrimeTime Women will be spending more time with their girlfriends and will have expanded influence on immediate and extended families. Therefore, they will have a lot more opportunities to use their word of mouth. Marketers should care *and* beware! Word of mouth can be used to spread both good and bad brand experiences around this large network of PrimeTime Women and the many people they influence. And don't overlook "Word of Mouse." PrimeTime Women are still coming online faster than any other segment and their primary use once there is e-mail.

One More Communication Key: Beware of the One False Note

PrimeTime Women are very sensitive to what I call "the one false note" syndrome. They will ferret out the fake, the phony, and the contrived in any communication. For example, I recently saw a print ad for a car in which a couple was driving down the road, and the wife was pointing a camera out of the car window. The headline was, "Bill cleverly convinced Mary that sightseeing was best done on the fly." Well, every woman knows that the point of the story is that Bill just didn't want to stop. In her head, Bill "told" Mary rings true, while "convinced" does not. No way. The "one false note" syndrome is about making sure the ad or marketing message reflects the way a woman sees the situation, not the way a man does. I work with many companies in a variety of industries helping them identify and weed these "false notes" out of their communications.

For your handy dandy convenience, here's a summary of my GenderTrends principles and how they change for PrimeTime Women.

PrimeTime Women Principles: The Differences Between PrimeTime Women and Younger Women

- "My" Time

- Yearning to Leave a Legacy

- Craving Authenticity

- Love the Skin They're In

- Appearance—PrimeTime Personal Best

- More Time for Girlfriends

- No Time to Lose

- Managing Major Milestones

- Zeroing in on the Details That Matter

- Always Learning

- The Perfect Answer *Now*

- She Knows What She Likes

- The Story of Her Life

- Humor Helps Her Handle Life's Hurdles

- PrimeTime Word of Mouth: The Marketing Mega Multiplier

Applying these insights boosts the impact of your marketing programs and communications in two ways:

1. It aligns your messages and media with the way PrimeTime Women think, feel, and make decisions, which makes them more likely to respond positively to your brand.

2. It enables you to approach your consumer in ways your competition has likely never considered—unless they're already ahead of you, in which case, you'd better hurry to catch up!

The Circle

Whereas the GenderTrends Star captures what the woman buyer brings to the equation, the Circle represents what the company brings (see Figure 7.2). Here, the keystones surrounding the Circle

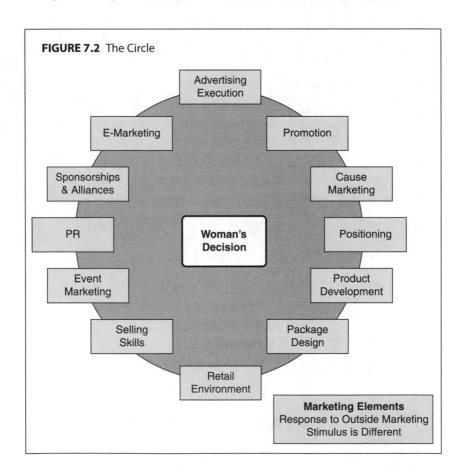

FIGURE 7.2 The Circle

Advertising Execution

E-Marketing

Promotion

Sponsorships & Alliances

Cause Marketing

PR

Woman's Decision

Positioning

Event Marketing

Product Development

Selling Skills

Package Design

Retail Environment

Marketing Elements
Response to Outside Marketing Stimulus is Different

represent the 12 elements of the marketing mix: advertising, promotion, public relations, and so on.

Some marketers may not use all the marketing elements—for instance, some may not include event marketing in their plans. However, regardless of which elements you use, the Circle illustrates that PrimeTime Women respond differently than men do, and than younger women do, to every one of these elements. Combined with the Star, the Circle provides a structure for organizing your thinking about these differing reactions, as well as a tool to help you plan your marketing approach.

The Compass

The GenderTrends Compass (see Figure 7.3) helps you visualize the concept that each of the four Star Points of female gender culture has a potential impact on each of the 12 marketing elements in the marketing mix. For example, Star Point One, women's differing Social Values, can and should change the way you develop your advertising, e-marketing, sponsorships and alliances, and other elements that you build into your marketing plan. Alternatively, as you are developing your advertising, for example, you should be looking at it relative to all four Star Points: Social Values, Life/Time Factors, Decision Styles, and Communication Keys. As you rotate the Star inside the Circle and align each Star Point against the applicable marketing element, you'll create a systematic way to apply your gender and age learnings to the realities of the consumer marketplace.

The Spiral Path

The fourth component of the GenderTrends Marketing Model, the Spiral Path (see Figure 7.4), represents the consumer's decision process, which can be simplified into five stages: Initiate Action, Research & Select, Decide & Buy, Own & Ask, and Rave or Rant.

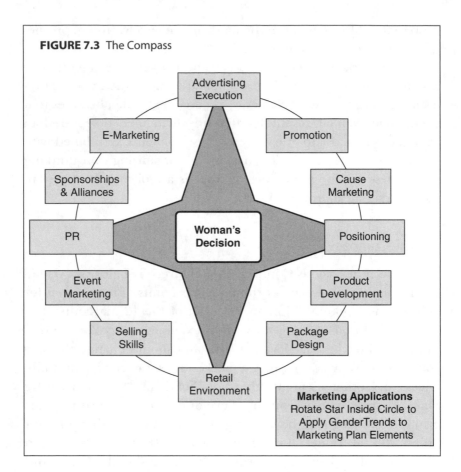

FIGURE 7.3 The Compass

Marketing Applications
Rotate Star Inside Circle to Apply GenderTrends to Marketing Plan Elements

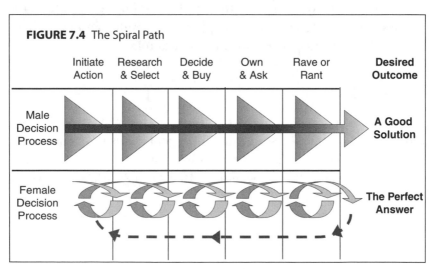

FIGURE 7.4 The Spiral Path

The Differences between Men and Women

There are four key disparities in how women and men advance through their purchase path:

1. Women start the process differently—asking around.

2. Women pursue a different outcome—The Perfect Answer.

3. Women seek more information and investigate more options— the Spiral Path.

4. Women's influence on your sales success doesn't end with their purchase.

The GenderTrends Marketing Model shows a woman's purchase decision process as a Spiral Path for a specific reason. A man will proceed fairly linearly from one stage of the decision process to the next. A woman, however, gathers more information and input at every stage of decision making and purchasing, often circling back to previous stages in the process.

The PrimeTime Spiral Path

Here are the two key points to keep in mind when applying the Spiral Path for PrimeTime Women:

1. It becomes shorter and simpler (there are fewer loops back). (See Figure 7.5.)

2. There is *no difference* between PrimeTime Women and younger women in terms of loyalty or willingness to try something new.

Shorter and Simpler

• PrimeTime Women will still be asking around, using word of mouth even more than before. But now they'll be asking peers with a greater inventory of experience to draw on. So that will immediately get them farther and faster into the process than when they were younger and asking less experienced peers.

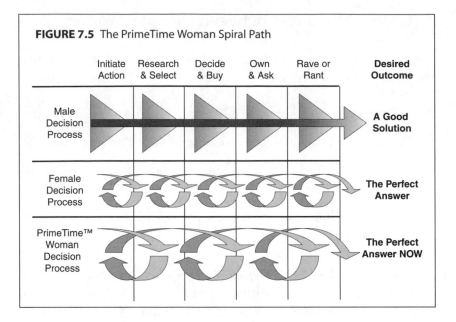

FIGURE 7.5 The PrimeTime Woman Spiral Path

- PrimeTime Women themselves have greater experience with their own decision process. They've been there, done that once or many times before, so they know what they like and have an existing framework into which they can quickly integrate new options and considerations. They have more experience with products and services, so they don't need to loop back and revisit previous stages of the decision path as many times in order to make their decisions.

- As a result, the shape of the Spiral Path does change, getting shorter and simpler, with fewer loops, on its way to The Perfect Answer *Now* for PrimeTime Women.

PrimeTime and Loyalty

First, let's look at brand loyalty among women relative to men. Because a woman does so much more due diligence on her first decision to buy a product new to her, she generally has a stronger disposition to return to that brand, that retailer, and that salesperson for the next purchase (assuming, of course, the decision has turned out to meet or exceed her expectations). She has invested more time and effort than a man would, in evaluating and weeding out the options, so if she has had a positive first experience with the brand, she has more confidence that she made the right choice. Whereas a man is likely to start with a clean slate in approaching the next transaction, a woman will remain loyal to her previous purchase.

Relative to younger women, though, there is no indication that as conventional wisdom would have it, PrimeTime Women are any less likely to try new brands and products. Conventional wisdom and "common knowledge" say that older consumers are very brand loyal and that it's a waste of time to try to get them to switch or try new brands. Hence, all of the marketing money is spent on the "youth" who are still forming their supposed lifelong loyalties. The reality is that, when it comes to brand loyalty, older consumers are pretty much the same as younger consumers. Studies have shown that they are just as willing to stay with a brand as younger consumers—and just as willing to switch.

- A Roper ASW and AARP study in 2002 revealed that the same percentage of older consumers and younger consumers agreed that *"In today's marketplace, it doesn't pay to be loyal to one brand."*

  - 55 percent of those age 45+

  - 58 percent of those under 45[3]

- According to Yankelovich Inc., the same percentage of older consumers as younger consumers agree that it's "not risky" to buy an unfamiliar brand.

  - Sixty-seven percent of consumers over 50 agreed with that statement.

  - Sixty-four percent of respondents aged 16 to 34 agreed.

  - Seventy percent of people aged 35 to 49 did as well.[4]

- According to a 2004 survey by Leo J. Shapiro & Associates LLC for *DSN Retailing Today,* brand switching was as prevalent among older consumers as it was within the total population.

  - When asked if they would probably switch brands of consumer electronics, PrimeTimers 50–59 were more likely than average to say they would try something new (48 percent and 40 percent respectively).

– PrimeTimers were also somewhat more likely than average to agree they would try another brand of health-and-beauty product (56 percent and 51 percent, respectively).[5]

• ACNielsen, Nielsen Media Research, and Nielsen/NetRatings just released results from a study of Baby Boomers Down Under (yes, they are called Boomers in Australia, too, but they've been divided into two subgroups, Life Jugglers and Life Surfers). The results showed that both Life Jugglers and Life Surfers are just as likely to switch brands as any other demographic.[6]

Forget the stale stereotypes of PrimeTime Women being married to their brands for eternity. There are some things PrimeTime Women do hold onto dearly for life—girlfriends, lifelong learning, nurturing the next generation, and inner strength—but not brands. PrimeTime Women have changing needs and want brands and products to meet these changing needs. Targeting younger people does not secure you their business for life. Targeting older people is not a futile attempt to get old folks set in their ways to try something new. On the other hand, targeting older consumers *is* a way to win the hearts, minds, and business of the people who have the most money.

CHAPTER EIGHT

Tailoring Your Marketing to PrimeTime Women

How to Win the Hearts, Minds, and Business of Boomer Big Spenders

Insights and understanding are all well and good, but their value to marketers comes from translating them into action. How can your new understanding of the opportunity and of PrimeTime Women give you a competitive advantage and increase your sales and share?

- **Improve the relevance and appeal of your products, services, and store offerings**

  - **Current Products:** Be the first to recognize the opportunity and market to PrimeTime Women. With your competitors distracted by their irrational obsession with young consumers, you can be the first to go after the consumers with the most money and the greatest growth opportunity. It's just that simple.

  - **New Products:** Be the first to research, understand, and serve PrimeTime Women's emerging needs as they move into midlife, changing physically and developing new lifestyles. Boomers, the first cohort of PrimeTime Women, are the largest generation in history and, as women, radically different from all the women who came before them. Consider: you have a large segment of prosperous consumers who have needs that have never been explored before. Smells like opportunity to me, and it should to you, too.

- **Boost the effectiveness of your marketing programs and communications**

    - **Greater ROI:** Get more bang out of every buck in your sales and marketing budgets by developing and tailoring your marketing programs to better align with PrimeTime Women's gender culture.

    - **Communications Impact:** Boost the breakthrough, relevance, and appeal of all your marketing communications by both reflecting and speaking to PrimeTime Women's real priorities and interests.

The GenderTrends Compass

When you rotate the Star inside the Circle to align each Star Point against a marketing element, you create the Compass, our GenderTrends guidance system for applying gender-savvy principles to the realities of the consumer marketplace. The Compass provides direction for each element in your marketing mix, from promotion to PR, from e-marketing to event marketing.

The 12 elements of the marketing mix that I'll be discussing in this chapter are show in Figure 8.1.

Incidentally, just because you don't currently use a particular marketing element doesn't mean that the thinking behind it won't help your business. Some of my best ideas come from transplanting one industry's seeds into another industry's flowerpot. That said, which marketing tools you choose to use will vary by the type of business you are in—products, services, or retail; large corporation or small business enterprise.

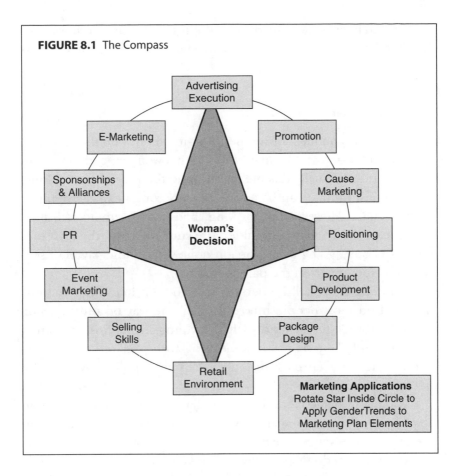

FIGURE 8.1 The Compass

Advertising Execution

E-Marketing

Promotion

Sponsorships & Alliances

Cause Marketing

PR

Woman's Decision

Positioning

Event Marketing

Product Development

Selling Skills

Package Design

Retail Environment

Marketing Applications
Rotate Star Inside Circle to Apply GenderTrends to Marketing Plan Elements

Tool #1: Advertising Execution

Two key considerations in advertising are how to connect with your consumer and how to differentiate from your competition amidst all of that clutter out there in mass media land. Therefore, most advertising executions are judged on the following criteria:

- Is it breakthrough?
- Is it relevant?
- Is it likable?
- Is it believable?

You can boost your advertising's ability to meet these criteria and thus its effectiveness with PrimeTime Women by applying the Gender-Trends insights below.

People Power

It's not only about showing people—it's about who they are and how they come across. The main thing is that women need to be able to "read" them. Usually this means showing their facial expressions; but done just right, it can be a tone of voice, or an expressive bit of body language. However, just showing "body parts" with no face associated (e.g., the slope of a shoulder, the curve of a calf, the twist of a wrist) isn't quite going to get the job done without the payoff of seeing what kind of person the parts belong to.

By no means do all the people have to be PrimeTime Women. Women find most people interesting in one way or another. For example, the State Farm ad with the young man whose car ends up in a pond ("the map left something to be desired . . ."), and whose male State Farm agent is also the town's police diver is very engaging.

As a matter of fact, they don't even have to be actual people. The new Charles Schwab campaign, which is very realistically drawn animation, captures very subtle facial expressions—terrific people power.

Actually, they don't even have to be *human*. The GEICO gecko is one of the most engaging "people" on TV; he has lively expressions, realistic mannerisms, and a great accent . . . How do you not love a guy like that?

Authenticity and Commonality

So then what do I mean when I say the people need to be "authentic?"

Women are more likely to believe claims that relate to someone with whom they have more in common. This idea is captured perfectly by the clever AOL microsite produced by Dove Calming Night Lotion, which features Felicity Huffman of "Desperate Housewives"—the most harried housewife on Wisteria Lane, and definitely one of the most authentic Boomer women on TV. The microsite features three "webisodes," or Web films, which show Huffman escaping a stressful parenting situation by taking a hot shower with Calming Night body wash or body bar. When she goes to sleep, Huffman dreams of visiting classic TV moms such as "Leave it to Beaver" mom June Cleaver, "The Munsters" mother Lily Munster, and "The Brady Bunch" mom Carol Brady. It looked like Felicity Huffman was really interacting with the characters! The webisodes created quite a stir on the Web, as Boomer women forwarded the link to friends, and, more importantly, Dove mailed more than 500,000 samples out in the first two weeks of the campaign. The Calming Night Lotion campaign is part of Dove's larger "CEO" program, in which Dove and AOL partnered to recognize the many "Chief Everything Officers" who keep American households running. Dove excels at creating powerful connections with women by tapping into the "commonality and authenticity" principles.

One of my favorite ads and a nice example of the principles of authenticity and commonality with PrimeTime Women is this print ad from PaineWebber shown in Figure 8.2. It shows a woman, probably in her late 50s, sitting to the right of her 30-something daughter. The copy reads, "You're psyched about the future. You're full of new ideas. You're looking to start a business. You're the one on the right." The dynamic that drives this ad is the surprise of the "punch line." It is so rare to see an ad that acknowledges the oft-overlooked vitality and aspirations of PrimeTime Women that actually coming across one that does creates a genuine sense of delight and satisfaction. "Hey—they actually got it! Finally!"

Keep in mind the principles of "Craving Authenticity," "Love the Skin You're In," and "PrimeTime Personal Best" when it comes to portraying PrimeTime Women in ads. Use models who look like they could be your next-door neighbor—lovely, but perhaps not so impeccably perfect and turned out that she looks like she just came from a Ralph Lauren fitting. Go for the feel of a "candid," rather than a studio shot. Use casual environments, relaxed poses, and open, accessible facial expressions.

FIGURE 8.2 PaineWebber: Authenticity and Commonality

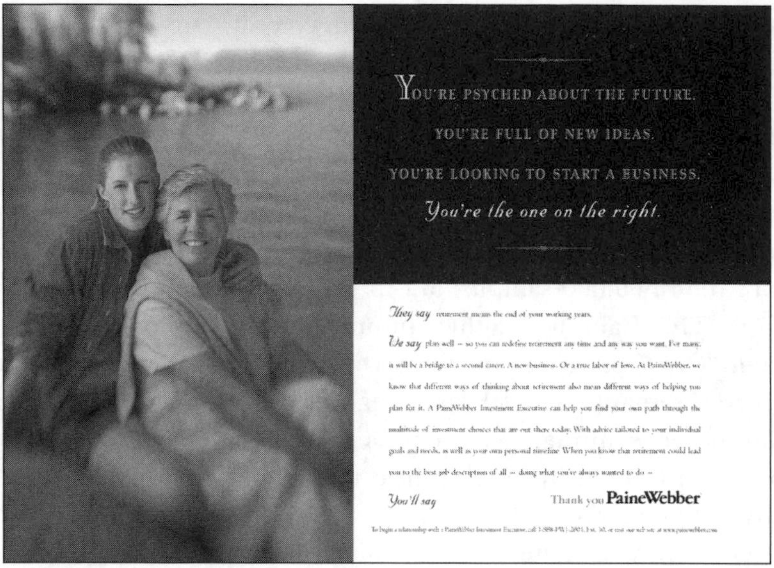

Photographer: Jamey Stillings

J. Jill does an excellent job of using "authentic" PrimeTime Women models in their communications materials, as does Eileen Fisher. The ad in Figure 8.3 is just one in Eileen Fisher's campaign using real women of all ages, PrimeTime Women included, in casual poses with fresh faces and natural smiles.

To touch back on the Charles Schwab campaign again, I find it exceptional in capturing a feeling of authenticity, even though it's animated. The writing does a superb job of conveying the feeling that these are a real woman's real words. You get the feeling it was written by a movie writer, not a copywriter, which actually isn't a bad frame of reference for this whole discussion. Does your copy "feel" like *When Harry Met Sally*, *Must Love Dogs*, or *The Devil Wears Prada*? Or like the eternally cheerful Stepford Wives being chipper about peanut butter or laundry detergent?

FIGURE 8.3 Eileen Fisher: Authenticity

Photo courtesy of Eileen Fisher, Inc.

Procter & Gamble has always done a nice job of recognizing their customers in their ads, and their latest for Pantene (shown in Figure 8.4) is a good example of showing a PrimeTime Woman who is aging beautifully, clearly not denying her age, and is looking her personal best.

FIGURE 8.4 Pantene: PrimeTime Personal Best

Joshua Jordan

Social Situations

The usual practice in executing advertising targeted to the 50+ crowd is to depict PrimeTime Women as part of an older couple. There's nothing wrong with that except that it is virtually the only context in which they are shown. The fact of the matter is that in their pursuit of "my time," PrimeTime Women are going to be spending a fair amount of time pursuing their own interests, perhaps in a classroom. Or hanging out with their girlfriends, as portrayed in a recent Boniva (an osteoporosis drug) ad showing a lively conversation among four friends—a welcome change from all the overly calm and flowery ads so common in the pharmaceutical category. So avoid the "couple" cliché. Another context in which they'll want to spend more time is the extended family, with kids and grandkids. The ad shown in Figure 8.5 for Armstrong floors does a nice job of realistically portraying a PrimeTime Woman and her family in an approachable "that could be me" situation.

Finally, could we please retire the overdone "classic" images of retirement? Enough already with all of those sunset beaches and Adirondack chairs and people playing golf! Remember that Prime-Time Women are still working and most don't plan to retire. Their PrimeTime (and PrimeTime Plus) years are going to be filled with jobs, travel, sports, grandkids, volunteering, classes, and lots of activities, so if you're showing "retirement," you're shutting yourself out of most of the PrimeTime market.

Celebrities

In most instances, using conventional celebrity advertising to reach PrimeTime Women won't work. Consumers in PrimeTime have less of a need to aspire up and impress others and are no longer as driven by materialistic values such as fame and fortune.

This is not to say that all celebrity usage is ineffective. It's that there is a different dynamic at work than operates with celebrities in the world of younger people. For PrimeTimers, it's not about emulating famous stars and wanting to belong—be cool, be in, be hip. PrimeTimers are past being inspired by people whom they're supposed to *want* to be like. Instead, they're drawn to people whom they already *do* like.

So celebrity endorsements in PrimeTime can have an impact if they draw on likeability, authenticity, and trust. Oprah, for example, is one celebrity whom PrimeTime Women identify with and respect. Paradoxically, the reason she is so successful, or "aspirational," is

FIGURE 8.5 Armstrong: Social Situations

Ad courtesy of Armstrong World Industries, Inc.

exactly because she is so approachable. Women relate to her because she's not perfect: she struggles with her weight all the time, she gets emotional, she makes mistakes—just like the rest of us.

Other celebrities' appeal is based on a combination of respect for their achievements and likeability: celebrities like Chris Evert,

Peggy Fleming, spokeswoman for Lipitor, Jimmy Carter for Habitat for Humanity, and Paul Newman for his "charitable proceeds" line of products. Regis Philbin for Osteo Bi-Flex, on the other hand, pretty much embodies "anti-authenticity" when he is pictured in a polo get-up and says, "I don't play polo, but if I did . . ."

Motivations

PrimeTime Women have many things that they care about more than when they were younger, things that are on their minds, ideas and issues that motivate them now. For example:

- **Family/personal legacy:** PrimeTime Women are looking for ways to leave a legacy, to create something that can be handed down for generations that tells their descendants "this is who I am." A recent television commercial for Bank of America has tapped into this insight nicely. It starts out by showing a Prime-Time Woman discussing the evolution of her family business. She tells us that she didn't inherit anything but a work ethic. As her assets grew more complicated, she sought out the help of the private bank of Bank of America. The commercial cuts to her pregnant daughter and a family gathering in the kitchen to conclude that "I can preserve the value of what I've built without compromising the family values that built it." This successful PrimeTime Woman is passing down her family contribution through her business and through the decisions she makes with Bank of America.

- **My Time:** PrimeTime Women finally have some time to themselves and are relishing the opportunity to pursue their dreams and explore new possibilities. Whether it's taking a class in jewelry making, going back to school to get her master's, teaching underprivileged inner city children how to read, or going on a trip to China, she is ready to spend her newly released time and money on some well-earned "my time." The example shown in Figure 8.6 from Avis captures her sense of adventure and "why not now?" The image shows a PrimeTime Woman on safari with her husband and observes, "Discovery isn't just a channel."

FIGURE 8.6 Avis: "My Time"

Impax Marketing Group for Avis Rent a Car System, LLC

(The ad is also a good example of transforming a conventional product appeal into one based on having a great *experience*.)

- **Milestones:** Life events, or milestones, are key triggers in the decision-making process for many industries, from health care to financial services. PrimeTime Women are experiencing their share of life events in the second half of life. Raymond James, a financial services company, recently launched a new print campaign focused on milestone marketing. One print ad features a profile shot of "Joan," an attractive attorney who is 54 and has a son at a private college in Chicago. She would like to retire soon and open a coffee house called "Joan's Place." The ad continues on another page with smaller profiles and captions that list other milestones in midlife: retiring early, caring for two generations, saving for the twins' college, and so forth. The ad in Figure 8.7 shows that Raymond James understands

FIGURE 8.7 Raymond James: Milestones

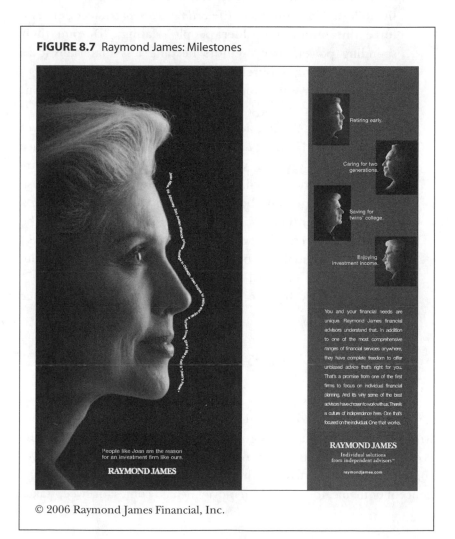

what PrimeTime Women are going through in these new life stages—sure to engage their interest through the relevance of the message.

- **Experiences:** Joe Pine and Jim Gilmore, authors of *The Experience Economy,* believe most people in today's consumer economy are becoming jaded about the next great product or service. The experts on the Mature Market would layer on the observation that, by midlife, it's not about "what I have" or "establishing myself socially" anymore. It's about "Now that I realize I only have one life to live, I intend to experience it to the fullest." The authors of the *Selling to Seniors* newsletter reinforce this notion for older people, stating: "Despite their spending power, many seniors become less materialistic as they age, looking to purchase experiences rather than things." More than they want more "things," PrimeTime Women want to collect experiences.

  The Toyota Avalon ad in Figure 8.8 (produced by Curves as an advertorial in their *diane* magazine) conveys the experience of a girlfriends' getaway weekend in New York. There is beautiful scenery and a small shot of the car, collaged like postcards from a trip. The body copy is written like an entry in a travel journal and works in subtle but relevant mentions of the Avalon's features. The ad is not focused on the product features, or the usual and boring car benefits (miles per gallon, rpm, computer onboard technology, suspension, and torque). It is focused on the PrimeTime Women and their experience with the car.

Tool #2: Promotion

Promotions motivate sales and drive awareness. There are two kinds of sales motivators: the time-limited offer, that is, an incentive with an expiration date, designed to get you to "buy *now*"; and the continuity program, that is, a reward for buying more product over time. The awareness driver is the creativity and/or excitement of the concept or theme, for example, a movie-themed contest or sweepstakes.

FIGURE 8.8 The Toyota Experience

Toyota advertorial used with permission; *diane* magazine copyright 2005

Incentives

Loyalty program rewards, sweepstakes and contest prizes, and discounts such as "buy one, get one free" are all examples of promotional incentives. It's time to think outside the box on incentives for

PrimeTime Women, who have "been there, done that" and are jaded on t-shirts and ball caps as prizes. Break through the promotional clutter with some unique PrimeTime-oriented incentives such as:

- **Experiences:** Offer experiences instead of products or price discounts.

  - *Spa Services:* While large corporate promotions are more frequently offering trips to Canyon Ranch, small businesses could offer a day of pampering at the local day spa. Or offer at-home experiences that were once only available at out-of-the way or exclusive locations. For instance, in the UK, the Powderpuff Girls will send a team of professional makeup artists in sexy but prim Agent Provocateur-inspired uniforms to ordinary homes, preening lady guests with a VIP hair and makeup session—fantastic prize for a "Big 5-0" birthday party promotion. (Remember that milestone marketing!) PrimeTime Women in Southern California can have Spa on Location stop by: it's a 36-foot mobile spa RV that parks in front of customers' homes. The onboard treatment center provides massage therapy, facials, manicures, and pedicures.

  - *Makeovers:* A PrimeTime Woman wants to be her "personal best." Having a hair, wardrobe, home, hobby, or fitness makeover could be just what she is looking for to jump-start her leap into "my time."

  - *Vacations:* Offer a soft adventure travel weekend or a week of white water rafting, fly fishing, cross-country skiing, hiking, etc. Or, why not offer PrimeTime Women the chance to take a cruise on the Volga River and learn about the art and literature of Tsarist Russia?

  - *"Live Your Fantasy":* A tie-in with Vocation Vacations would be a profound and life-changing promotion that would certainly break through the clutter and resonate with PrimeTime Women contemplating what to do with the second half of their lives. Vocation Vacations, an Oregon-based enterprise, offers people the chance to "test drive" their dream jobs. An office manager/computer technician test-drove life as a cattle rancher. A veterinary technician tried out the world of a pastry chef. A social services senior vice president learned what it was like to be a wine retailer. These vacations sometimes translate into permanent career changes—and they always translate into some serious mind-altering experiences for the lucky "testers."

Or try Signature Days. I heard about this company because it was featured as a participant in the extravagantly over-the-top Oscars gift bags. Chicago-based Signature Days is a company that offers over 1,500 unique gift experiences: hang gliding, bullfighting, snowboarding lessons, screenwriting boot camp, helicopter rides, paintball fights, dance lessons, sailing, tours of Napa Valley, wine tasting, riding in a NASCAR race car, scuba diving, having your own personal chef, and so on. A big spender can splurge on a seven-day yoga and chocolate retreat in Mexico. I can hear PrimeTime Women everywhere saying "Sign me up!"

- **Girlfriends:** As we've discussed, girlfriends are one of the most important aspects of PrimeTime Women's lives. So, incentives that let a PrimeTime Women give the gift of fun to her girlfriends—something they can all share in together—what could be better? For an incentive with huge motivation and widespread word of mouth, take any of the experience promotions mentioned above and make them for two, three, or four people. Kimpton Hotels has done a nice job with their girlfriends getaway weekend program, which features unique packages such as "Downtown Divas," where guests receive chocolate-covered strawberries and Veuve Cliquot champagne, town car service to and from the hotel to Nordstrom, a Nordstrom personal shopper, a pint of Haagen-Dazs ice cream at turn down, and more.

Word of Mouth

One of the key benefits of a breakthrough promotion is word of mouth. Women, especially PrimeTime Women, are big practitioners of this marketing multiplier. Here are some tactics guaranteed to generate positive word of mouth among this influential target:

- **Random acts of kindness:** The key to this tactic is to "surprise and delight" your target audience. For example, a couple of years ago, after he'd finished unloading the groceries in my kitchen, the Peapod delivery man surprised me with a lovely bouquet of red roses. "Wow," I said, "They're beautiful. Unfortunately I didn't order any roses, so I guess they must be for someone else." Turns out, because it was Valentine's Day, Peapod had decided that all customers who happened to have a grocery order scheduled for delivery that day would get a dozen lovely red roses. It wasn't an incentive, a reward I claimed for ordering more or ordering sooner. It was a sweet surprise, totally unexpected and forever remembered.

  Or you could offer a small service. For example, sponsor a Nail Taxi parked outside a corporate office at lunch time, and offer PrimeTime Women some special treatments. This cute and clever mobile nail boutique offers manicures on the move and will show up at customers' homes, offices, hotel suites, and hospital rooms. Right now the Nail Taxi is only operating in the Washington, DC, area, but it hopes to expand to ten other U.S. cities by May 2007.

- **Change the prize structure:** Rather than have one big prize (a new car!) and then a bazillion small prizes (T-shirts, ball caps, free product samples), consider spreading the wealth out across the top tier of prizes and offering fewer trivial, lower-level prizes. The goal is to give as many people as you can something "talk-worthy" rather than throwing your money into low value prizes that aren't worth mentioning. The costs can be exactly the same, but the prize structure is flatter and more interesting to consumers.

- **Include a friend:** "Tell a friend" is creating some reason for your prospect to talk about your brand, advertising, or other marketing program. Sometimes all it takes to get tongues wagging is a clever concept, a witty tag line, or a particularly apt use of humor. Remember the microsite for Dove's Calming Night

Lotion? "Sell a Friend" is offering your immediate prospect an incentive she can pass along, such as Swiffer's inclusion in their new mop kit of a $5 coupon for another kit. "Now, why would I want a coupon for something I just bought?" I wondered at first. Then I realized—if I liked the kit, Swiffer wanted me to have a reason to recommend it to a girlfriend. And of course "Bring a Friend" is a way for you to motivate more women to accept your invitation by adding a social component, as well as boosting the attendance and traffic at your event by extending the reach of your list to other qualified prospects.

Tool #3: Cause Marketing

Cause marketing is a marketing partnership between a business and nonprofit entity for mutual benefit. The marketing entity gets increased visibility and an emotional "feel good" factor that helps drive consumers to its brand and differentiate itself from the competition. The cause gets money raised from the joint effort as well as increased awareness in mass channels that it would not otherwise be able to achieve or afford on its own.

I coined the term *corporate halo* in reference to women's propensity to be the "guardians of civilization" and therefore much more active in cause marketing efforts. Corporate halo is a bigger idea than cause marketing; it's more than just a business partnership—it is the sum of a company's acts of social responsibility and community citizenship for the benefit of the whole community. And companies can make their corporate halos shine a little brighter with Prime-Time Women, who are actively looking for ways to make the world a better place and leave a legacy.

Events

Events that have a charitable spin will always be a stronger pull for PrimeTime Women than younger women. Since PrimeTime Women have more time and money on their hands, they are seeking more ways to get involved, to be actively altruistic. An example of a good corporate halo/legacy event might be a tree planting picnic sponsored by one of the new hybrid cars. Interested PrimeTime Women could bring a friend or two to plant a tree, enjoy some live music over lunch, and leave with a seedling memento of the occasion in her goody bag.

One of the most emotionally powerful and successful events is the Susan G. Komen Breast Cancer 3-Day Walk. It is the kind of program that PrimeTime Women are looking for—an event that requires not just money but also their time and energy and that involves being with and helping other "Girlfriends." I have heard from many 3-Day Walk participants that this is one of the most grueling yet fulfilling things they have ever done in their lives. The ad in Figure 8.9 not only supports this great cause but also shows that this organization "gets" PrimeTime Women who are in a process of transition to a new identity in a new life-stage. The copy reads: "I passed up the old me 10 miles ago." I just heard a great 3-Day Walk radio ad as well. All of these women are talking about how life-changing and amazing this walk is. One woman in particular summarizes it like so: "I kept waiting for someone to make a difference . . . then I realized that I am that someone." She's talking like a true PrimeTime Woman.

Products

I am excited to see the new Red "syndicated brand," developed by U2 singer Bono and combining the strengths of Motorola, The Gap, Emporio Armani, Nike's Converse, and American Express. Red's mission is to help Africa; the companies will develop and sell specific Red products, and a portion of the sales will benefit The Global Fund to fight AIDS, tuberculosis, and malaria. Some commentators in the marketing press seem to think Red's best prospects will be teens and twenty-somethings, probably because they can't imagine that Red's "coolness quotient" would appeal to anybody but youth. Yet the consumers who would be most responsive to this concept are PrimeTime Women. Of course, who buys more Red depends not only on the concept, but on the products they offer. Let's hope the Red companies are not so foolish as to offer only products that appeal to youngsters without a lot of disposable income.

FIGURE 8.9 Breast Cancer 3-Day Walk: Corporate Halo Event Marketing

Breast Cancer 3-Day Walk benefiting the Susan G. Komen Breast Cancer Foundation

Promotions

Make the most of promotions with a charitable bonus, and PrimeTime Women will take the time to act and buy. BMW is in its tenth year of The Ultimate Drive promotion, in conjunction with the Susan G. Komen Breast Cancer Foundation. For every mile of a test drive, BMW will donate $1 on the driver's behalf for breast cancer research, education, screening, and treatment programs.

Online

An interesting example of not-for-profit leveraging the unique properties of the Internet comes from a site called Kiva. The online organization enables individuals to make modest "microloans" to entrepreneurs in developing countries. Through Kiva's Web site, donors are able to choose a business to sponsor and can immediately make contributions in increments of as little as $25 toward the amount the business needs. At the end of a flexible 6- to 12-month period, lenders are repaid, without interest. Throughout the loan repayment, donors can communicate directly with the businesses they choose to sponsor. They also receive regular e-mail updates, photos, and progress reports. A fishmonger, a medicine shop, and several family-run produce stands are among the 13 enterprises in Uganda that Kiva's microfinance investment model currently supports. I love their tag line: "Loans that change lives." It's guaranteed to appeal to PrimeTime Women's heightened drive to make a difference. Tying in with causes like Kiva's would be a smart marketing move.

While many companies have gotten into the cause marketing act, few have publicly touted their actions. If PrimeTime Women don't know about your good deeds, how do you expect them to reward your company for its acts of kindness? Therefore, it is imperative for any cause marketing program to be supported with awareness-driving activities.

Tool #4: Positioning

When developing positioning against the PrimeTime Woman target, your big opportunity is to go beyond functional benefits to focus on the emotional benefits. It's not about what a brand or product *does*, but about how it makes PrimeTime Women *feel*. If you can unearth that insight into PrimeTime Women's emotions and develop positioning and subsequent marketing materials that elicit that emotion, you win. My colleague Tom Peters says it best: "Branding is ultimately about nothing more (and nothing less) than heart. It's about passion . . . What you care about. It's about what's inside—what's inside you, what's inside your company."[1]

Be Experiential

Powerful PrimeTime positioning should center on experiences that are emotionally fueled. Remember that PrimeTime Women are looking to use their new freedom and passion to acquire more experiences than things.

This exercise may help you clarify your thinking about how to use the emotional and experiential benefits that resonate with Prime-Time Women.

- Emotional benefits in the auto industry:

    - Features: What it is—a chassis of reinforced steel

    - Benefits: What it does—protect the occupants of the car

    - Emotions: How it makes her feel—secure, relaxed, confident

- Experiential benefits in the travel industry:

    - Features: What it is—a trip to Thailand

    - Benefits: What it does—get away from work, relax for two weeks

    - Experience: How it makes her feel—excited, curious, ready to discover and explore

Most positionings in these categories focus on either the product feature level or, sometimes, the human benefit level, but rarely are these translated into the experiential level, which is the best way to tap into PrimeTimers' motivational machinery.

Don't Be Afraid to Be "the Boomer Brand"

Being a "Boomer brand" is not about being an "old person's" brand or "rich person's" brand.

Some brands have decided it's okay and perhaps even "cool" to position themselves as Boomer brands. Witness Cadillac rocking and rolling with Led Zeppelin. Or Miller High Life claiming that it is now the "beer for grown-ups." American Express's new Ameriprise Financial Services company was created just for Boomers.

"I'm Pink and I'm Proud"

There is a very interesting recent development with PrimeTime Women, and it's the "reclamation of pink." It's okay to be pink again. In fact, PrimeTime Women are reclaiming their femininity in many ways.

PrimeTime Women have already proven themselves in their careers and roles they have played for the past 30-plus years. They no longer have to wear blue chambray shirts and gray suits and play squash with the boss. PrimeTime Women are taking back their female strengths and expressing themselves, pink blouses and all. Just look at PINK magazine, a brand new business women's magazine. Its vision and mission is summed up by founding editor and CEO Cynthia Good as follows:

> Ask most driven, focused, passionate, career women what they think or feel about the word pink and you'll get an earful. Only the most confident men wear it. And until recently, ambitious career women avoided it like the plague.
>
> It's not just about color. Throughout your life pink has been symbolic. Since the day you were born and a pink cap was placed upon your head, the color partly defined who you were and who you felt you could or could not become. At times pink was confining, girlish, degrading, liberating or all of these.
>
> But today a growing number of women who are at, or heading for the top, are comfortable with their own pinkness—the color, the attitude, and the opportunity it represents. They are embracing their femininity along with their strength, their compassion and resilience, power and passion. PINK exists to promote this new generation of women who are making a significant impact on the world through their work and their lives—while being true to themselves.

Tool #5: Product Development

There are over 20,000 new products launched every year. Only 10 percent are still on the market and profitable after three years. The reasons for new product failure are well understood and outlined on the next page. You can use the GenderTrends principles to reduce the chances that your product will fail, and to gain a powerful advantage over your competitors.

- **Overestimation of market size:** Not a problem with PrimeTime Women

- **Design problems:** Remember that details make the difference

- **Incorrectly positioned, priced, or advertised:** There are lots of ideas in this chapter to help you avoid these mistakes

- **Pushed despite poor marketing research findings:** Listen to your PrimeTime Women consumers!

- **Development costs:** Think about adapting current products to PrimeTime Women's new needs

- **Competition:** Hurry before they get to this golden bull's-eye!

It's important to note that women in general are suspicious of "designed just for women" products. PrimeTime Women are no exception. In fact, they may be even more suspicious because of their experience with many past disappointments using this approach. Nonetheless, PrimeTimers, PrimeTime Women included, need products that not only have functionality, style, and ease of use but that also meet their changing and emerging needs. Here are some ideas.

Changing Needs

PrimeTime Women's changing life-stages and needs spell opportunity for new product development. For example:

- **Packaged goods: size, taste, and ingredients.** Make the sizes smaller to accommodate smaller households and smaller appetites. Pillsbury has developed smaller portions and menu ideas focused on the "empty nest" milestone, but with a twist: the *joys* of "dinner for two" again. In one TV spot, the male half of a fiftyish couple dabbles in new food and exercise regimens as his female partner affectionately looks on. As the couple settles down to a dinner that includes Pillsbury frozen rolls, she remarks that she can only tolerate so much experimentation, "at least at the dinner table" (wink, wink). And the packaging has been modified too, so that smaller portions are available, and the rest can be saved for later. Downsize: Yes. Upside: Definitely!

FIGURE 8.10 Pillsbury: Marketing to Empty Nesters' Changing Needs

Reprinted with the permission of General Mills, Inc.

PrimeTime Women are leaving the nest themselves and traveling and exploring the world, so travel size products for everything from health and beauty aids to packaged goods to medications will be flying off the shelves and into the suitcases of PrimeTime Women.

Increase nutritional value because PrimeTime Women are paying greater attention to their health and to their spouses' as well. We have been seeing this trend in the cereal aisle for some time, with products enhanced per the nutritional concerns of older people (Antioxidants, fiber, Omega-3, calcium) rather than those of kids (vitamins and minerals). I'm not sure why this trend hasn't expanded faster into other food categories, but I expect it will any day now.

Add flavoring/seasoning to foods in order to address PrimeTimers' diminished taste buds; even offer customized seasoning and spice packets, as mentioned in Chapter 4.

- **Everyday devices: function and design.** OXO, Ford, Vital Radiance, and even a couple of consumer electronics companies have all developed or adapted products to meet PrimeTime consumers' changing needs. GreatCall is a new wireless company that targets Baby Boomers with a phone manufactured by Samsung. The phone has big buttons, a bright screen, easy-to-read text, and loud and clear sound.

One version, perhaps for the PrimeTime Woman's parents, is simplified even further, its number keys have been replaced by three emergency buttons: one for 911, a second for the operator, and a third for a personalized direct dial number. Operators are an important element of GreatCall's services; besides looking up numbers or placing calls for customers, operators can program a phone's contact list over the network (so now they don't have to ask their grandkids to do it!).

Emerging Needs

Here are some more new product ideas that cater to PrimeTime Women's emerging needs and wants:

- **Self expression.** A good way to tap into PrimeTime Women's new zest for exploration and self-expression is via customized "design-your-own" products. What about Web sites or stores that allow PrimeTime women to create their own unique jewelry—rings, necklaces, bracelets? Or take the concept right to PrimeTime Women's homes, like the company Gems to Jewels has done. At hostess workshops, a Gems to Jewels instructor teaches mothers, daughters, girlfriends, or whoever wants to show up how to design and create "heirloom-quality" jewelry from semiprecious stones, sterling silver, and gold. Look for growth in all types of creativity-driven arts and crafts—ceramics, painting, sculpture, home décor, woodworking, fabric weaving, and wearable art.

- **Caregiving/proactive health care.** The health care field in particular can surely create many products and services to help caregivers and proactively healthy PrimeTime Women. A good example is the new company and service called OnFile. With OnFile, you can store all of your medical information online in one convenient place. Each profile contains the essential information about an individual's medical status, such as emergency contacts, allergies, medications, preexisting conditions, family history, immunizations, physician's information, and even living will and power of attorney information. In an emergency, medical personnel can access this information via a member card with an access code and ID.

Tool #6: Package Design

The three main strategies behind successful package design are:

1. shelf appeal and stopping power,

2. functionality, and

3. differentiation/added value.

Shelf Appeal and Stopping Power

Use the PrimeTime Women principles of people power, craving authenticity, and storytelling to create impact at shelf. For example, why not break out of the health and beauty monotony of white box packaging and show PrimeTime Women on labels for skin care products? I loved the Vital Radiance makeup line made especially for enhancing PrimeTime skin. I would have liked to see them feature the beautiful PrimeTime Women that already appeared in their ads and on their Web site on the Vital Radiance packaging as well.

Functionality

Legibility is a huge issue for package labels, and not just for PrimeTime customers. I would love it if I could go to the store and find an eye cream with the list of ingredients and application instructions in anything larger than mousetype. Who can read those bottles? One smart marketer has created a solution: CVS/Pharmacy offers magnifiers on cords hanging from shelves to help consumers read the labels. Another great idea would be lift-up extendable labels. Advil is already using these, but other manufacturers who need more space can use these labels in order to enlarge type to make it readable.

Ease of use is another key functionality factor. Some marketers are getting the message. There are now Folger's coffee cans with a peel-back foil lid, Sherwin-Williams created twist-and-pour paint cans just in time for PrimeTime Women to remodel their homes, and Starkist Tuna's plastic pouches are great for ease of opening, portion control, and portability of healthy food on the go. Tylenol recently introduced a new easy-to-open bottle that's actually preferred over any other arthritis cap. Target has created clever pill bottles with color-coded caps for each member of the family to know whose medicine is whose. It would be smart for the makers of CDs, DVDs, and videos to get on board and create more functional and easy-to-open packaging as well.

Differentiation/Added Value

Details make the difference for PrimeTime Women. These details add value, differentiate from the competition, create word of mouth, and generate repeat visits from PrimeTime Women. Many PrimeTime Women love to shop at (well, actually get gifts from) Tiffany's and the Red Envelope. Do you know why? The packaging! We're all familiar with the ubiquitous blue box. Red Envelope delivers baubles lusciously wrapped in volumes of tissue paper with special notes about the origin and meaning of the gifts inside.

Tool #7: Retail Environment

The retail environment is critical. It's where the sale happens—or not. The 5 S's of effective retail design are store design, sales staff, signage, services, and safety. We'll discuss each in detail below.

Store Design

There are three key factors that should be taken into account in store design:

- **Aesthetics:** Buying lingerie can be even more sensitive than trying on swimsuits. One way to help soothe the senses is through design aesthetics. And one store to pay attention to when it comes to design with PrimeTime Women in mind is

Soma, a sister store to Chico's that sells undergarments. PrimeTime Women don't want to shop at Victoria's Secret anymore. And the department stores offer less than appealing lingerie options as well. Soma by Chico's aims to fill the gap. In Soma, which means "body" in Greek, Chico's transferred its signature design style for elegant older women to beautiful lingerie, active wear, and sleepwear. Soma's design team put a lot of thought into the dressing rooms and fitting area. Original artwork, decorative lighting, lush furnishings, and a vanity with a large illuminated mirror behind it have transformed the most frequented areas of the store into warm and spacious personal dressing rooms. An upholstered wardrobing panel provides the backdrop for "staging" outfits. A combination of fluorescent and incandescent lighting was carefully chosen—with illumination projected toward the customer and not down on her, to give a more flattering reflection.[2]

- **Experience:** I am a big fan of Best Buy and its customer centricity program, which identified Best Buy's best customers and then went about redesigning its retail experiences with these consumers in mind. Best Buy's new concept store aimed at PrimeTime Women looks to be a similarly smart move. It's called eq-life and is targeted to women 35-plus who seek well-being and innovation. The name "eq" is a shortened version of "equilibrium." Eq-life nurtures balance through three outlets: health, technology, and wellness. In a single visit, customers can fill a prescription, attend a yoga or Pilates class, and shop the latest heart monitors, MP3 players, exercise equipment, or other products. PrimeTime Women can also consult the Health Notes information kiosk, or maybe research a topic with eq-life's resources and relax with a cup of Caribou Coffee. And they can end their experience with a soothing visit to the spa and salon. I love their experience-focused tagline: "Enter seeking balance, leave feeling fulfilled. life, meet balance."

- **Functionality:** Women shop by "outfit." They view any individual item as part of a larger context. Department stores have this figured out: whereas men's apparel is usually organized by type (shirts, jackets, slacks, etc.), women's apparel is usually organized by outfits. Women who come in intending to buy a new pair of slacks generally leave with a coordinating blouse, sweater, and perhaps a jacket as well. The same principle can be applied to other retail contexts as well. For example, home improvement stores have taken a strong interest in women customers over the past several years. These traditionally male environments are starting to merchandise their bathroom and kitchen fixtures and décor items as coordinated collections. The big idea? Find ways to group related products together, both "anchor" items and accessories. You'll sell more products, and you will find PrimeTime Women willing and interested, because they value their time more and will be attracted to one-stop shopping.

Sales Staff

When it comes to making the sale, it all comes down to the sales staff for PrimeTime Women. Make sure your sales staff are well trained and adapt your recruiting efforts to maximize effectiveness with your PrimeTime Women customers.

- **Training:** Women like to get their information from people rather than from brochures. When it comes to training, make sure that your sales staff are well-versed in not only the product features but also in how the product can fit into people's lives. PrimeTime Women don't want to know the number of gigabytes or the processing speed—they want to know whether it will help them run their lives more smoothly. Train sales personnel to ask customer-oriented questions that are oriented to PrimeTime Women's lifestyles, how they plan to use the product in their lives, and so on.

- **Recruiting:** Having sales staff that can relate to PrimeTime Women would be a huge competitive advantage and differentiator. Hire PrimeTime Women to work in your stores. They not only provide empathy and commonality with your key

PrimeTime Women customers, but they are also looking for work that can provide them with a social outlet and flexible options. Take the example of Chico's, the women's apparel shop. Many a PrimeTime Woman (and her husband) like to shop there because the sales associates are not only friendly but are also the same age as their customers. They have more empathy in their little fingers than a 20-year-old salesgirl has in her entire slim body. One retail environment that could use a dose of PrimeTime Women's Social Values is the office supply industry, especially since there are so many PrimeTime Women business owners. The 22-year-old boys who generally work in these stores are just about at the opposite end of the spectrum when it comes to these motivating principles.

Signage

If PrimeTime Women don't know where to go in the store to find what they need, they are likely to make their shopping trips short and walk out the front door. Make sure signage is large and clear. And use some gender-savvy principles and insights to make it capture the attention of PrimeTime Women:

- **People Power:** Use images of people on signs to tap into PrimeTime Women's strong people orientation. The signage can be in the front windows to draw customers in off the street, as Gap has successfully done. Or it can be in the store to show people enjoying the products, as at Best Buy.

- **Suggestive Selling**: Signage can be used to cross/upsell PrimeTime Women who are in the market for related products. Suggest a wine with the cheese selection in grocery stores, or garden services with flower displays in landscaping stores, or new DVDs just released at the popcorn section in discount stores.

- **Legibility:** We've already discussed the legibility issue with package labels. Make sure your signs are readable too. Small type and reversed-out light type on dark backgrounds won't capture PrimeTime Women's attention. Make sure directional signs are legible from near and far, especially signs that point to key locations such as restrooms, checkout, and customer service.

Services

Marketers can serve PrimeTime Women's critical needs by going beyond customer service to customer *services*.

- Why don't hardware stores offer a "wintering" service in which they would bring rock salt and other necessary (and heavy!) supplies to PrimeTime Women's homes at the start of cold-and-snow season?

- Why don't outdoor and garden retailers branch out into home delivery of potted plants and flowers, soil and mulch, and other products—cumbersome, heavy products—that PrimeTime Women want as spring rolls around?

- A PrimeTime Woman named Adrienne Simpson of Stone Mountain, Georgia, just started a new moving company that helps the 50+ market not just pack and move but also set up their new homes. Her company can even set up the new home just like the old home for sight-impaired persons who need that consistency.

- Consumer electronics companies and home improvement stores should combine forces to take advantage of the tremendous amount of money being spent by midlifers on upgrading their current and second homes. Empty nesters and Baby Boomers are finding a new purpose for vacant rooms instead of selling their four-bedroom homes. They are installing "specialty rooms and spaces": home theaters, game rooms, exercise rooms, outdoor living areas (with every comfort and all possible technology), dance rooms, basketball courts, yoga rooms, home spas, bar rooms, and so on. Don't let PrimeTime Women be Do-it-Yourselfers. Do it for them!

Those are just a few examples of ways that companies could go beyond customer service (the price of entry onto the playing field) to "customer *services*" (the much more appreciated competitive edge that will score you a goal).

Safety

PrimeTime Women want to shop in a safe and secure environment, especially if they are on their own. Make sure that the parking lot, entryway, stairs, and escalators are clean, ice-free in the winter, and made safer with handrails and railings. Make sure the parking lot is well-lit and provide "greeters" who not only say "hello" when they arrive, but who also walk PrimeTime Women customers to their cars when they are done shopping.

Tool #8: Selling Skills

Face–to-face selling with PrimeTime Women customers takes place not just in retail but also in insurance, investments, auto, home sales, remodeling, banking, and so on. It's time to roll out the welcome mat, and here are some helpful tips.

Hospitality

If she has come to your place of business, have the good manners and good sense to make sure she's comfortable. If it's warm out, offer her a cold drink. If it's cool out, offer her some coffee. Offer a place of privacy to discuss her needs. Make sure there is seating in a waiting area. And let her use the ladies' room before or after her visit. Treat her like you would a guest in your own home.

Listen

Recognize that women often communicate via the "story of their lives." A lot of salesmen are puzzled by this "life story" thing that women do. *If she wants to buy a car, a hammer, or an insurance policy, why is she telling about how her twins just left for college, when they bought their house, or how her dad is doing with Alzheimer's?* Because she's telling you what she is going to use your product or service for, in the context of her life, in the context of the people in her life, and in the context of her needs. That's how women think and communicate, in both contextual and people terms. They are not making small talk. You need to listen for cues to her needs, wants, and worries.

- **Nonverbal cues:** In face-to-face selling, it's important to recognize what PrimeTime Women are trying to tell you with their face and body language. When women listen to another person, male or female, they use furthering phrases ("I see . . . "), make acknowledgment noises ("umhum"), and do a lot of "face work"—smiles, nods, and empathetic expressions—to show they're tracking with the conversation and to encourage the speaker to continue. In the male gender culture, nodding means "yes." In female culture, it means "go on, I'm listening." Nodding comes naturally to women—it's the default position. What you want to watch out for is when she stops nodding. That means "Stop. I've been waiting to say something for the past 10 minutes, but you haven't taken a breath."

- **Details matter:** Many men jump in prematurely with an answer. They listen to the first few things and figure they should stay focused on the "important" stuff. But women have a longer list—they care about all the same things as men, and then some. This is the deciding factor. Cutting her off before she gets through her list is a bad idea.

Presenting Your Products

Present the human benefits, not the product features, in the context of the lifestyle needs that she already told you. Don't use the canned pitch; personalize your pitch based on what she's telling you. Offer options for her to consider—but make it only two options because the PrimeTime Women's purchase process is shorter and simpler now—with the pros and cons of each, so she can feel that she has a comprehensive grasp of specifics and has done "due diligence."

Follow-Up

PrimeTime Women's decision process is shorter than younger women's, but just because she doesn't buy after the first conversation doesn't mean that she is not interested. It probably just means she's busy. Be sure to follow up in the way that indicates that it's for *her* benefit, not yours: "I was thinking about you today when I read an article on second homes" versus "We're coming up on the end of the month, and I really need to close all my open business."

Small Thank-You Gift

Saying thank you with a small gift can lead to a big payoff. Thanking PrimeTime Women for their business with something to surprise and delight them will lead to word of mouth and many positive recommendations to their friends and expanded networks. This is a much better way to ensure referrals than by asking for them. A small thank-you gift can be anything from a beautiful Tiffany key chain attached to the keys of her brand new car to a bottle of wine at the close of the sale of her new house to a gift certificate for a romantic dinner at a local restaurant upon the completion of financing the kids' college educations.

Selling to Couples

Selling to couples can be tricky business. When the couple is buying something for *her*—*her* car, *her* computer, *her* new kitchen, if the salesman talks to the husband, he gets one warning, often from the husband. If he continues, she leaves. There is no room for mistakes here. When the couple is buying for *him,* you still need to talk to *her.* Whether it's a big screen TV or a yacht, the PrimeTime wife needs to be sold to also. There once was a young yacht salesman who figured out how to sell to couples. He said that he doesn't target the husband; he already wants the boat. He sells to the wife because she's the one who needs to be convinced. And he became one of the most successful yacht salesmen in his company using this strategy. The moral of the story is that PrimeTime Women have enormous influence on conventionally male big-ticket items as well.

Tool #9: Event Marketing

Event marketing works to attract customers and build brands through borrowed interest and affinity. The benefits of event marketing are:

- *visibility* at the event and prior to the event via PR and advertising;

- *traffic-building* at retail, or lead generation for nonretail businesses;

- *face-to-face networking* as you meet and connect with your prime prospects; and

- *hands-on interaction with your product.* From computers to refrigerators, from cosmetics to energy drinks, consumers are more likely to buy when they have had the chance to sample and try.

PrimeTime Women are more likely to be responsive to event marketing because

- they have more time and money than when they were younger and

- older consumers are in the market for great experiences.

Fun, Learning, Social

Here are the key insights to leverage in event marketing to appeal to all women, and to PrimeTime Women in particular.

Fun. Make the event about more than just distributing information and products; make it fun and memorable and interactive. Make the topic more appealing by renaming and repositioning; for example, turn a "conference on health foods" into a "Fit & Fabulous Health & Wellness Expo." Provide entertainment such as a concert. Provide an interactive activity such as jewelry shopping, a sailing excursion, or wine tasting.

Learning. Women in general, and PrimeTime Women in particular, are into lifelong learning. Provide an educational experience for them. Offer a mini seminar in how to buy art, or about mother-daughter relationships, or on "amazing things invented by women, such as Kevlar," or about computers.

When it comes to choosing your topics for fun and learning, it is important to align with the interests and inclinations of PrimeTime Women vs. younger women. There should be less mating, dating, kids, and career-building and more health, wealth, self-actualization, what to do with the second half of your life, and personal and public legacy.

Social. There are two kinds of socialization that can be leveraged via event marketing.

- Bring a friend: PrimeTime Women are always looking for interesting activities to do with girlfriends, so they will welcome a unique event to attend.

- Make a friend: Chemistry and bonding at all-women events is radically different from mixed or mostly male events. This was quite evident in our Girlfriend Groups. By the time the focus groups were over, these PrimeTime Women who had been strangers just two hours ago were exchanging phone numbers, agreeing to meet for coffee, and talking about their families and their passions like old friends.

There are two kinds of event marketing, solo and syndicated.

Solo

With solo events, you create your own event and therefore have total control over branding and the brand experience. The event will provide you with solo visibility and an uncluttered effect on consumers.

The Nike Women's Marathon is a great example of a strongly branded and executed solo event. While it is not necessarily targeted to PrimeTime Women, many of the participants fit this profile, based on what I have seen on the Web site. I've included this example of event marketing because it is a best practices case study of leveraging several GenderTrends principles.

- *Corporate halo:* The race benefits the Leukemia & Lymphoma Society, the world's largest voluntary health organization dedicated to funding blood cancer research.

- *Storytelling:* The Nike Women's Marathon Web site features amazing stories from real women that are mind-changing and life-affirming. The hundreds of stories are listed as links with a memorable first line for each story such as "Began running in my 70s," "In memory of my son Nick," "Set an example for healthy living," and "Training with six other women." You can't help but click on them all!

- *Motivations:* The Nike Women's Marathon captures many female motivations to participate. Some love to run just for the heck of it, some seek goals to accomplish, some run in honor of survivors, some run in memory of loved ones, some run to bathe in the beauty of San Francisco, some run to lose weight and gain a fitness routine for life, some run to be social and to train with friends. No matter the reasons, the Nike Women's Marathon has got them covered.

- *Female-friendly surprise and delights:* This event would be just an ordinary marathon without the specific female-friendly spin Nike has added to every element. Take the Chocolate Mile, for instance, where Ghirardelli gives out chocolate treats for an entire mile. And the feet pampering pedicare stations midway make tired feet finish the race. And finally, each woman who crosses the finish line gets a beautiful silver necklace from Tiffany (blue box and all).

The Office Depot Success Strategies for Businesswomen Conference is also a great solo event. It is an annual conference targeted to women business owners. Here are some highlights:

- The keynote speakers are inspirational accomplished women with a message (e.g., Barbara Walters, Hillary Clinton, Lily Tomlin, Christine Todd Whitman, B. Smith, Barbara K, and Katie Couric).

- There are breakout sessions that feature action-oriented learning that women business owners can take home and apply.

- There are a lot of networking opportunities.

- There is some fun mixed in too—from the shopping expo where participants can buy from other women business owners to the silent auction to benefit Count Me In, a nonprofit organization that provides nationwide access to micro loans, business consultation, and education for women entrepreneurs.

- Office Depot does more corporate halo as well; it sponsored Dress for Success, a nonprofit organization that offers interview suits, confidence boosts, and career development to low-income women seeking employment, and women business owners were invited to bring donations of jewelry, scarves, and accessories.

Syndicated

With syndicated events, you join a national or local conference, tour, or expo and share branding and costs with other sponsors of the event. These are much more affordable and much more turn-key.

On a national level, there are events like the Rolling Stones and Jimmy Buffet concert tours, Special Olympics, the Susan G. Komen Breast Cancer Walk, and the American Heart Association's Go Red events, which have taken place throughout the country. This year's big event was Rhapsody in Red, Celebrating How Women Go Red, the first-ever cause-related event/party during New York's Fashion Week, featuring Sigourney Weaver as the hostess.

On a local level, one of the most impressive marketing events I am aware of comes from Berkeley Hall, a luxury golf community located in South Carolina. Tom Swanson, a marketing consultant, helped Berkeley Hall develop a program called Just Rewards, a series of seminars and outings for women only. Swanson told the real estate developer, "Focus on the wives, not on the husbands." The husbands are already sold on Berkeley Hall—it's the wives that need convincing. The strategy behind the event was to expose newcomers to the many benefits and beauty of the community, while creating an experience that would form strong friendship bonds among the 300 or so women attending the event. The Just Rewards program featured fun and learning; women could get a cooking lesson from the chef of a very exclusive restaurant with a months-long waiting list. Ten lucky women could also get hair and wardrobe makeovers by stylist to the stars Jose Eber. In between, there was lunch, kayaking, biking, spa treatments, and so on. There was plenty of time for bonding, and the whole event culminated with a moving poetry reading by poet laureate Maya Angelou. A very select group of additional sponsors were invited to participate in the event, selling only via subtle signage, mind you; Mercedes had its new SUV tranport guests to various community facilites, while a wine distiller got the restaurant and food contracts.

Tool #10: Public Relations/Product Publicity

The goals of PR and product publicity are to ensure a company has a strong public image and that the public is aware of and understands a company's products and services.

PR consists of

- press coverage generated to promote a company's corporate image, highlighting all of its good points, and

- crisis management to explain the situation from the company's point of view, talk about what action is being taken, and to accept responsibility for the bad news.

Product publicity consists of

- press coverage to increase a product's visibility as well as add credibility via a third party endorsement, and

- "on the street" type programs that create word-of-mouth buzz and augment a product and brand's personality and street credentials.

In order to generate press coverage that not only compels an editor or publisher to use it but also motivates the reader to read it, you can't just write press releases about your product. It's got to be a human interest story about your prospect, about "authentic" Prime-Time Women. Here's how to make your story more relevant for PrimeTime Women.

- **Use storytelling and anecdotes:** Build commonality with your audience by sharing secrets and surprises that make them feel "she's just like me."

- **Capture their emotions and feelings:** When you quote, make the speakers "excited," "relieved," "surprised," etc.

- **Focus on "real" people:** Use some descriptions that will dimensionalize them. Don't just say, "Susie Cook, 56, said _____." (and please not "Susie Cook, perky redhead,") but perhaps "Susie Cook, 56 and an avid cyclist and Bruce Springsteen fan . . . "

- **Provide a lot of information:** PrimeTime Women are lifelong learners and keep physical, mental, and electronic drawers full of magazine and newspaper clippings of information they "might just need someday," for gift giving, party planning, travel itineraries, etc.

- **Community/civic activism:** Why not create a PrimeTime Women's advisory panel? Your company can get some of the healthiest, wealthiest, most active, educated, and influential PrimeTime Women in your community (and beyond) on a board to aid in product development, respond to surveys, test products, react to marketing campaigns, and generally have a voice in how your company can meet their needs. Look for local PrimeTime Women business owners as examples and mentors who can help lead your company down the Prime-Time path. This not only makes for a great PR story, but it also creates word of mouth among their PrimeTime Women peers.

- **Expert testimonials and credentials:** Remember that Prime-Time Women are searching for The Perfect Answer *Now* and will be doing "due diligence" and comparison shopping in order to get there. One of the ways to get them to the Perfect Answer *Now* is through expert testimonials and credentials. Doctors can answer menopausal questions and make recommendations with authority. Life planning experts can do Q&A in editorials regarding how to make the transition smoothly to a PrimeTime Woman. Psychologists can elaborate on "why" PrimeTime Women are experiencing the different developmental phases in their lives. Financial experts can speak to the financial tools and solutions PrimeTime Women can use to balance their portfolios. Dietitians can delve into the different health and wellness needs of PrimeTime Women. Travel experts can suggest some wonderful PrimeTime pleasurable pursuits. All of these experts can be great assets in your PR plan.

Tool #11: Sponsorships and Alliances

The key benefits of sponsorships and alliances are

- visibility,

- affinity, and

- cost efficiency.

Sponsorships

- **Visibility:** One of the most powerful advantages to sponsorship is the increased exposure gained from the borrowed interest of the big-name event or program being sponsored. But note that PrimeTime Women have different interests than younger women. It's no longer about sponsoring the latest Disney movie release or McDonalds Happy Meal. Try sponsoring relevant concerts (Barbra Streisand, Eric Clapton, Paul McCartney), museum tours (Jacqueline Kennedy: The White House Years dress exhibit), and sports events (Nike Women's Marathon).

- **Affinity:** By affiliating with something she cares about, a brand can gain PrimeTime Women's affection and become a brand she cares about as well. This is where PrimeTime Women's desire to create and leave a legacy becomes a powerful insight. The cause marketing ideas discussed earlier in this chapter are great ways to create affinity with PrimeTime Women who want to improve people's lives, be it their own offspring or other people's.

Using the more personal notion of legacy, wanting descendants to know "who I am," companies can sponsor programs that inspire PrimeTime Women to create and share their life stories. Saturn sponsors the NPR initiative called StoryCorps. What started as a booth in New York's Grand Central Station has transformed into two mobile story booths on wheels, crisscrossing the country, collecting the stories of everyday Americans. StoryCorps' mission is to instruct and inspire Americans to record one another's stories in sound. They have made it as easy as possible by helping customers ask the best questions. At the end of the hour-long session and with a $10 donation, customers get a copy of their interview on CD. StoryCorps will also add each interview to the StoryCorps Archive, housed at the American Folklife Center at the Library of Congress, with the goal of it becoming nothing less than an oral history of America. StoryCorps' vision sounds like it's perfect for Prime-Time Women: "We've found that the process of interviewing a friend, neighbor, or family member can have a profound impact on both the interviewer and interviewee. We've seen people change, friendships grow, families walk away feeling closer, understanding each other better. Listening, after all, is an act of love."[3] What if "time keepers" such as Timex or Citizen sponsored StoryCorps or another type of "family history/ life story" service and offered a lifetime of "time"? That would be an emotionally charged sponsorship that PrimeTime Women would certainly care about.

- **Cost efficiency:** One benefit of multisponsor programs is syndicated budgets; by everyone chipping in and sharing costs of building visibility/awareness, everyone gets more bang for the collective buck.

Alliances

On a smaller scale, companies can get many of the same benefits of sponsorships through alliances with other noncompeting companies with similar PrimeTime Women prospect profiles and compatible brand personalities. The benefits of alliances are

- *Visibility:* Expand reach by cross-marketing via each other's customer communications—direct mail inserts, Web site links, mention in collateral, in promotions, etc.

- *Affinity:* Select a partner with established positive equity with PrimeTime Women (Curves, New Balance, Chico's, etc.).

- *Cost efficiency:* Share costs of joint marketing initiatives.

There are many considerations and options for choosing companies to partner with to reach PrimeTime Women.

Partner for Borrowed Interest.   Look for companies that have something in common.

- Tie in with wine and champagne companies that give Prime-Time Women tools for celebration.

- Align with toy companies that give grandparents the thrill of spoiling their grandchildren.

- Partner with hospitality companies (e.g., hotels and cruise lines) that bring PrimeTime Women closer to their families, to their friends, and to their dream vacations.

- A great example of a borrowed interest alliance that worked well with PrimeTime Women comes from William Blair, the financial services company, and Tiffany, the jeweler. Tiffany provided the venue, catering, and an Elsa Peretti trunk show. William Blair delivered attendance of a select group of highly affluent women. There was no selling involved, strictly networking and getting to know potential customers. The women were invited to tell a friend and bring a friend. Each company benefited from the cachet of the other and the opportunity to build relationships with a highly qualified group of PrimeTime Women prospects.

Partner for Concept Compatibility. Tie in with health and beauty companies that cater to PrimeTime Women's changing wellness needs. For example, what if Dove Calming Night lotion partnered with the manufacturer of "Hot Mama Menopause Pajamas" to create a "Cool Nights" promotional program? That may sound like a crazy "niche" idea. But remember, 100 percent of women go through menopause. That's more than 50 percent of the booming 50+ population. PrimeTime Women are not a niche!

Partner for Reach and Credibility. A recent study shows that 86 percent of 50+ consumers say that endorsements from a senior organization such as AARP influence their purchasing decision.[4] Home Depot is one of the first to jump on board, with its partnership with AARP to create workshops, products, and in-store marketing materials.

Other powerful PrimeTime Women's organizations to partner with are the established businesswomen's organizations such as the National Association of Women Business Owners (NAWBO) and the National Association for Female Executives (NAFE). Current corporate partners of NAWBO are American Express, Wachovia, Wells Fargo, Principal Financial Group, Office Depot, Guardian Life Insurance of America, Mirrasou Winery, Verizon SuperPages, Wal-Mart, the U.S. Postal Service, UPS, AT&T, AXA, and CNA. Current corporate partners of NAFE are AXA Advisors, Geico, Motorola, Office Depot, Office Team, the WNBA, bizwomen.com, and the National Women's History Museum. However, don't just offer discounts. Develop creative and interactive programs that allow PrimeTime Women to benefit from these networks of extraordinary women.

Tool #12: E-marketing

The unique capabilities of e-marketing are:

- *Linkage/Targeting:* Consumer choice is optimized online, and therefore advertising, PR, and search capabilities can all be much more highly targeted.

- *Low cost:* E-marketing can deliver depth of information, customized information such as entry pages and recommendations, added value via wish lists, comparison tools, etc.—all with a relatively small marketing investment.

- *Immediacy:* Consumers can buy, download, read right now because e-marketing operates on "my time."

- *Referability:* Consumers can forward Web pages, e-mail newsletters, wish lists, etc.

- *Multimedia:* You get sound, video, animation, games, live action Web cams, etc., all on one multimedia screen.

- *Interactivity:* Live chat customer service, community functions (e.g., chat rooms, social networking), online surveys and consumer research, education, engagement, games, and user reviews all contribute to the growing interactivity of e-marketing on the Internet.

- *Multi-user networking:* Consumers can share photos, jokes, videos, and play real-time games with multiple friends (and strangers).

Younger generations have a tendency to look down their noses at their elders when it comes to acceptance and use of new technology. Contrary to popular opinion, when it comes to computers, PDAs, and the Internet, PrimeTimers are all over it. Younger Prime-Timers (50–59) grew up with computers, and the Internet has become an essential part of their lives. Elder PrimeTimers adapted later, but are rapidly coming online. Here are the latest usage stats and projections:

- Almost 92 percent of Boomers own a computer.[5]

- By 2008, 74 percent of 50- to 64-year-olds will be online, a steady rise from the 62 percent who were online in 2003.[6]

- Over the next 15 years, the 50- to 64-year-old online market will grow 50 percent and the 65+ market will grow 32 percent, while the 18–40 market will grow only 3 percent.[7]

- Forty-two percent of those over 55 say they've bought something online.[8]

The majority of PrimeTimers are already eagerly availing themselves of the benefits of the Internet, as shown in the chart below.

Activity	51–59 year olds	60–69 year olds
Use e-mail	94%	90%
Get health info on at least one topic	84	68
Product research	79	74
Go online	75	54
Get news	70	74
Online purchase	67	65
Make travel reservations	64	59
Use government sites	60	55
Do job research	54	31

Source: Pew Internet, Generations Online, December 2005

Expect to see acceleration, as PrimeTime Women wander the Web filling their newly free time and wielding their newly fat wallets. PrimeTime Women, not men, are driving the growth trends on the World Wide Web. While women in general are catching up to men in Internet usage, PrimeTime Women in particular have surpassed men: 66 percent of women ages 50–64 are online vs. 63 percent of men the same age.[9] According to Leslie Harris in *After 50: How the Baby Boom Will Redefine the Mature Market*, Boomer women are substantially heavier users of the Internet than their male counterparts; 21 percent of women who are Internet subscribers are online for more than 20 hours per week, while no men indicated that use frequency.[10]

Why Online

PrimeTime Women use the Internet specifically for the following:

- **Connectivity:** It's all about creating community. PrimeTime Women want to connect with family and friends via e-mail, photo sharing, Web cameras, etc. They especially want to create a bond with their grandkids, given their desire for leaving a personal legacy. The marketing manifestations of this insight are chat rooms, community pages, user groups, social networking sites, etc. I predict that there will be a new and uniquely PrimeTime version of MySpace.com, focused on PrimeTime users who have new interests and activities they want to share and new problems and challenges they want help solving. (As we go to press, the enormously successful founder of Monster .com, Jeff Taylor, just announced the launch of his next company, Eons.com, a "50+ media company inspiring a generation of boomers and seniors to live the biggest life possible." It has received a lot of press and is being touted as a MySpace-style social networking Web site for PrimeTimers. The site boasts all the functionality of kids' networking sites, including the chance to blog, join groups, and meet people. The truly PrimeTime highlights are: a Longevity Calculator, obit alerts, a group dedicated to walking, and a daily jigsaw puzzle to keep mature brains thriving. So, my prediction has already come true.)

- **Commerce:** PrimeTime Women like the convenience and comparison shopping of the Internet and also look for peer reviews and user recommendations as part of their online purchase process.

- **Research:** PrimeTime Women are pursuing new interests, passions, and dreams; they are facing new challenges and the fear of the unknown in certain life-stages. They are also buying new products in new categories based on new needs, and therefore are making new and different brand choices as well. The Internet provides them with a useful research tool to guide them in their second adulthood.

- **Dating:** Match.com and eHarmony.com have huge 50+ communities. That's largely because more Boomers are single than any previous cohort of 40- to 60-year-olds. According to the U.S. Census Bureau, 29 percent of adults age 45 to 59 were unattached in 2003, compared to only 19 percent in 1980.[11] People over 50 make up Match.com's fastest-growing segment, with a 300 percent increase since 2000. Some sites cater primarily to PrimeTimers, such as PrimeSingles.net.[12]

- **Gaming:** According to Peter D. Hart of Research Associates, some 19 percent of gamers are over 50.[13] There are even Web sites dedicated to PrimeTimer games, such as geezergamers .com. Wouldn't it be great for game developers to create real-time games for grandchildren and grandparents to play so Grandma Katie and her grandson can connect by having a game of Monopoly at 4 PM every Thursday?

Insights

Women respond to different Web site elements and approaches than men. Consider the following in your e-marketing.

- **People power:** Show images of your customer and of your company to put a human face on your Web site and dimensionalize yourself and your products and services. In addition, focus on consumer benefits, not product attributes. Does a PrimeTime Woman care if a Web cam has a 1.3 megapixel CCD image sensor? No way. She cares if the images of her grandchildren will be crystal clear on the Web cam when she "calls" them every Sunday morning. Women prefer to get their information from people rather than static brochures that don't answer all of their questions. Offer "Help" with online live chats with customer service or a 1-800-number that is easy to find right away. One consumer electronics site that is using people power positively is Philips Electronics. While most electronics sites feature giant images of their products with nary a consumer in sight, the Philips site is full of images—great visuals from the World Cup, which it sponsors, romantic images of landmarks around the world, which it lights—and, accompanying an image of an adorable infant, Philips promotes its "sense and simplicity" campaign which is more than a brand promise; it is actually a company mission to make simplicity the goal of Philips' technology. As can be expected, iPod's Web site carries on with its iconic "silhouettes" marketing campaign in which consumers can easily see themselves dancing and swaying to the beat.

- **Storytelling:** Use the latest and greatest technology to tell your brand's story. Video clips and audio downloads of testimonials bring customers' stories to life like never before. Target recently launched a new section on their Web site sure to appeal to PrimeTime Women. It's called "Every Day Stories," and it features real and personal accounts of people in the many Target communities who are being helped by the various Target charitable programs. Take Allison's story, for example. She is a breast cancer survivor and found a special Target in Times Square that is devoted to benefiting the Breast Cancer Research Foundation. Or read PrimeTime Woman Gail's story. Through a Target grant, she is turning the wasted space behind her classroom into a mural to help tell the town's history and leave a legacy. The stories are told by "turning pages" in a bright red covered "book" on Target's Web site.

- **Due diligence/comparisons:** Many shopping portals and search sites offer price comparison charts so consumers don't have to search 10 different sites to compare prices themselves. Doctors Foster & Smith pet supplies have a Web site that provides a comprehensive yet easy to understand product/brand comparison for every category from heart worm to flea and tick control.

- **Integration/In Context:** So many Web sites try to sell products photographed against a black and white background. Why not show the product "in situ," with a PrimeTime Woman actually using it? I can't tell you how many times I have logged off of eBay or other sites because I couldn't tell about the size and usefulness of a product the way it was shown online.

- **Commonality/word of mouth:** Boomerwomenspeak.com is an online community of PrimeTime girlfriends and is the number one hit for the key phrase "Baby Boomer Women" in search engines. By the end of 2005, it was receiving between 1.1 and 1.6 million hits per month. The site has grown mainly through networking, which helps it get linked to many others, as well as through word of mouth. As site founder Dotsie Bregel says, "They share their experiences and encourage, inform, and inspire one another on a whole host of areas important to women, including parents, retirement, careers, health, sex, even cosmetic surgery and more." Based on the success of her first site, Bregel launched the National Association of Baby Boomer Women (*www.nabbw.com*), which offers networking opportunities, personal and professional advice, and product and service discounts.[14]

  Another great Web site that caters to PrimeTime Women is thirdage.com. Trendsetting founder and president Sharon Whitely was inspired by the French term "Troisième Âge," which refers to the concept of lifelong learning, self-development, and fulfillment, and the period of life following young adulthood yet preceding "seniorhood" and retirement. The site has everything from health alerts to relationship advice, from online classes in finances and computers to beauty advice. At the center of ThirdAge.com is a vibrant community where ThirdAgers can voice their opinions, recount experiences, and share advice in chat rooms and discussion boards. Subjects range from contemporary and political issues to specific life-stage concerns.

- **Research:** Like most women, PrimeTime Women not only want to share with each other, they are more than ready and willing to share with marketers as well. W Network, the Canadian television network dedicated to bringing women the best entertainment that television has to offer, conducts regular surveys with its panel of more than 2,300 women of all ages and usually gets about a 55 percent response rate. Fascinating results from their latest survey were shared at the *Strategy* magazine "Understanding Women" conference, about women's views on home, career, friends, and parenting. Your company can share the results of the surveys and even offer occasional "Surprise and Delight" sampling to get these PrimeTime Women to give you their opinions.

Some of the Web sites our PrimeTime Women research participants mentioned as favorites are: redenvelope.com, itunes.com, talbots.com, potterybarn.com, realsimple.com, amazon.com, netflix.com, evite.com, expedia.com, orbitz.com, google.com, foodtv.com, coolrunning.com, and zappos.com.

* * *

The GenderTrends Model helps you enhance the impact of every element in your marketing mix with all women. In the next chapter you will see two stellar examples of companies who have taken the GenderTrends insights and created fully integrated marketing plans that have been hugely successful with PrimeTime Women. Be inspired!

In Depth and Integrated Case Studies— Best Practices in Marketing to PrimeTime Women

People ask me all the time: "Marti, what are some examples of companies that are doing a good job marketing to PrimeTime Women?" Reasonable question . . . but one to which I have very few good answers.

Of course, five years ago, I had the same conundrum when people would ask me who was doing a good job marketing to women in general. "Well," I would say, "there are a few companies that are doing an interesting initiative here, a progressive program there . . . But as for companies that have made a *commitment* to marketing to women, and really gotten their organization behind a comprehensive effort? Not so many."

Today, there are lots. I like to think I helped with that a bit. Once you looked at the numbers, there could be no question of the market opportunity. But people didn't have any thinking or guidelines about whether or how to market to women differently.

As a marketing opportunity, PrimeTime Women is up against the dual barrier that not only are companies unsure of how to market to them, very few of them even recognize PrimeTime Women as the "golden bull's-eye" target market that it is.

When I went searching for case studies to illustrate exceptional marketing to PrimeTime Women, I was once again hard pressed to come up with many comprehensive, fully integrated examples, let alone exceptional examples. As you've seen throughout this book, there are a number of companies that have dipped a toe into the water—created terrific ads or an excellent event or a strong corporate halo program—but few that have jumped into the big pool with a splash.

That said, there are two companies that stand out as truly exceptional—Curves fitness franchise and MassMutual financial services. They have taken all of the lessons from Chapter 8 and applied them to their marketing plans with brilliant results. Each of these companies has a strong understanding of the PrimeTime Woman prospect and has created a comprehensive, well–thought-out, well-executed marketing plan.

Notice that I say "plan," by the way, not "initiative." The distinction is that each of these companies focuses on women as an integral part of their corporate DNA. Their female-targeted programs and communications are built into the company strategy and growth plan, not this year's "program du jour."

As you will see, every element of their marketing programs tie tightly together, so the total effect to the PrimeTime Woman consumer is "one look, one voice." The consistency of their message and brand personality is as much a part of their success as the strength of the individual elements.

So let's jump in and learn the best practices of two very smart companies.

Curves Gets PrimeTime Women's Marketing in Shape

Opportunity

PrimeTime Americans are flocking to exercise clubs and activities in droves. More than half of health club members are over 40;[1] 25 percent of members are people over 55, which is a 120 index versus the total population (meaning people over 55 are 20 percent more likely than average to belong to a health club).[2] People over 55 are the fastest-growing segment of health club members,[3] and the number of "frequent participants" over 55 zoomed 33 percent from 1998 to 2004, vs. zero growth in the 18–34 year old group.[4]

PrimeTime Women in particular are seeking out more ways to stay in shape. They are more conscientious when it comes to both nutrition and wellness behaviors and, as discussed in Chapter 4, more likely to exercise regularly than either midlife men *or* younger women.

According to the International Health, Racquet & Sportsclub Association, the latest numbers for gym membership among women aged 45 to 64 show a 51 percent rise between 2000 and 2004.[5]

Curves is the first fitness and weight-loss facility dedicated to providing affordable, one-stop exercise and nutritional information for women, primarily women over 35. Launched in 1995 by Diane and Gary Heavin (pronounced "haven," which seems particularly appropriate to the concept they created), today Curves is the largest fitness franchise in the world with over 9,500 locations. A core part of the company's mission is to "strengthen women," a memorial to Gary Heavin's mother, who died prematurely of hypertension when he was 13.

While Curves is not focused exclusively on PrimeTime Women, most of their membership falls within this range, and their wonderfully empathetic and "authentic" marketing does a great job of including PrimeTime Women in all aspects of the club.

Strategies

Gary and Diane realized that many women, especially those over 35, didn't feel comfortable working out in any of the health club facilities available at the time, which were either trendy venues filled with sleek young "hardbodies" in unitards or "manly man" gyms where power, sweat, and testosterone ruled. The couple resolved to change the entire exercise category for women, PrimeTime Women included.

Curves Changed the Size, Scope, and Affordability of Fitness Clubs. They made smaller clubs, with less equipment, so they were affordable not only for women to join as members but also for women to buy and run as franchisees.

Curves Changed the Accessibility of Fitness Clubs. They started out offering their unique program in small towns that had no other fitness facilities and have now expanded to bigger cities as well.

Curves Changed the Format. They created a unique 30-minute "round robin" of machines designed specifically for women and requiring no complicated adjustments to move from one piece of equipment to the next. Women spend five minutes at each station and zip through an effective aerobic and strength training workout.

Curves Changed the Atmosphere. Curves is all about building community. The laughter, conversation, and sense of support that is seen at a typical Curves is different from any other health club.

Curves Also Changed the Way Franchises Work. Curves International Inc., the corporate office, provides extensive support to its franchisees around the world. It offers free training, classes in sales and other business strategies, and provides mentors at the start and throughout a franchisee's ownership experience.

Marketing Tactics

Positioning. The very name of this company, "Curves," speaks to the "craving authenticity" principle—it celebrates the shape of "average women." Curves has been built with a truly empathetic positioning, as a place where women of all ages and sizes can feel comfortable working out in a unique, noncompetitive, supportive atmosphere. As the Curves Web site says, "Only one place can give you the strength of over 4 million women."

Advertising. Curves' vivacious and energetic advertising showcases many PrimeTime Women principles in action—people power, girlfriends, warmth, commonality, empathy, and authenticity. Part of the Curves appeal is its use of real women rather than models, including PrimeTime Women. There are no wannabe actresses with perfect skin and 24-inch waists—just real women, which is welcome and reassuring to prospective Curves members. In fact, Curves used size 14 women in its advertising well before Dove did. It's easy for PrimeTime Women to see themselves joining, fitting in, and having fun at Curves.

Product. The 30-minute round robin "circle" system is built around easy-to-learn hydraulic resistance machines, so there are no cumbersome weight stacks to change or manage. This system is truly unique and leverages many PrimeTime Women insights:

- *Saves Time:* Women are busy, and this half-hour program is certainly a welcome change from the intensive hour-long (or more) classes many gyms offer. Curves has figured out how to save women time.

- *Community:* Women can stop by anytime, but most have a routine—they come in after taking the kids to school, at their lunch hour, or after work—so they tend to see the same women there each time they go. This builds a sense of community.

- *Empathy:* The circle is key. As it says on Curves' Web site: "One of the reasons Curves works is that we are women in a circle. For centuries women have sat in circles and shared their wisdom and support. Here we exercise in a circle and, whether we talk to each other or not, we are face to face supporting each other by our energy and our presence. In this circle as with circles of yore, we are not alone." (See Figure 9.1.)

- *Girlfriends:* All of this results in close friendships. Often, Curves members get together socially outside of the facility. In addition, Curves members make it a point to visit Curves locations in other cities and even in other countries, to share the sisterhood. One woman on a "round the world" trip visited 27 Curves locations on her travels!

Promotion.

- *Partnerships:* In 2005 and 2006, Curves joined forces with the "Got Milk?" marketers to promote the Great American Weight Loss Challenge. The promotion employs the principles of storytelling, girlfriends, empathy, and female-friendly prizes to make Curves' marketing more compelling to women everywhere.

FIGURE 9.1 Curves: The Circle

Curves International, Inc.

The campaign promoted drinking "24 ounces in 24 hours," a clever way to update the way you say "three 8-ounce glasses of water a day"—and featured a promotion to win one of 24 shopping sprees worth $2,400 and a 24-month Curves membership.

A promotional brochure alongside the milk display in grocery stores featured three women's "journals" of their weight loss journey. Part of the weight loss plan was focused on exercise, and Curves was featured in their storytelling "journals" along with a coupon for one free week at Curves.

- *Merchandise Incentives:* Curves has a tiered system of Curves-branded merchandise rewards as incentives for members to persist in striving for their goals—items such as clothing, lotion, candles, water bottles, T-shirts, socks, and sweat bands. These products are available only to members who have reached certain goals, so they are exclusive, very sought after, and publicly worn with pride.

- *Team Contests:* Throughout the year, Curves has different challenge periods during which members form teams that compete for prizes. Sometimes teams win by losing pounds, sometimes by losing inches, collecting labels, or other tactics. This brilliantly leverages women's sense of community (whereas for men it would be leveraging their sense of competition), because any woman who might be tempted to let herself slip on her own goals for a few days is going to think a lot more seriously about letting her team down.

Word of Mouth. Members become Curves' best advocates when they invite friends to join them. The Buddy Referral program offers members "Bring a Friend" coupons for one week of free workouts so members can invite friends to give the club a try. Curves' phenomenal conversion rate of 80 percent—8 out of 10 referrals sign up to join as members—reflects the appeal of the concept and the persuasiveness of the "member ambassadors."

Web Site. Curves' public Web site exemplifies how to leverage social values to communicate with PrimeTime Women, as it taps into people power, storytelling, warmth, authenticity, empathy, and inspiration. The video testimonials on the Web site feature PrimeTime and younger members describing warmly and naturally how wonderful their Curves experience has been. In addition, the Web site features images of women who are real Curves members and recounts the stories of not only their achievements but also the hardships they faced en route to their goals. These stories and their credibility are what makes the Curves experience so tangible and believable.

Mycurves.com. Curves just launched this new private, members-only Web site that extends all that is good about the Curves experience to the online environment. It provides success stories, articles, and recipes, and offers interactive tools to help members reach their goals—such as a calorie burn calculator and shopping lists. MyCurves.com will help members find the support they need when they're not at Curves, from other members across the country, and on the other side of the world.

Product Extensions. Curves has been so successful that it has been proud to launch several product extensions that carry its name and values.

- *"diane" Magazine:* An award-winning quarterly magazine just for members, "diane" features people power, storytelling in the form of real success stories, and helpful articles on everything from caregiving to friendships, from depression to making a difference after Hurricane Katrina.

- *Curvestravel.com:* It's a new company to provide travel services and special deals and discounts to Curves members. With free access to www.curvestravel.com, members can take advantage of special offers and hot deals on vacation packages, cruises, hotels, and rental cars online, as well as group trips.

- *Apparel for Sale:* High-quality Curves branded apparel items are available for purchase by Curves members. These attractive, well-made clothing articles are visible signs of membership. They tap members' sense of community by allowing them to recognize each other outside of the facilities, and they serve as "signage" and invite inquiries about the club from nonmembers.

Alliance—Fitness-Functional Products from Avon. Avon has created exclusive Curves-branded products for women that are meant to be fun as well as functional: a heart rate monitor watch, fitness pedometer, flexibility mat, and thermal waist trimmer, as well as apparel and footwear. The social network of both companies help women embrace and support each other on the journey to "real" wellness.

Corporate Halo Sponsorships. Curves is proud of its corporate donations to worthy causes and takes its community passion down to the franchise level. Every March, when food supplies are lowest in food banks across the country, Curves franchisees do their own food drive and in 2006 gathered more than 11 million pounds of food. Moreover, Curves founders Gary and Diane Heavin announced shortly after Hurricane Katrina hit that they would match donations up to $1,000 per club from their Curves franchisees. More than 2,700

Curves franchises from eight different countries responded by collecting and donating $1.5 million.

Results

Before I tell you about the business results, let me tell you a story of Curves' success in achieving two elements of Gary and Diane's vision to "strengthen women."

First, 90 percent of Curves franchisees are women, and the company has created a profitable and rewarding business opportunity for over 5,000 women business owners.

Second, Curves has provided a women's health opportunity that simply isn't available anywhere else. Here is the story of one remarkable member. Rosa Mustelier was admitted to the ER in early 2004 after suffering continual cold symptoms for years. She could hardly breathe, and at 5 feet and 411 pounds, it wasn't really all that surprising. Doctors told her that her lungs were filled with fluid and that what she needed most was to lose weight. She went home, looked in the Yellow Pages, and found Curves. At first, Rosa was very shy and self-conscious; she'd put her purse right by the front door, and if anyone so much as looked at her she'd grab it and run. She had a hard time with the workout and started slowly on the circuit in order to build up her endurance. Soon she was able to complete the entire circuit. But she still wasn't losing weight; in fact, she was gaining. Julie Preston, the club owner, asked Rosa what she was eating and found out that her diet consisted of one boiled chicken breast for breakfast, one for lunch, and one for dinner. Julie helped Rosa combine the exercise circuit and the Curves weight management program, and she lost 100 pounds in her first five months! But Rosa didn't stop there. She recently got married, and her seamstress told her to stop losing weight because she couldn't size her wedding dress down any more. Rosa is a busy woman who works three jobs— taking care of the elderly, running them to their doctor's appointments and performing other errands for them—but she still finds time to squeeze in her Curves workouts three times a week. Rosa has now lost 231 pounds, 167 inches, and 12 dress sizes! This is a company that changes women's lives.

It took McDonald's 25 years and Subway 26 years to open 6,000 franchises; Curves did it in only seven. Curves is the largest fitness franchise in the world, the 8th largest of any kind in the United States, and the 10th largest in the world. There are more than 4 million members, representing 50 states and 42 foreign countries. In January 2006, Curves received the following accolades in *Entrepreneur* magazine's 27th annual elite Franchise 500 rankings: the No. 1 Fitness Franchise, the No. 1 Low Cost Franchise, the No. 5 Fastest Growing Franchise, the No. 3 Top Global Franchise and the No. 3 Best Franchise overall. The Curves 2004 marketing campaign, "The Power to Amaze," received an EFFIE award and was so successful that it exceeded all measurement metric goals by at least 200 percent, according to Curves' president Mike Raymond.

FIGURE 9.2 Curves: Changing Women's Lives

Curves International, Inc.

MassMutual Helps PrimeTime Women Secure Their Futures

Opportunity

The premise of this book is that PrimeTime Women are perched atop the intersection of the two most powerful consumer opportunities in the world: 50+ households that have most of the money, and women heads of household who spend, save, and invest it. It should come as no surprise that the financial services industry was among the first to wake up, sit up, and get busy.

Households where the head of household is over 50 own up to 79 percent of all financial assets in America.[6] They control 80 percent of all of the money in savings accounts,[7] and 66 percent of all dollars invested in the stock market.[8] Their enormous economic clout will continue to escalate based on increasing income, high net worth, and inheritance of even more assets.

The "power of the purse" also means the power of the credit card, the stock market, the checkbook, and all other financial instruments. In 85 percent of U.S. families, women handle the checking account.[9] Women manage 75 percent of family finances[10] and control or influence 53 percent of family investment descisions.[11]

PrimeTime Women have increasing control over all financial decisions, including long-term asset accumulation like retirement accounts and trusts. Among Boomer women, 80–90 percent have sole or joint responsibility for managing finances in savings accounts, investment accounts, IRAs, 401(k)s, annuities, life insurance, and so on.[12] It's a complicated undertaking and a big responsibility, but unlike previous generations of women, they are equipped with the education, earning power, and work experience to handle it.

Looking ahead to their 70s and 80s, PrimeTime Women will be outliving their husbands by an average of 15 to 18 years, during which time they will have sole control over the jointly accumulated assets of their PrimeTime years.

Strategies

MassMutual Financial Group, a global financial services organization, recognized the PrimeTime Women's market as ripe for potential, and for the moment, poorly served. I say "for the moment" because a good number of their competitors have already initiated programs targeted to "women" in general. It seems likely it won't take them long to locate the low-hanging fruit: PrimeTime Women.

MassMutual's objectives in developing a women's financial program have been

- to break through competitive clutter,

- to establish MassMutual as a trustworthy, useful, and accessible source of financial advice, and

- to motivate women to take action on their financial needs.

MassMutual has made its women's financial program more than just a "niche" initiative. It named its department "Women's Markets" as opposed to "The Women's Initiative" to position their efforts as a long-term commitment, not a short-term program. The department's strategy is summed up on their Web site: *"We understand that, while women share the same goal as men of achieving financial security, they have unique wants, needs and concerns, which shape the way they approach developing a financial strategy, insurance and investing."* MassMutual's efforts center on providing financial education, tools, and support in an understanding environment.

While MassMutual does not focus on PrimeTime Women exclusively, they understand the power of the PrimeTime purse and have concentrated much of their communications and visual materials on the realities of PrimeTime Women.

Marketing Tactics

Positioning. MassMutual's promise statement is captured in their tagline: "You Can't Predict. You Can Prepare." This sentiment is well aligned with PrimeTime Women's experience coping with the unexpected bumps, bounces—and bonuses—of life and creates a bond-building moment of affinity: "Boy, ain't that the truth."

Events/Educational Seminars. One of MassMutual's key tactics is its series of educational financial seminars. The umbrella theme for the seminars has been the memorable imagery from its popular and successful advertising campaign entitled "Never Kissed a Frog. Never Had To." In contrast to other companies' financial seminars, Mass-Mutual set out to differentiate itself through its attitude and format. From the invitations to the advertising, from the refreshments to the giveaways, from the location to the way the information is presented, MassMutual transformed its seminars to be more appealing to women and tapped into their values of people power, authenticity, girl-friends, empathy, emotions, and milestone marketing.

The latest event is called "Pearls of Wisdom:"

- *Invitations:* To differentiate itself from the conventional pre-sentations of competitors' seminars, whose invitations all look like formal, engraved wedding invitations, and to ensure the invitation got opened, MassMutual's envelope featured an illustration of the famous frog—wearing pearls. Inside, the invitations feature visuals of women, including PrimeTime Women. The language used is warm and empathetic and not "sales" focused at all. (See Figure 9.3.)

- *Format and Positioning:* Inside the invitation it says that Pearls of Wisdom is an "entertaining, educational seminar for you" and invites women to join "a circle of like-minded women to share ideas and financial strategies for taking care of the peo-ple who matter most in your lives."

  – The circle is a point of differentiation and interest to women: it's not going to be a "seminar" where everyone sits class-room style facing a presenter—it's going to be a discussion among a group of women who share common interests.

  – The "take care of people who matter most in your life" appeal is focused not on "me," but on "we," as often you can get

FIGURE 9.3 MassMutual Invitation to Seminar

women to take action faster when the need is not for themselves, but for the people they are responsible for.

- *Bring a Friend:* The invitations also invite women to bring their mothers, sisters, or friends.

- *Personalize the Presenter:* And included in the invitation is a photo and short bio of the female financial advisor who will be leading the discussion—not the usual list of financial degrees and accomplishments but personal information about her interests and how she likes to spend her time, a little about her kids, if she has any, and perhaps a note about her philosophies on money, saving, and investing.

- *Storytelling:* The seminar is delivered by the presenter and illustrated by an interactive DVD or CD from which the presenter can choose short videos of 19 women telling their stories, the challenges they are facing, and how these issues impact them financially. The women in the presentation come from all walks of life and include PrimeTime Women.

- *Commonality:* The presenters don't use all 19 stories, of course; to make it easier for them to present the ones most appropriate to a particular audience, the stories are grouped by audience segment. For example, there are three or four stories each for women business owners, for retiring PrimeTime Women, and for professional women. The women in the audience can relate to the Pearls of Wisdom stories and storytellers because they are real. Then, the financial advisors can discuss the financial issues and solutions revealed in the stories in context. This then allows women in the audience to open up with "me too" stories and questions.

- *Female-Friendly Customization:* "Pearls of Wisdom" has been customized so that it can be given in front of any size audience in any location. Some innovative financial advisors have further enhanced the female-friendly atmosphere.

  - For example, one financial advisor had the first "Never Kissed a Frog. Never Had To" seminar in conjunction with a local wine shop and invited women to come for the seminar and for a tasting of Frog's Leap wine.

  - Another financial advisor created a "Fiscal and Physical Fitness" seminar and partnered with a local health club for some fitness and nutrition tips. The seminar was given in the advisor's home, where her chef/husband prepared a gourmet meal for all of the women attendees.

– At the Danskin Women's Triathlon, which MassMutual sponsors, the company puts on a breakfast seminar right before the popular expo on the day before the race. At the seminar, the women triathletes not only get some financial education, they also get a free breakfast, some fun giveaways, an extra $10 donation to the Breast Cancer Research Fund, and their race packet, which means they don't have to wait in line with thousands of other women to get their race information.

Needless to say, MassMutual's unique seminar settings and approach translate into a significantly higher conversion rate than the conventional methods. Inside the company, the top financial advisors—now including men as well as women—are eager to receive and apply the Pearls of Wisdom seminar kits. At the beginning of 2006, MassMutual's corporate headquarters had 1,500 kits to give its financial advisors; by summer they were down to 50.

Online Audio Seminar. The online audio seminar is perfectly formatted with women in mind, as women prefer to get their information from people rather than static pages. So, it is a delight to find that the "Ten Questions" seminar is hosted by Susan Sweetser, a MassMutual second vice president and head of women's markets. Consumers can see her face and her bio right on screen and can connect with her immediately: "I know her." This is much more powerful and motivating than having an anonymous actress present the information. Susan cares about her customers, and it shows. (See Figure 9.4.)

Web Site. MassMutual's Web site does a wonderful job of warming up PrimeTime Women with its use of many PrimeTime Women principles and insights.

- *Visuals:* Images of women, couples, and PrimeTime Women are all used on the Web site, which taps into women's people-orientation and is a strong point of differentiation from the many face-

FIGURE 9.4 MassMutual: Susan Sweetser/Online Audio Seminar

less, hyper-linked, too-much-copy-on-the-screen Web sites out there. These people are "authentic" and look like they are real customers of MassMutal rather than models. (See Figure 9.5.)

- *Focus on the Prospect, Not the Product:* Unlike many financial institutions, MassMutal focuses on the prospect, not the product, as evidenced by the use of customer images, the innovative "Ten Questions" audio seminar, and the use of life events as guideposts to help women decide where to go on the site.

- *Milestone Marketing:* MassMutual has recognized that very often it's a major milestone that triggers a woman's need or decision to act on a financial matter. The Web site lists 16 different events (such as starting a business, needing elder care, and becoming empty nesters), any of which PrimeTime Women might encounter, then goes into detail about which products or services might be beneficial for each milestone. This marketing is very targeted to PrimeTime Women's specific and critical needs.

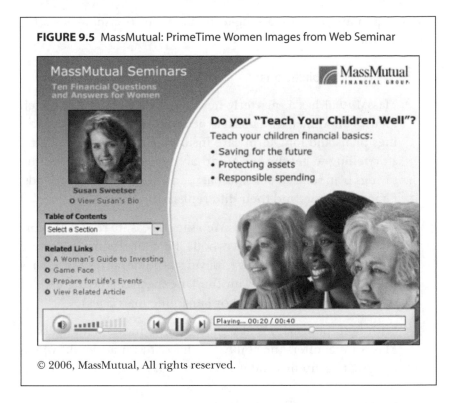

FIGURE 9.5 MassMutual: PrimeTime Women Images from Web Seminar

Sales Process. MassMutual learned through research with women on their advisory boards that selling to women is a completely different process than selling to men. The company took its learnings and developed training programs for their financial advisors to help them succeed with women customers, PrimeTime Women included. For example, women want to learn from a partner, a teacher, someone who can help them make informed decisions. Women don't make decisions in a vacuum—they want context, contingencies, and lots of information; and they will use their hearts and intuitions as well as their minds. They also won't give referrals right away, because women need to make sure the relationship is working before they give access to people they care about. Advisors had to learn how to understand the emotional side of the decision process and earn women's trust.

Women also are not likely to want to meet right after one of MassMutal's financial seminars, so MassMutual gave its financial advisors different follow-up strategies to use. MassMutual trained its advisors that the focus should not be on how to close the sale but on how to open and develop a long-term client relationship—it's a beginning, not an ending.

Newsletter/Publications

- MassMutual has a quarterly newsletter called *Intuition,* which focuses on women's financial issues. It covers topics such as savings plans and long-term care insurance and uses compelling storytelling to get the key points across. For instance, with the savings plan subject, MassMutual used a story about two friends, Grace and Kate, and their different savings strategies.

- MassMutual distributes on its Web site the easy-to-read *A Women's Guide to Investing,* which covers both "Planning for the Expected" (such as paying for college, buying a home, investing for retirement) and "Coping with the Unexpected" (taking care of others, widowhood, second or late-in-life marriages).

- With both publications as well as other educational materials, MassMutual offers the ability to "share it with a friend," which is a great girlfriends and word of mouth tactic.

Women's Advisory Boards. With the support and assistance of MassMutual's corporate office, a number of their local agencies across the country have developed Women's Advisory Boards (WABs) in their communities. These local boards provide some of the top women in each city with an outlet for their desire to contribute in a meaningful way. A substantial side benefit of this initiative is that, because the board members are so engaged with and committed to their efforts, they tend to talk about them and seek to enlist others in their programs. So in effect, MassMutual has a cadre of some of the most influential women in the city spreading the word of MassMutual's good works, essentially acting as brand ambassadors. Most influential women tend to be in the PrimeTime Women age group, and so are their friends.

Corporate Halo. MassMutual supports an extensive portfolio of philanthropic efforts tied into their mission to empower and educate women financially. Moreover, they also communicate their support of these programs right on the first page of the women's section of the Web site, a smart way to alert PrimeTime Women to the company's strong commitment to corporate citizenship.

- MassMutual created "LifeBridge" to provide completely free life insurance for lower-income parents to help protect their children's education. Its goal is to give away $1 *billion* dollars of free life insurance, in the form of 20,000 10-year term policies, each with a death benefit of $50,000—no strings attached. By the end of 2005, MassMutual issued more than 4,600 policies—more than $230 million in free coverage—and sadly paid out two death benefits. Thanks to LifeBridge, the children of the mothers who died will have funds available to help pay for their education.

- MassMutual also supports the Breast Cancer Research Foundation, Girl Scouts USA, the All-American Girls Professional Baseball League, the Danskin Women's Triathlon Series, the Executive Women's Golf Association, the Office Depot Success Strategies for Business Women Conference and many other programs aligned with PrimeTime Women's values and priorities.

By supporting efforts that have the potential to make a local impact, MassMutual is accomplishing two key things. First, the programs provide a community rallying point—a sense of immediacy and personal connection. Second, it gives its local agents a relevant business-building platform to use in engaging attention and interest on a grass-roots level.

Workplace Environment. Not only does MassMutual talk the talk of "doing well by doing good," they walk the walk. In 2005, *Working Mother* magazine named MassMutual one of the best 100 companies for working women. MassMutual provides a number of options to help employees achieve a strong work-life balance, including flexible schedules, near-site childcare facilities, an on-site credit union, convenience store, dry cleaner, tailor, jewelry and shoe repair, a barbershop, and a hair salon. MassMutual also has a strong commitment to employee health, offering state-of-the-art fitness centers, medical clinics for employee visits, and an employee assistance program.

Results

"MassMutual strives to be the best provider of financial services for women, whether they are launching a new business, running an existing one, or organizing their own personal finances," says Susan Sweetser. Her Women's Markets division has the unbridled support of upper management at MassMutual because "It's not just that it's the right thing to do. They see the business case."

2005 was a strong year for MassMutual; it produced a double-digit increase in assets under management and strong performance in businesses throughout the organization. In addition to improving efficiencies, reducing costs, and maintaining a prudent investment approach, MassMutual's management credits expanded product offerings and a top tier and dedicated sales force and employee base, along with innovative market approaches, like the Women's Markets program, for helping to produce the strong annual results.

MassMutual is attracting more long-term PrimeTime Women customers by understanding their needs, anticipating their changing demands, and providing products and services to meet them. Mass-Mutual is also doing it in a way that is different from any other financial services company out there. As Sweetser says, "We have a heart. We really are a different company."

CHAPTER TEN

Notes to the CEO

If you've gotten this far in the book, I'm thinking I've done my job of convincing you that PrimeTime Women are indeed the golden bull's-eye of target marketing. So now you're eager to go and get other people in the organization excited about the opportunity, particularly that person with the purse strings in the corner office. Given you normally get about 30 minutes of that person's time to make a case, even one as important as this one, how do you present the opportunity in a nutshell?

To help you with that, I'm closing the book with an Executive Summary, the seven building blocks of the PrimeTime Women business case.

PrimeTime Women—they're in the prime of their lives, and they are marketers' prime marketing opportunity.

PrimeTime Women—The Executive Summary

1. Women control most of the consumer spending decisions worldwide, and in the United States, most of the corporate and small business spending decisions as well.

In the consumer sector, women bring in half or more of the income in 55 percent of U.S. households. In 27 percent of U.S. households, single women are the sole earner, and 30 percent of working wives out-earn their husbands. Women operate as the "Chief Purchasing Officer" in almost all households, and are estimated to make 80 percent of all household buying decisions. This includes handling the majority of purchasing in such traditionally male categories as investments, automotive, consumer electronics, and home improvement.

In corporations, they constitute 50 percent of managers and professionals, 58 percent of purchasing agents and managers, and 53 percent of wholesale and retail buyers. In addition, they make most of the decisions on office equipment, services and supplies, and employee financial and insurance plan providers.

In the small business arena, women have accounted for 70 percent of all privately held startups over the last 15 years. Their growth in numbers, employees, and revenues has outperformed the general economy by two-fold, three-fold and four-fold, respectively.

Women are different from men, and their buying decisions are based on different attitudes, priorities, and decision styles. To be effective in marketing to them, companies need to apply different messages, media, and communication approaches. The insights and principles of the GenderTrends Marketing Model set forth in my first book, *Marketing to Women,* will help companies reap significant competitive advantage, resulting in sales and share boosts, as well as increases in customer satisfaction among both men and women.

2. PrimeTime Women—women 50–70 years old—control spending for the households with the most money.

With the aging of the Baby Boomers, the population of consumers over 50 is growing astronomically fast (up 45 percent from 2000 to 2020), while the population under 50 is actually declining (down 2 percent 2000–2020). These consumers have enormous economic clout. They're in their peak earning years and expect to continue working well into their 70s.

They already control 79 percent of the financial assets in the United States and will keep accumulating more, as they continue to bring in two paychecks, and add to that some inheritance money from their parents. They have the greatest discretionary spending power of all consumer segments, because their expenses decline when their kids launch their own households. On a *per capita* basis, consumers over 50 spend 2.5 times what the average person spends.

Women over 50 exert greater spending influence than women under 50, as they handle more of the household decisions independently of their husbands; as their children consult them on spending decisions in their own newly established households; and as they become an increasing percentage of the older population.

3. Boomer women are the first generation of PrimeTime Women and are *radically* different from any generation of women in history.

This is the dawn of PrimeTime. Thirty years ago you couldn't call the ages between 50 and 70 years old "PrimeTime." Advances in awareness, knowledge, and practice of new health, wellness, fitness and nutrition behaviors has extended life expectancy by more in the past 100 years than in the 1,000 years preceding it. More important, the quality of life has been substantially enhanced; in effect, rather than an extra ten years being added to the end of life, they have effectively been added to the *middle* of life. Both men and women in their 50s and 60s report these to be the happiest decades of their lives.

At the same time, Boomer women have shattered the mold of how women have lived their lives for all the generations before them. They are the first generation of women to attend college in numbers about equal to their brethren; the first to enter the workplace *en masse*, with the majority bringing home a paycheck of their own; the first to have control of whether and when to have children, which significantly affects job seniority and career progress; and the first to win regulatory rights that give them control of their own financial matters equal to men. Relative to previous generations of women, these are far from small, incremental changes. They are a radical transformation of women's role in the household, political, and economic infrastructure of our society.

This represents a watershed opportunity for marketers. Never before have consumer households had such substantial spending power, driven by the advent of two-paycheck households, and the increased longevity to accumulate spending power over time. Never before have there been so many consumer goods available and relevant to fulfill wants and desires beyond basic food, clothing, and shelter needs—goods like travel, consumer electronics, telecommunications, financial instruments, entertainment, and many more. And never again will marketers have the opportunity to be first to market with this new cohort of high-spending consumers.

4. Most marketers are missing the boat and the opportunity because they're trapped in their own outdated stereotypes.

First of all, we in the Western world suffer from a bad case of youth myopia. On an emotional level, as a culture, we aspire to the characteristics of young people—energetic, high-spirited, physically strong, impulsive, and colorful; and we are ignorant about the true qualities of older people—experienced, resilient, even-tempered, patient, intuitive. We let ourselves be buried in all the baggage that comes along with the only terms we have had for the midlife market: "middle-aged," "mature," "aging," and "senior" all carry connotations of dumpy, frumpy, sober, and slow. Not surprisingly, none of those descriptions sound particularly appealing to today's marketers, even those at senior levels of management who may themselves be PrimeTimers and ought to know better.

Second, marketers either truly believe, or proffer as a rationalization, the explanation that young people are the prospects with the most lifetime sales potential. "Get 'em while they're young," they say, "and they'll buy your brand for life." Nonsense. That may actually have been true back when there weren't that many brands to choose from in the 1950s, and when most brands enjoyed a substantial and perceptible point of difference versus their competitors.

That was 50 years ago, folks. In today's marketplace, where consumers are confronted by an excess of choice, and many categories are seen as collections of fairly interchangeable commodities, everybody tries new stuff all the time. And in fact, the research shows that older people are actually *at least as* likely to try something new than younger people—probably because their needs, preferences, and priorities are changing and they are looking for new options.

Moreover, anyone who thinks "Well, at least younger people have lots more purchase cycles in them than older people do," might want to do their homework and check their facts. They might be surprised to learn, for example, that of the 13 cars that an average household buys over its "lifetime," seven—the majority—are bought after the head of household reaches 50.

It baffles me when I read that marketers are *worried* that their customer base is "older," that they are desperate to reach younger consumers, that they are willing to pay substantially more for media that reaches younger people, that programmers and content developers are scrambling to develop properties to deliver younger audiences. Twenty-somethings and thirty-somethings are lovely people, but as prospects, they have a fraction of the spending power of the generation ahead of them. Personally, if I were a marketer looking for a competitive advantage, while the rest of the market duked it out over the young buyers that have no dough, I would court the consumers who have the most moolah. Call me crazy.

5. To effectively market to the PrimeTime Woman, you have to understand who she really is.

PrimeTime Women regard their 50s and 60s as the prime of their lives. Unlike PrimeTime men, they don't experience midlife as a crisis; to them it's more like a liberation. What psychologists have characterized as the "empty nest," supposedly a time of loss and sadness, PrimeTime Women experience as "the next quest," when after decades of suppressing their own preferences and passions in favor of focusing on family needs, they are finally free to return to themselves, to experience "My Time." They're healthy, strong, and energetic, and the launch of the kids frees up time and money to pursue old passions and explore new possibilities.

Menopause, far from being the mysterious mood monster that takes over their lives, is well under control, and actually brings a bonus—post-menopausal zest, as Margaret Mead called it, a boost in energy experienced as increased creativity and productivity.

PrimeTime Women are mentally strong, and getting stronger every day. And their new awareness of their mortality gifts them with both a greater appreciation for life and a stronger sense of legacy, the urge to contribute and give back.

Thanks to hormone shifts, combined with their greater life experience, they feel more assertive, confident in themselves, resilient and capable of handling whatever life throws at them. PrimeTime brings more peace, equanimity, strength, confidence, appreciation, and perspective.

They're at a stage of human development when they experience greater drives for authenticity, to find and behave as their "real selves," rather than their youthfully created "social selves," and they feel free to exempt themselves from many of the social constraints and conventions that bound them when they were younger.

Contrary to popular opinion, PrimeTime Women are not in denial about their age or appearance, not fighting tooth and nail to retain or reclaim their "lost" youth. Sure, gravity happens; everything is a little less firm, a little less smooth, a little more bumpy here and there. But unlike their younger selves when they were in their 40s, Prime-Time Women have made peace with their appearance.

They care about looking their personal best and are glad to avail themselves of help from nutrition, exercise, clothing, hair color, and cosmetics, but marketers who think they are desperate to look 20 are completely missing the point. The PrimeTime Woman redefines beauty on her own terms, and it is anything but skin deep. Instead, it comes from a combination of her external physical features, which she is comfortable with, and her internal self-confidence, which radiates strength and serenity. She thinks she looks great, and she doesn't appreciate marketers who tell her she doesn't measure up.

6. Marketers who understand the new dynamics of the PrimeTime consumer market, and the new dimensions of the PrimeTime Woman, have many ways to leverage these insights into major business opportunities.

The first opportunity is simply to recognize PrimeTime Women as a high-opportunity market segment, and instead of "worrying" about having too many older consumers, count yourself lucky and court these big spenders before your competitors figure it out. And before you invest the billions it takes to open foreign markets, jumping the hurdles of unfamiliar customs and alien regulations, make sure you haven't overlooked the customers in your own backyard.

Second, develop new products to serve PrimeTime Women's emerging needs as they move into midlife, changing physically and developing new lifestyles. You have a large segment of prosperous consumers who have needs that have never been explored before. Opportunity? I think so.

Third, use your new insights to boost the effectiveness of your marketing programs and communications. Get more bang out of every buck in your sales and marketing budgets by developing and tailoring your marketing programs to better align with PrimeTime Women's gender culture. And enhance the breakthrough, relevance, and appeal of all your marketing communications by both reflecting and speaking to PrimeTime Women's real priorities and interests.

Don't make the catastrophic mistake of thinking this opportunity applies only to those industries conventionally thought of as "senior categories:" hearing aids, medicines, fiber products, recreational vehicles, orthopedic shoes, and anti-aging potions. This book has provided myriad examples of industries that can and will grow based on PrimeTime Women's opening up to new activities, interests, needs, and priorities.

7. PrimeTime Women are the healthiest, wealthiest, most educated, active, and influential generation of women in history. This is *their* PrimeTime. And it's your prime marketing opportunity.

PrimeTime is the Promised Land, and PrimeTime Women hold the key. It is a moment of marketing opportunity unparalleled in history. Never before. Never again. Don't miss your chance to win the hearts, minds, and business of Boomer big spenders—PrimeTime Women.

The Best Resources
in the Business

Publications

American Demographics magazine, now part of *Advertising Age* magazine, *http://adage.com/americandemographics/*

Baron-Cohen, Simon, *The Essential Difference: The Truth About the Male and Female Brain*, Perseus Books Group, 2003; *The Essential Difference: Male and Female Brains and the Truth About Autism*, Basic Books, a member of the Perseus Books Group, reprint 2004

Brizendine, MD, Louann, *The Female Brain*, Morgan Road Books, 2006

Cavanaugh, John C., *Adult Development and Aging*, 5th edition, Thomson Wadsworth, 2006

CD Publications, *Selling to Seniors' Guide to Senior Marketing*, CD Publications, 2002; CD Publications also offers a monthly newsletter called *Selling to Seniors;* each issue of Selling to Seniors contains case studies of successful sales approaches, highlights of research studies, and reports on demographic trends, including ways to effectively segment the mature market in order to increase advertising effectiveness. *www.cdpublications.com/pubs/sellingtoseniors.php*

Cohen, Gene, MD, PhD, *The Mature Mind*, Basic Books, 2005

Coyle, Jean M., *Handbook on Women and Aging*, Praeger Publishing, 1997, 2001

Crowley, Chris & Henry S. Lodge, MD, *Younger Next Year for Women*, Workman Publishing Company Inc., 2004, 2005

Dailey, Nancy, *When Baby Boom Women Retire*, Praeger Publications, 1998, 2000

Diamond, Jed, *The Irritable Male Syndrome: Managing the 4 Key Causes of Depression & Aggression*, Rodale Press, 2004; *Male Menopause*, Sourcebooks, 1998

Doress-Worters, Paula B., and Diana Laskin Siegal, *The New Ourselves, Growing Older*, Touchstone, 1994 edition

Dychtwald, Ken, *Age Power: How the 21st Century Will Be Ruled by the New Old*, Tarcher/Putnam, 1999

Fitzgerald, Kathleen, *Divas, Dames & Dolls*, Hill Street Press, 2005

Freedman, Marc, *PrimeTime: How Baby Boomers Will Revolutionize Retirement and Transform America*, Public Affairs, 2002

Gillon, Steve, *Boomer Nation: The Largest and Richest Generation Ever and How It Changed America*, Free Press, a division of Simon & Schuster, Inc., 2004

GRAND magazine, Currier Palmer Publishing, St. Petersburg, FL

Green, Brent, *Marketing to Leading-Edge Baby Boomers: Perceptions, Principles, Practices & Predictions*, Paramount Market Publishing Inc., 2006

Hales, Diane, *Just Like a Woman: How Gender Science is Re-defining What Makes Us Feel Female*, Bantam, 2000

Harris, Leslie, *After Fifty: How the Baby Boom Will Redefine the Mature Market*, Paramount Market Publishing, Inc. 2003

Alspaugh, Nancy and Marilyn Kentz, *Not Your Mother's Midlife: A Ten-Step Guide to Fearless Aging*, Andrews McMeel Publishing, 2003

Marketing to Women newsletter, EPM Communications, Inc., a publishing, research, and consulting firm founded in 1988 by Ira Mayer and his wife and partner, Riva Bennett, *www.epmcom.com/html/women/MTW/*

More magazine, published by Meredith Corporation, Des Moines, IA

Morgan, Carol and Doran Levy, *Marketing to the Mindset of Boomers and Their Elders*, Attitudebase, The Brewer House, 2002

New Strategist Publications: *American Women: Who They Are & How They Live*, 3rd Edition (New Strategist Publications, Inc., 2006); *Older Americans, The Baby Boom, Gen X, The Millennials*, 4th Editions (New Strategist Publications Inc., 2004)

Nyren, Chuck, *Advertising to Baby Boomers*, Paramount Market Publishing, Inc., 2005

Peters Tom and Marti Barletta, *Tom Peters Essentials: Trends*, DK Publishing Inc., 2005

Rowe, John, MD, and Robert L. Kahn, PhD, *Successful Aging*, Dell Publishing, a division of Random House Inc., 1998

Sax, Leonard, MD, PhD, *Why Gender Matters: What Parents and Teachers Need to Know about the Emerging Science of Sex Differences*, Broadway, 2006

Sheehy, Gail, *New Passages: Mapping Your Life Across Time*, Ballantine Books, a division of Random House Inc., 1995

Sheehy, Gail, *Sex and the Seasoned Woman*, Random House Inc., 2006

Shellenbarger, Sue, *The Breaking Point: How Female Midlife Crisis is Transforming Today's Women*, Henry Holt and Company, LLC, 2004

Stein, Murray, *Midlife: A Jungian Perspective*, Spring Publications, 1983

Tréguer, Jean-Paul, *50+ Marketing: Marketing, Communicating and Selling to the Over 50s Generations*, Palgrave Macmillan, 1998, 2002

Wolfe, David, *Ageless Marketing*, Kaplan Publishing, 2003

Organizations

AARP. AARP is a nonprofit, nonpartisan membership organization for people age 50 and over. AARP is dedicated to enhancing quality of life for all as we age. AARP leads positive social change and delivers value to members through information, advocacy, and service. Publishes magazine, policy, and research reports, and the AARP bulletin online. *www.aarp.org/*

Focalyst. Focalyst is a joint venture between AARP Services Inc., a wholly owned subsidiary of AARP and The Kantar Group, the leading source of data, analysis, and advice about Baby Boomers and older consumers. *www.focalyst.com/index .html*

Center for Women's Business Research. The CWBR is the go-to source on the trends, characteristics, achievements, and challenges of women business owners and their enterprises. *www.womensbusinessresearch.org/index.php*

JWT Mature Market Group. Founder Lori Bitter developed a 45+ expertise in research and consulting for the J. Walter Thompson ad agency. Publishes LiveWire! newsletter. *www.frnht.com/clients_aquent/JWTSC/mmg/about/mmg_home .html*

The Boomer Project. Started in 2003 by Matt Thornhill, the Boomer Project is a marketing research and consulting company focused on Baby Boomers and marketing. *www.boomerproject.com/.* Sign up for the newsletter.

ThirdAge Inc. President and CEO Sharon Whiteley created ThirdAge Inc. as an online media and direct marketing company focused exclusively on serving the needs of midlife adults—generally those in their 40s, 50s, and 60s—and those who want to build a genuine relationship with them. *http://thirdage.com/ index.html*

Web Sites and Links

The Mature Market.com, international daily news on the Mature Market by Senior Strategic Network—Worldwide Experts Network of the Mature Market. *http:// thematuremarket.com/SeniorStrategic/index.php.* Sign up for the newsletter.

Second50Years.com provides information about the mature market, making it easier and more affordable for businesses of any size to stay on top of best marketing practices, news, and the demographics of Baby Boomers and Seniors. *www.second50years.com/.* Sign up for the newsletter.

Women and Diversity: WOW! Facts. The Business Women's Network in Washington, DC publishes this wide-ranging and interesting collection of independent facts from myriad sources on everything from the women's market to health, philanthropy, politics, and sports. Also available in print as a book of the same name. *www.ewowfacts.com/chap.html*

Endnotes

Introduction

1. Gail Sheehy, *New Passages* (New York: Random House Inc., 1995); *Sex and the Seasoned Woman* (New York: Random House Inc., 2006).

2. Michael J. Silverstein, *Treasure Hunt: Inside the Mind of the New Consumer* (New York: Penguin Group, 2006), pp. 40–41.

3. *American Women*, 3rd Edition (Ithaca, NY: New Strategist Publications, Inc., 2006), p. 158.

4. The Women's History Project, 1998, *www.legacy98.org*.

5. Nancy Gibbs, "Midlife Crisis? Bring It On!", *TIME* (May 16, 2005; retrieved online May 2, 2006).

Chapter 1

1. 2005 White House Conference on Aging

2. Patricia Winters Lauro, "Aiming at the over 50 traveler, a Minneapolis agency stresses mystery and avoids stereotypes," *The New York Times*, July 25, 2001, p. 10; U.S. Census Bureau estimates.

3. JWT Mature Market Group, Industry Facts, 2006.

4. U.S. Census Bureau, 2005 Estimates.

5. U.S. Census Bureau, 2005 Estimates.

6. Ken Dychtwald, *Age Power* (New York: Tarcher/Putnam, 1999), p. 155.

7. John Cavanaugh, *Adult Development & Aging*, 5th edition (Belmont, CA: Thomson Wadsworth, 2006), p. 80.

8. Bureau of the Census, Marital Status and Living Arrangements, March 2000 (updated).

9. Sarah Mahoney, "The Secret Lives of Single Women," *AARP* (May & June 2006): 62–106.

10. National Association of Realtors, as quoted in *The Wall Street Journal*, "Single Women Become Force in Home Buying," by Jennifer Lisle, November 24, 2004.

11. *Older Americans*, p. 114; *The Baby Boom*, p. 89, *Gen X*, pp. 89–90; *Millennials*, pp. 166–67 (Ithaca, NY: New Strategist Publications, 2004).

12. *The Baby Boom*, p. 108; *Older Americans*, p. 133 (Ithaca, NY: New Strategist Publications, 2004).

13. *Older Americans* (Ithaca, NY: New Strategist Publications, 2004), p. 114.

14. *The Baby Boom,* p. 108; *Older Americans,* p. 133 (Ithaca, NY: New Strategist Publications, 2004).

15. *The Baby Boom* (Ithaca, NY: New Strategist Publications, 2004), p. 152.

16. "American Consumers: The Word's Biggest Spenders," *American Demographics* (January 10, 2006).

17. Peter Francese, "U.S. Consumer—Like No Other on the Planet," *Advertising Age* 77, no. 1 (January 2, 2006).

18. *Older Americans* (Ithaca, NY: New Strategist Publications), p. 361.

19. U.S Census Bureau, 2005 Estimates.

20. Ken Dychtwald, *Age Power* (New York: Tarcher/Putnam, 1999), p. 20; *AARP*.

21. Gary Onks, SoldOnSeniors Inc.

22. Gary Onks, SoldOnSeniors Inc.

23. Ken Dychtwald, *Age Power* (New York: Tarcher/Putnam, 1999), p. 20.

24. "Age 50+Demographic Not a Homogenous Group," The Media Audit, April 15, 2003.

25. AARP State of 50+ in America Report, 2004.

26. Paul Hodge, "Living Younger Longer: Baby Boomer Challenges," 2005 White House Conference on Aging, Policy Hearing Committee, October 1, 2004.

27. $14 trillion from Carol M. Morgan and Doran J. Levy, PhD, *Marketing to the Mindset of Boomers and Their Elders* (AttitudeBase, 2002), p. 133; $25 trillion from The Allianz American Legacies Study as quoted in "The Greatest Generation Shares the Wealth," *Christian Science Monitor* (August 1, 2005); $41 trillion from "Great Expectations," *American Demographics* (May 1, 2003)—sociologist Paul Schervish, director of the Institute for Social Welfare Research at Boston College, calculated the sum of all American inheritances to be distributed over the next half-century.

28. Nancy Dailey, *When Baby Boom Women Retire* (Praeger Publishers, 1998, 2000), p. 39.

29. Deloitte Research Study, Wealth with Wisdom, 2006.

30. Gary Onks, SoldOnSeniors, Inc.

31. Ken Dychtwald, *Age Power* (New York: Tarcher/Putnam, 1999),p. 20.

32. Gary Onks, SoldOnSeniors, Inc.

33. *Older Americans,* 4th Edition (Ithaca, NY: New Strategist Publications, 2004), p. 265.

34. *Older Americans,* 4th Edition; *The Baby Boom,* 4th Edition; *Gen X,* 4th Edition (Ithaca, NY: New Strategist Publications, 2004).

35. *http://cyberatlas.internet.com/bigpicture/demographics/.* Accessed August 29, 2000.

36. "Older Consumers Buy Stuff, Too," *The Wall Street Journal,* April 6, 2004.

37. *The Baby Boom,* 4th Edition; *Older Americans,* 4th Edition (Ithaca, NY: New Strategist Publications, 2004).

38. Brookings Institution, May 25, 2000.

39. *American Women,* 3rd Edition (Ithaca, NY: New Strategist Publications, 2006), p. 7.

40. Ibid., p. 36.

41. Peg Tyre, "Poker Buddies for Life," *Newsweek,* Feb. 20, 2006, p. 61.

42. *American Women,* 3rd Edition (Ithaca, NY: New Strategist Publications, 2006), p. 158.

43. *American Women,* 3rd Edition (Ithaca, NY: New Strategist Publications, 2006).

44. Center for Women's Business Research, 2004.

45. Center for Women's Business Research, "Women Business Owners in Non-traditional Industries: Changing Traditional Views," October 2005.

46. Joan Hoff, *Law, Gender, & Injustice: A Legal History of U.S. Women* (New York: New York University Press, 1991), p. 281, as quoted at *Sunshine for Women* at *www.pinn.net~sunshine/main.htm.*

47. The Women's History Project, 1998, *www.legacy98.org.*

48. *American Women,* 3rd Edition (Ithaca, NY: New Strategist Publications, 2006), pp. 104–106.

49. Ibid.

50. Todd Hale, "The Relevance of the Aging Population," *Consumer Insight,* February 20, 2006.

51. Securities Industry Association, e. 1998.

52. Consumer Electronics Assocation, 2004.

53. Lowe's, per CEO Robert Tillman, cited on Forbes.com and quoted in Tom Peters presentation, June 1 2003.

54. "American Women," *Road & Travel* magazine, on roadandtravel.com, 2005; Jean Halliday, "Ford aims at women's market as it lines up ad space for '98," *Automotive News,* July 14, 1997.

55. Conde Nast/Intelliquest Survey, as quoted in *Ad Age,* 1997.

56. *The Baby Boom,* Fourth Edition; *Older Americans,* Fourth Edition; *Gen X,* Fourth Edition (Ithaca, NY: New Strategists Publications, 2004).

57. *American Women,* 3rd Edition (Ithaca, NY: New Strategist Publications, 2006), p. 178.

58. John Cavanaugh, *Adult Development & Aging,* 5th Edition (Belmont, CA: Thomson Wadsworth, 2006).

59. Gail Sheehy, *New Passages* (New York: Random House, Inc., 1995), p. 6.

60. *The Wall Street Journal,* 1997.

61. AARP State of 50+ in America Report, 2004.

62. *American Demographics,* March 2003.

Chapter 3

1. Gail Sheehy, *New Passages* (New York: Random House, Inc., 1995), p. 255.

2. Susan R. Sherman, "Images of Middle-age and Older Women," in *Handbook on Women and Aging,* New Ed Edition, ed. Jean M. Coyle (Westport, CT: Praeger Publishing, 2001), p. 18.

3. Elizabeth W. Markson, "Sagacious, Sinful or Superfluous? The Social Construction of Older Women," in *Handbook on Women and Aging,* New Ed Edition, ed. Jean M. Coyle (Westport, CT: Praeger Publishing, 2001), p. 58.

4. Suzanne Degges-White, "Midlife Transitions in Women: Cultural and Individual Factors," *ADULTSPAN Journal,* Spring 2001.

5. Dr. Gene Cohen, "The Myth of the Midlife Crisis," *Newsweek,* January 16, 2006, *www.msnbc.msn.com/id/10753221/site/newsweek/.*

6. John Cavanaugh, *Adult Development & Aging,* 5th Edition (Belmont, CA: Thomson Wadsworth, 2006), pp. 342–349.

7. Suzanne Degges-White, "Midlife Transitions in Women: Cultural and Individual Factors," *ADULTSPAN Journal,* Spring 2001.

8. David P. Schmitt, "Is there an early-30s peak in female sexual desire? Cross-sectional evidence from the United States and Canada," *The Canadian Journal of Human Sexuality,* Vol. II, Issue 1, 2002.

9. Dianne Hales, *Just Like a Woman: How Gender Science is Re-defining What Makes Us Feel Female* (New York: Bantam, 2000), p. 75.

10. Sourced from *www.femininezone.com/articles.php?a=read&aid=189*. Used by permission from Jed Diamond, June 2006.

11. Carol Orsborn, "From Trend Victim to Wise Woman: A Motivational Map for Marketing to Baby Boomer Women," Imago newsletter, November 18, 2005.

12. Jeffrey Kluger, "The Surprising Power of the Aging Brain," *TIME*, January 16, 2006, pp. 85–87.

13. Suzanne Degges-White, "Midlife Transitions in Women: Cultural and Individual Factors," *ADULTSPAN Journal*, Spring 2001.

14. University of Michigan Institute for Social Research study as quoted in "Men doing more; women doing less—Housework," *USA Today* magazine, December 2002, by the Society for the Advancement of Education.

15. Nancy Gibbs, "Midlife Crisis? Bring It On!", *TIME*, May 16, 2005, retrieved online May 2, 2006.

16. Melissa Healy, "The Healthy Bond," *Chicago Tribune*, May 18, 2005.

17. Jean Pearson Scott, "Family Relationships of Midlife and Older Women," in *Handbook on Women and Aging*, ed. Jean M. Coyle (Westport, CT: Praeger Publishing, 2001), p. 373.

18. Gail Sheehy, *New Passages* (New York: Ballantine Books, 1996), p. 221.

19. Chris Crowley & Henry S. Lodge, MD, *Younger Next Year for Women* (New York: Workman Publishing Company, Inc., 2005), p. 3.

20. Marion Winik, "Who Says getting older has to be scary?," *Health*, April 2004.

21. AARP Foundation, Women's Leadership Circle Study, "Looking At Act II of Women's Lives," April 2006.

22. Gail Sheehy, *Sex and the Seasoned Woman* (New York: Random House, 2006), p. 7.

23. Gail Sheehy, *New Passages* (New York: Ballantine Books, 1996), p. 151.

24. Gail Sheehy, *Sex and the Seasoned Woman* (New York: Random House, 2006), p. 17.

25. David Wolfe, *Ageless Marketing* (Chicago: Dearborn Trade Publishing, 2003), pp. 45, 234–235.

26. David Wolfe, *Ageless Marketing* (Chicago: Dearborn Trade Publishing, 2003), p. 45, 102, 93.

27. Gail Sheehy, *Sex and the Seasoned Woman* (New York: Random House, 2006), p. 17.

28. John W. Rowe, MD, and Robert L. Kahn, PhD, *Successful Aging* (New York: Dell Publishing, 1998), p. 134.

29. *Columbia Dictionary of Quotations* (Columbia University Press, 1998).

30. AARP Survey on Lifelong Learning, July 2000.

31. Nancy Gibbs, "Midlife Crisis? Bring It On!", *TIME*, May 16, 2005, retrieved online May 2, 2006.

32. "The Home Depot and AARP Launch Nationwide Workshops," *www.aarp.org*, posted September 29, 2005.

33. John W. Rowe, MD, and Robert L. Kahn, PhD, *Successful Aging*, (New York: Dell Publishing, 1998), p. 27–28, 137, 154, 123–24.

34. Vira R. Kivett, "Rural Older Women," in *Handbook on Women and Aging*, ed. Jean M. Coyle (Westport, CT: Praeger Publishing, 2001), p. 359.

35. "UCLA Researchers Identify Key Biobehavioral Pattern Used By Women To Manage Stress," *Science Daily*, May 22, 2000, *www.sciencedaily.com/releases/2000/05/000522082151.htm*.

36. "UCLA Study On Friendship Among Women: An alternative to fight or flight," ©2002 Gale Berkowitz, article on Melissa Kaplan's Chronic Neuroimmune Disease site, *www.anapsid.org/cnd/gender/tendfend.html.*

37. Mary Jane Solomon, "Crimson Tide," special to the *Washington Post* (Friday, October 22, 2004), p. WE29.

38. David Wolfe, *Ageless Marketing* (Chicago: Dearborn Trade Publishing, 2003), p. 215.

39. Sue Shellenbarger, *The Breaking Point* (New York: Henry Holt and Company, LLC, 2004), p. 152.

Chapter 4

1. John Cavanaugh, *Adult Development & Aging,* 5th Edition (Belmont, CA: Thomson Wadsworth, 2006), p. 198–99.

2. Harvard Men's Health Watch, April 2006.

3. John W. Rowe, MD, and Robert L. Kahn, PhD, *Successful Aging* (New York: Dell Publishing, 1998), pp. 129–130.

4. *www.nerve.com/screeningroom/books/interview_malcolmgladwell/,* retrieved September 19, 2006.

5. John W. Rowe, MD, and Robert L. Kahn, PhD, *Successful Aging* (New York: Dell Publishing, 1998), p. 131.

6. Ibid., p. 44, 304.

7. John Cavanaugh, *Adult Development & Aging,* 5th Edition (Belmont, CA: Thomson Wadsworth, 2006), p. 271.

8. Dr. Gene Cohen, *The Mature Mind* (New York: Basic Books, 2005), p. 5.

9. Jeffrey Kluger, "The Surprising Power of the Aging Brain," *TIME* (January 16, 2006), pp. 85–87.

10. Dr. Gene Cohen, "The Myth of the Midlife Crisis," *Newsweek* (January 16, 2006), *www.msnbc.msn.com/id/10753221/site/newsweek/.*

11. Dr. Gene Cohen, *The Mature Mind* (New York: Basic Books, 2005), p. 5.

12. John Cavanaugh, *Adult Development & Aging,* 5th Edition (Belmont, CA: Thomson Wadsworth, 2006), p. 298.

13. Dr. Gene Cohen, "The Myth of the Midlife Crisis," *Newsweek* (January 16, 2006), *www.msnbc.msn.com/id/10753221/site/newsweek/.*

14. Dr. Gene Cohen, "The Myth of the Midlife Crisis," *Newsweek* (January 16, 2006), *www.msnbc.msn.com/id/10753221/site/newsweek/.*

15. Jeffrey Kluger, "The Surprising Power of the Aging Brain," *TIME* (January 16, 2006), pp. 85–87.

16. Claudia Wallis, "How to Tune Up Your Brain," *TIME* (January 16, 2006).

17. Tara Parker-Pope, "This is Your Brain on Menopause," *More* (December 2005/January 2006).

18. Scott LaFee, "Myelin's role doesn't diminish as people age," *San Diego Union-Tribune* (February 8, 2006).

19. John Cavanaugh, *Adult Development & Aging,* 5th Edition (Belmont, CA: Thomson Wadsworth, 2006), p. 232.

20. Dr. Gene Cohen, *The Mature Mind* (New York: Basic Books, 2005), pp. 17–18.

21. andropausecanada.com; New Zealand Menopause Institute, nzmenopause .co.nz; Dr. Gabe Mirkin, radio host, author of The Healthy Heart Miracle; Empowering Women's Wisdom, Dr. Christiane Northrup, DrNorthrup.com; womens-meopause-health.com.

22. Connie Lauerman, "Ways of Worrying," *Chicago Tribune* (January 18, 2006).

23. Michele Miller blog, December 5, 2005.

24. Jeffrey Kluger, "The Surprising Power of the Aging Brain," *TIME* (January 16, 2006), pp. 85–87.

25. Dr. Gene Cohen, *The Mature Mind* (New York: Basic Books, 2005), pp. 17–18.

26. Tara Parker-Pope, "This is Your Brain on Menopause," *More* (December 2005/January 2006).

27. Fred Warshofsky, "Aging in the New Millennium," quoted in grandtimes .com, from *Stealing Time, The New Science of Aging*, 1999.

28. John Cavanaugh, *Adult Development & Aging*, 5th Edition (Belmont, CA: Thomson Wadsworth, 2006), pp. 234, 311–319.

29. Robert Sanders, Media Relations, "Brain hormone puts brakes on reproduction," *UC Berkeley News* (February 6, 2006).

30. Murray Stein, *In Midlife, A Jungian Perspective* (Putnam, CT: Spring Publications, 1983).

31. Louann Brizendine, MD, *The Female Brain* (New York: Morgan Road Books, 2006), pp. 137–149.

32. Dr. Abraham Kryger , "Sex Hormones," renewyouth.com.

33. andropausecanada.com.

34. Dianne Hales, *Just Like a Woman: How Gender Science is Re-defining What Makes Us Female*, (New York: Bantam, 2000), p. 75.

35. John Cavanaugh, *Adult Development & Aging*, 5th Edition (Belmont, CA: Thomson Wadsworth, 2006), p. 375.

36. AARP Women's Leadership Circle Study, January 2006.

37. Carol Morgan and Doran Levy, "To Their Health," *Brandweek*, January 19, 1998.

38. Paula B. Doress-Worters and Diana Laskin Siegal, *Ourselves, Growing Older*, 2nd Ed. (New York: Touchstone, 1994), p. 396; "Facts About Hearing Loss," Disability Initiative: Fact Sheet, AARP, 1992.

39. John Cavanaugh, *Adult Development & Aging*, 5th Edition (Belmont, CA: Thomson Wadsworth, 2006), p. 48.

40. "Buzz off, adults: Mosquito copy is teens' cell secret," *Chicago Tribune* (June 12, 2006).

41. Study by U.S. National Institute for Occupational Safety & Health, June 2006.

42. John Cavanaugh, *Adult Development & Aging*, 5th Edition (Belmont, CA: Thomson Wadsworth, 2006), p. 48.

43. Ibid., pp. 46–48.

44. Ibid., pp. 46–48.

45. Ibid., pp. 52–53.

46. "Decline in Taste and Odor Discrimination Abilities with Age, and Relationship between Gustation and Olfaction," *Chemical Senses Journal* 25:3 (2000) pp. 331–337.

47. Ibid.

48. Barbara Pease and Allen Pease, *Why Men Don't Listen and Women Can't Read Maps: How We're Different and What to Do About It*, (New York: Broadway, 2000), p. 35.

49. John Cavanaugh, *Adult Development & Aging*, 5th Edition (Belmont, CA: Thomson Wadsworth, 2006), p. 66.

50. Medline Plus, U.S. National Library of Medicine, and National Institutes of Health, 7/23/04; "Relationships between physical performance measures, age, height and body weight in healthy adults," *Age and Aging*, Oxford University Press, May 2000.

51. Medline Plus, U.S. National Library of Medicine, and National Institutes of Health, July 23, 2004.

52. Dr. Richard Berger, "Innovative Options—Minimally Invasive Quad-Sparing Knee Arthroplasty," *Orthopedic Excellence* 1:1 (2003–4); "Surgery for shoulder arthritis: Joint Replacement & Other Options," Mayo Clinic, Nov. 3, 2004 .

53. *Corporate Design Foundation Journal* 2:1, *http://cdf.org/journal/0201_oxo.php; www.OXO.com,* "Our Roots".

54. Ford Motor Company, "'Third Age Suit Helps Ford to Understand Mature Drivers," January 7, 1999.

55. 2005 MRI Doublebase/Simmons Spring 2005 NHCH Adult Full-Year Unified Study, 2004, Provided by DDB Chicago.

56. "Crisis? Study says midlife is the best of times." Sentinel Wire Services, *The Holland Sentinel* (February 16, 1999).

57. "Study of Women's Health Across the Nation (SWAN)," Inter-University Consortium for Political and Social Research, 1995–1997.

58. American Society for Aesthetic Plastic Surgery, 2006.

59. Amy Wallace, "True Thighs," *More* (September 2002), p. 90–95, as quoted in David Wolfe's *Ageless Marketing* (Chicago: Dearborn Trade Publishing, 2003), p. 19.

60. Simmons Spring 2005 NHCH Adult Full-Year Unified Study.

61. Nancy Gibbs, "Midlife Crisis? Bring it on!" *TIME* (May 16, 2005).

62. Nancy Berkley, "Welcoming Women Golfers," *PGA Magazine,* March 2004.

63. Retrieved from *www.spanx.com.*

64. The Center for Interactive Advertising @ The University of Texas at Austin, *www.ciadvertising.org/studies/student/99_fall/theory/maddux/polykoff/polyintro.htm.*

65. Ibid.

66. Alison Stewart, "Media Bombards Women with Mixed Weight Messages," *Consumer Health Journal* (October 2003), *www.consumerhealthjournal.com/articles/women-and-weight.html.*

67. Samuel Solley, "Dove Extends 'Real Women' Work to Sponsorship," *Brand Republic* (January 5, 2005).

68. Ibid.

Chapter 5

1. Rebecca Clay, "An empty nest can promote freedom, improved relationships," *Monitor on Psychology* (April 2003), p. 40.

2. Del Webb survey, 2004, retrieved from *www.pulte.com* (or *www.delwebb.com*).

3. Rebecca Clay, "An empty nest can promote freedom, improved relationships," *Monitor on Psychology* (April 2003), p. 40.

4. Ibid.

5. Ken Dychtwald, *Age Power* (Putnam/Tarcher, 2000), p. 88.

6. Joan Raymond, "A New Chapter: The Joy of Empty Nesting," *American Demographics* (May 30, 2000).

7. Eileen Ambrose, "Retiring to the Nest," *The Baltimore Sun* (February 29, 2004).

8. "Baby Boomers Reclaim Independence in the Empty Nest but Many Expect Parents to Move In or Kids to Come Back," *www.seniorjournal.com/NEWS/Housing/4-06-29Survey.htm* (June 29, 2004).

9. "Mom and Dad, I'm Home—Again," *BusinessWeek Online* (November 3, 2003), *www.businessweek.com/magazine/content/03_44/b3856124.htm.*

10. Shawn T. Taylor, "Grannies Set Pace For Growing 50+ Travel Crowd," *Chicago Tribune* (June 22, 2005).

11. "Baby Boomers: From the Age of Aquarius to the Age of Responsibility," Pew Research Center, December 8, 2005.

12. John W. Rowe, MD, and Robert L. Kahn, PhD, *Successful Aging* (New York: Dell Publishing, 1998), p. 16.

13. John Cavanaugh, *Adult Development & Aging*, 5th Edition (Belmont, CA: Thomson Wadsworth, 2006), p. 106.

14. John W. Rowe, MD, and Robert L. Kahn, PhD, *Successful Aging* (New York: Dell Publishing, 1998), pp. 13–16.

15. Pamela Paul, "Make Room for Granddaddy," *American Demographics* (April 1, 2002).

16. The Maturing Marketplace, sample issue, Business Publishers Inc., Roper Starch Worldwide research, 1998.

17. "The Grandparent Study, 2002 Report," AARP, conducted by RoperASW, retrieved from *www.aarp.org.*

18. David Wolfe, *Ageless Marketing* (Chicago: Dearborn Trade Publishing, 2003,) p. 233.

19. "Grandparents: A $3.4 Billion Buying Force," NPD Study, November 20, 2003.

20. EPM Research Alert newsletter, EPM Communications, Inc., August 16, 2002.

21. "The Grandparent Study, 2002 Report," AARP, conducted by RoperASW, retrieved from *www.aarp.org.*

22. Pamela Paul, "Make Room for Granddaddy," *American Demographics,* April 1, 2002.

23. The Leisure Travel Monitor Report 2005, "Yesawich, Pepperdine, Brown & Russell," as reported in FloridaToday.com, May 6, 2005; picked up from *www.second50years.com/members/416.cfm*

24. Michele Melendez, "Nostalgia Propels Internet Essay on the Glories of Childhood," c.2003 Newhouse News Service, July 16, 2003.

25. Springwise, February 2006 newsletter.

Chapter 6

1. Alison Overholt, "The Labor-Shortage Myth," *Fast Company* (August 2004), p. 23.

2. *Older Americans,* 4th Edition (Ithaca, NY: New Strategist Publications, 2004), p. 167.

3. Anne Fisher, "How to Battle the Coming Brain Drain," *Fortune* (March 7, 2005).

4. Alison Overholt, "The Labor-Shortage Myth," *Fast Company* (August 2004), p. 23.

5. National Center for Health Statistics, Fast Facts Web site, "Life expectancy at birth, at 65 and 75 years of age by race and sex, 1900–2002 Health, United States 2005," table 27, *www.cdc.gov/nchs/fastats/lifexpec.htm.*

6. Beverly Kaye, Sharon Jordan-Evans, "The Boomer Bail Out," *Fast Company, www.fastcompany.com/resources/talent/bksje/081604.html,* retrieved September 13, 2006.

7. Alison Overholt, "The Labor-Shortage Myth," *Fast Company* (August 2004), p. 23.

8. *Roget's New Millennium™ Thesaurus,* First Edition (v 1.3.1), Copyright © 2006 by Lexico Publishing Group, LLC.

9. *Older Americans,* 2004, 4th Edition (Ithaca, NY: New Strategist Publications, 2004), p. 196.

10. Marilyn Gardner, "Seasoned Workers Snag Flex Jobs," *Christian Science Monitor,* accessed via moneycentral.msn.com.

11. Tim Knox, "Entrepreneurs Just Get Better With Age," matureresources.org.

12. Jim Hopkins, "The new entrepreneurs: Americans over 50," *USA Today* (January 17, 2005).

13. Center for Women's Business Research, 2004.

14. Stuart Elliott, "The Media Business: Advertising; A Public Service Campaign Airs to Persuade Retiring Baby Boomers to Become Volunteers," *The New York Times* (January 6, 2005).

15. "Staying Ahead of the Curve 2003: The AARP Working in Retirement Study," in *The Baby Boom* (Ithaca, NY: New Strategist Publications, 2004), p. 178.

16. A study by the Simmons School of Management reported in *The Breaking Point* by Sue Shellenbarger (New York: Henry Holt and Company, LLC, 2004), p. 152.

17. Abigail Trafford, "When Spouse Retires, Real Work Begins," Washingtonpost .com (October 25, 2005).

18. Del Webb 2005 Baby Boomer Survey conducted by Harris Interactive.

19. National Association of Realtors (NAR), 2004.

20. Lowe's research, per CEO Robert Tillman, cited on Forbes.com, and quoted in Tom Peters's presentation, June 1, 2003.

21. Lowe's internal research, as quoted in *Marketing to Women* newsletter (New York: EPM Communications, Inc., October, 2003); *DSN Retailing Today* (December 16, 2002).

22. *Marketing to Women* newsletter (New York: EPM Communications, Inc., 2004).

23. ACE Hardware, PDR, July, 2003, p. 41.

24. AARP, the-homestore.com.

25. Bill Jacobs, demographic analyst in Bonita Springs, Florida, quoted in *Chicago Tribune,* February 12, 2006.

26. "Baby Boomer Survey Shows Big Appetite for Real Estate," conducted by Harris Interactive for the National Association of Realtors, May 18, 2006.

27. NAR Second Home Owner Survey, May 16, 2006.

28. "Baby Boomer Survey Shows Big Appetite for Real Estate," conducted by Harris Interactive for the National Association of Realtors, May 18, 2006.

29. Nancy Dailey, *When Baby Boom Women Retire* (Westport, CT: Praeger Paperback, 2000), p. 39.

30. FDIC Outlook, April 2006.

31. Adam Geller, "Retired alumni become the newest college clique," *Chicago Tribune* (March 21, 2005).

32. Christine Vestal, "Retirees Boosting States' Rural Economies," stateline.org (published in *www.seniorjournal.com,* "Eying Baby Boomer Bonanza, States Woo Retirees," March 7, 2006).

33. Ibid.

34. Ibid.

35. Ibid.

Chapter 7

1. Gail Sheehy, *Sex and the Seasoned Woman* (New York: Random House, Inc., 2006), p. 14.

2. David Wolfe, *Ageless Marketing* (Chicago: Dearborn Trade Publishing, 2003), p. 294.

3. Ibid., p. 12.

4. Louise Lee, "Love Those Boomers," *Businessweek* (Oct. 24, 2005), *www.business week.com/magazine/content/05_43/b3956201.htm.*

5. Ibid.

6. The Senior Strategic Network, *Mature Market Newsletter* (June 14, 2006).

Chapter 8

1. Tom Peters, *Re-imagine!* (New York: DK Limited, 2003), p. 155.

2. Retaildesigncenter.com, November 15, 2005.

3. *www.storycorp.com.*

4. JoAnn Hines, "10 Packaging Tips that Sell Boomers," *Packaging Diva, www.rethinkpink.com,* March 28, 2006.

5. Leslie Harris, *After Fifty: How the Baby Boom Will Redefine the Mature Market,* (Ithaca, NY: Paramount Market Publishing, Inc., 2003), p. 50.

6. eMarketer.com, "Seniors Online: How Aging Boomers Will Shake Up the Market," June 2005, retrieved from second50years.com, *www.second50years.com/members/490.cfm?sd=32.*

7. Clickz, Facts and Resources About Senior Use of Internet, second50years.com.

8. emarketer.com, "Senior Media: The Internet: Seniors Shopping Online," second50years.com.

9. Pew Internet & the American Life Project report, "How Women and Men Use the Internet," December 2005.

10. Leslie Harris, *After Fifty: How the Baby Boom Will Redefine the Mature Market* (Ithaca, NY: Paramount Market Publishing, Inc., 2003), p. 50.

11. Barbara Kantrowitz, "Sex & Love: The New World," *Newsweek* (February 20, 2006), pp. 51–60.

12. Ibid.

13. Cliff Hahn, "Attack of the gaming grannies," Businessweekonline.com (October 19, 2005).

14. Jennifer Kalita, "Boomer Women: A Voice That's Getting Heard," second50years.com; Korky Vann, "Baby Boomer women find an online voice," *The Seattle Times* (October 21, 2005).

Chapter 9

1. J. Walter Thompson Mature Market Group, Industry Facts: Health Care.

2. *SUPERSTUDY® of Sports Participation,* January 2005, American Sports Data, Inc. (ASD), sponsored and published by Sporting Goods Manufacturers Association (SGMA) of Washington, D.C.

3. J. Walter Thompson Mature Market Group, Industry Facts: Health Care.

4. Source: *SUPERSTUDY® of Sports Participation,* January 2005, American Sports Data, Inc. (ASD), sponsored and published by Sporting Goods Manufacturers Association (SGMA) of Washington, D.C.

5. Louise Lee, "She's Not An Also-Ran Now," *BusinessWeek* (June 17, 2006), featured on rethinkpink.com newsletter, June 22, 2006.

6. Ken Dychtwald, *Age Power* (New York: Tarcher/Putnam, 1999), p. 20; AARP.

7. Gary Onks, SoldonSeniors, Inc.

8. Ken Dychtwald, *Age Power* (New York: Tarcher/Putnam, 1999), p. 20.

9. *American Women* (Ithaca, NY: New Strategist Publications, 1997), p. 28.

10. Women.com, P&G, Harris Interactive Study, 1999.

11. Securities Industry Association, e. 1998.

12. "Study on the Financial Experience and Behaviors Among Women," Prudential Financial, 2004–2005.

Index